A COURSE OF GERMAN *GESTECH*

THE MEDIAEVAL TOURNAMENT

R. Coltman Clephan

DOVER PUBLICATIONS, INC.
New York

Published in Canada by General Publishing Company, Ltd., 30 Lesmill Road, Don Mills, Toronto, Ontario.

Published in the United Kingdom by Constable and Company, Ltd., 3 The Lanchesters, 162–164 Fulham Palace Road, London W6 9ER.

Bibliographical Note

This Dover edition, first published in 1995, is an unabridged republication of the work originally published by Methuen & Co. Ltd., London, in 1919 under the title *The Tournament: Its Periods and Phases*. The frontispiece, originally in color, is here reproduced in black and white. For reasons of space, slight rearrangement of the illustrations has been necessary.

Library of Congress Cataloging-in-Publication Data

Clephan, R. Coltman (Robert Coltman)
   [Tournament, its periods and phases]
   The mediaeval tournament / R. Coltman Clephan.
      p.   cm.
   Originally published: The tournament, its periods and phases. London : Methuen, 1919.
   Includes bibliographical references and index.
   ISBN 0-486-28620-7 (pbk.)
   1. Tournaments.   I. Title.
CR4553.C5 1995
394'.7—dc20

                                                  94-47975
                                                   CIP

Manufactured in the United States of America
Dover Publications, Inc., 31 East 2nd Street, Mineola, N.Y. 11501

PREFACE

THOSE students of arms and armour who have Mr. Clephan's work on *Defensive Armour, Weapons and Engines of War* in their libraries will expect to find valuable material for study when they find his name as author of a work on the Tournament. And in this they will surely not be disappointed. It is perhaps a novel experience for one who has for some years seriously meditated such a work himself to be asked to introduce the work of another; but in the study of arms and armour all men are brothers, and I take leave to say that we of this brotherhood know little of the jealousies and divisions of opinion which beset the student in other historical details. The perusal of Mr. Clephan's work has shown me that it would have been impossible to undertake such a project without unattainable leisure, tireless energy, deep research and very real devotion to the subject. Mr. Clephan has dealt with the subject from a wide European point of view, and has amassed a vast amount of information from German sources which has, up till now, been denied to those unskilled in that language; and, with his copious notes and references, has made this material available for study, for which alone we must ever be deeply indebted to him.

The Tournament, as practised in Germany and towards the close of the sixteenth century in England, France and Italy, must have been a rather dull performance, as the minute regulations and the cumbersome equipment precluded that dash and intrepid onslaught which make the descriptions by Froissart and other writers of his time such excellent reading. Even the gorgeous displays of Henry VIII leave us rather cold when we find that the king invariably won, and that the queen could stop the tilting at her pleasure, which was presumably when her lord had had sufficient entertainment. We have only to note that the suit in the Tower made for Henry VIII to fight on foot in the lists weighs 93 lbs., to realize that no man could be strenuous or energetic in this equipment ; and when we find that the horse in the sixteenth century joust had to carry a dead weight of 340 lbs., it will be manifest that he could only amble gently along the tilt, and could not dash headlong down the lists, as the artist would have us believe. The whole subject of arms and armour teems with such disillusioning ; but to the earnest student these are taken with grace, because they are born of facts quarried out of masses of written and printed records with years of incessant perseverance and devotion.

After the pioneer work of Meyrick and Hewitt, the interest in arms and armour died down for over half a century, but in the last ten or fifteen years it has revived, and its resurrection may be traced to writers who, like Lord Dillon and Mr. Clephan, have striven to give us a real insight into the military life of nations, rather than highly-coloured fantasies which have no foundation in fact. If Mr. Clephan's researches cause us to modify our views on certain aspects of the Tournament, I feel quite certain that all who have previously written on these lines will admit the new light he has brought to bear. The audience he directly appeals to is small, but they will yield to students in no other branch of history or art in their keen devotion to their subject ; and I trust I may conclude, in their name, by wishing Mr. Clephan every success in the work before us, and, if I may enter into the spirit of his subject, " Good jousting."

CHARLES FFOULKES

OFFICE OF THE ARMOURIES
H.M. TOWER OF LONDON
29 *August*, 1917

INTRODUCTION

MOST of us owe our early impressions of the tournament to the delightful account of the " Gentle and Joyous Passage of Arms " of Ashby de la Zouche, in the county of Leicester, given by Sir Walter Scott in his fine romance *Ivanhoe*. But that eminent novelist, in presenting to his readers the picture of a *pas d'armes* of the times of the lion-hearted Richard, took a poet's licence by describing a jousting and *mêlée* such as belonged, in many details, to a time later than Richard's by some two and a half centuries. The knightly armour of the reign of King Richard was of chain-mail, while that of the times of Henry VI was, of course, a complete harness of plate. The first-named equipment is thus described by Sainte-Palaye : " *Une lance forte et difficile à rompre, un haubert ou haubergeon, c'est à dire, une double cotte de mailles, tissues de fer, à l'epreuve de l'épée, étoient les armes assignées aux Chevaliers.*"[1]

Sir Walter's account is thus hopelessly misleading in regard to its period, though admirably worked out in many other respects. There are ancient romances of great historic value, in that they give nearly contemporaneous details of the tournament of the fourteenth and fifteenth centuries, and represent many features which may be regarded as correct in the light of a close comparison with other records. That of *Petit Jehan de Saintré*, written by Anthoine de la Sale, in 1459, is one of these, and we owe much enlightenment to it.

There is great confusion among the works of chroniclers in regard to the dates of many tournaments, and often it is impossible to reconcile their statements. The differences are, however, usually but slight.

Mr. ffoulkes, in his Preface to this work, draws attention to the large amount of fable and exaggeration so often interwoven in many accounts given of the tournament, and to the necessity for presenting the subject historically in its true light. In order to do this one must discard much that has been written concerning it throughout the ages

---

[1] *Mémoires sur L'Ancienne Chevalerie*, l. 289.

and go back to original information, carefully sifted and compared, in order to arrive at some degree of truth.

As a rule, illuminations in MSS. must not be estimated at their face value, for, besides being often fantastic, they are rarely contemporaneous with the events they portray ; and the narrations of chroniclers were mostly written some time after the events in question, and often introduce details which really belong to a later age. Thus the illustrated *Froissart* in the British Museum,[1] which dates from about the end of the fifteenth century, pictures a joust at the tilt at the *pas d'armes* held at St. Inglevert in the year 1389, a tournament described in our chapter IV ; but a tilt or barrier placed between the combatants, along which they rode in opposite directions, was first employed about the end of the first quarter of the century following. Such anachronisms are very common in records of the tournament, so that care and discrimination are required in their interpretation.

The works of Meyrick and Hewitt are of great historical value, and they afford much information carefully gathered from original documents. This information has been copiously made use of by more recent authors with but a scant or even no acknowledgment. It should be remembered, however, that these eminent and devoted historians were pioneers, so to speak, and much has been learnt of the tournament since their day ; yet their labours form excellent foundations for the building up of a scientific superstructure.

The admirable version of *Freydal*, by Querin von Leitner, pictures the jousts of the Emperor Maximilian I, especially those of the last quarter of the fifteenth century. It presents a veritable mine of information concerning the tournament of that period, placing the technique of the subject on a sound basis. Even this account, however, is hardly contemporaneous.

The interest in the subject flagged for a season, and until some quarter of a century ago but little more was heard of it. It was Wendelin Boeheim, in his *Waffenkunde*, who set the ball rolling again ; and since his book was written a number of learned papers have appeared in England and Germany dealing with the tournament, though in French literature the subject has received but little attention. Among such papers those by Viscount Dillon, published in *Archæologia* and the *Archæological Journal*, are very important. This writer has

[1] Harl. MS. 4379.

corrected many mistakes made by the earlier authors and persistently handed down from one generation to another. Most of the writers would appear to have regarded as gospel truths all statements made by Meyrick. These mistakes are most difficult to eradicate from our literature, for their correction has been made in publications such as those mentioned above, which are unfortunately only read by a select few.

All these learned books and scattered papers treat the subject more or less sectionally, and, so far as I know, there has been no work of any importance published which attempts to deal with the subject as a whole from start to finish. This manifest want I have endeavoured to supply in the present volume.

My position for many years, up to the date of the war, as an official of the Verein für Historische Waffenkunde, gave me access to a mass of original information concerning what may be fitly termed the German period. Such information is not readily got at, and much of it has been embodied in the present volume. It is to such sources that we must turn for many details, more particularly for those of a technical nature. These records, however, mainly relate to tournaments of the last quarter of the fifteenth century (after the Burgundian Chronicles cease), to the whole of the sixteenth, and so up to the time when the institution fell into desuetude.

My thanks are due to Mr. Basil Anderton, M.A., the Public Librarian of Newcastle-upon-Tyne, for reading over parts of my MS. and for drawing attention to many books bearing on the subject of the tournament ; to Mr. Charles J. ffoulkes, B.Litt., F.S.A., Curator of the Armouries of the Tower of London ; to Mr. Frederick Walter Dendy, D.C.L., and Mr. Samuel T. Meynell, for some valuable suggestions ; and to the University of Cambridge for the loan of books.

R. COLTMAN CLEPHAN

Tynemouth,
    Northumberland

CONTENTS

CHAPTER IV

CHAPTER V

CHAPTER VI

CHAPTER VII

CHAPTER VIII

CONTENTS

APPENDICES

LIST OF ILLUSTRATIONS

BIBLIOGRAPHY

An Almain Armourer's Album.   Viscount Dillon, P.S.A.

Annales de Louis XII.

Antient Armour at Goodrich Court.   Skelton.

Antiquarian Repertory.

Archæologia, Vol. XI.   Copy of a Survey made of what remained of the Armoury of the Tower of London in 1660.

,,   XXXVII.   A list for the year 1631.

,,   XVII.   On the Peaceable Justs, or Tiltings, of the Middle Ages.   By Francis Douce, F.A.A.

,,   XVII.   Copy of a Roll of Purchases made for the Tournament of Windsor Park in the sixth year of King Edward the First.   Communicated by Samuel Lysons, F.R.S., V.P.

,,   XXIX.   Some Observations on Judicial Duels, as practised in Germany.   By R. L. Pearsall.

,,   XXXI.   Observations on the Institution of the Most Noble Order of the Garter.   By Sir Harris Nicholas, G.C.M.G.

,,   XXXI.   Account of the Ceremonial of the Marriage of the Princess Margaret, sister of King Edward the Fourth, to Charles Duke of Burgundy, in 1468.   By Sir Thomas Phillipps, Bart., F.S.A.

,,   LI.   A Letter of Sir Henry Lee, 1590, on the trial of Iron for Armour.   By the Hon. Harold Arthur Dillon, F.S.A.

,,   LI.   Arms and Armour at Westminster, the Tower, and Greenwich, 1547.   By the same.

,,   LVII.   On a MS. Collection of Ordinances of Chivalry of the Fifteenth Century belonging to Lord Hastings.   By Harold Arthur Viscount Dillon, Hon. M.A.(Oxon), President.

,,   LX.   Armour Notes.   By the same.

,,   LXIII.   Jousting Cheques of the Sixteenth Century.   By Charles ffoulkes, B.Litt. Oxon., F.S.A.

Arch. Journ. Vol. IV.   Illustrations of Mediæval Manners and Costumes from original documents.
Jousts of Peace, Tournaments and Judicial Combats.   By Albert Way.
Survey of the Tower Armory in the year 1660.

,,   ,,   XV.   Notice of a German Tilting-saddle of the Fifteenth Century, recently added to the Tower Collection.   By John Hewitt.

,,   ,,   XXI.   Tilting-helm of the Fifteenth Century in the Royal Artillery Museum, Woolwich.   By John Hewitt.

,,   ,,   XLVI.   The Pasguard, Garde de Cou, Brech-Rand, Stoss-Kragen or Randt, and the Volant Piece.   By the Hon. Harold Dillon, F.S.A.

Arch. Journ.   Vol. LV.   Tilting in Tudor Times.   By Viscount Dillon, Hon. M.A.Oxon., F.S.A.

  „   „   LV.   Additional Notes Illustrative of Tilting in Tudor Times.   By the same.

  „   „   LXI.   Barriers and Foot Combats.   By the same.

                  The Winchester Volume, 1845.

Armorial de la Toison d'Or.   National Library, Paris.

Armories of the Tower of London.   ffoulkes.

Ashmolean MSS.

Bayeux Tapestry, The.

Boeheim's Waffenkunde.

     „   Meister der Waffenschmiede Kunst.

     „   Album, Waffensammlung.   Vienna.

Boutell's Brasses.

Brantôme.   Par J. A. C. Buchon.

Carter's Painting and Sculpture.

Catalogues.   Catalogo Real Armeria de Madrid.

       „   The Imperial Collection at Vienna.

       „   Königliche Historische Museum, Dresden.

       „   Musée d'Artillerie, Paris.

       „   Königliche Zeughaus, Berlin.

       „   Sammlungen des Germanischen Museum, Nuremburg.

       „   Guida Officiale della Reale Armeria di Torino (Turin).

       „   Porte de Hal Collection, Brussels.

       „   National Museum, Munich.

       „   The Wallace Collection, London.

       „   The Armouries of the Tower of London.

Caxton's Book of the Order of Chyvalry and Knyghthode.

Chastelain's Chronique de Jacques de Lalain.

Chaucer's Knight's Tale.

Chronicle of Tours.

Chronicles of: William of Malmesbury.   Wace.   William of Newbury.   Roger of Hoveden.   William
    Fitzstephen.   Matthew Paris.   Robert of Gloucester.   Matthew of Westminster.   Père Daniel.
    Trivet.   Thomas of Walsingham.   Jocelin of Brakelond.   Hardyng.   Monstrelet.   Jean le Févre
    de S. Remi.   Hist. de Charles VI.   de Flandres.   de Charlemagne (in the Burgundian Library
    at Brussels).

Clark's History of Knighthood.

Clephan, R. Coltman.   The Defensive Armour, Weapons and Engines of War of Mediæval Times and of
        the "Renaissance."   1900.

           The Wallace Collection of Arms and Armour.   Published by the Verein für
           Historische Waffenkunde, Dresden.

           Armour Notes: With some Account of the Tournament.   Proceedings of the Society
           of Antiquaries of Newcastle, 1915.

Conquêtes de Charlemagne. A MS. in the National Library, Paris.
Cottonian MSS.
Coucy, Matthieu de. Histoire de Charles VII.

Ducange. Glossarium.
Dugdale's Origines Juridiciales.
Du Guesclin, Bertrand, La Vie de.

Eglington Tournament. The Tournament at Eglington, by James Aikman. 1839.
       ,,   ,,   The Grand Tournament, by James Bulkeley. 1840.
Ehrenpforte.
Excerpta Historica.

Favine. Honour and Knighthood. 1553.
ffoulkes, Charles. The Armourer and his Craft.
Freydal. Querin von Leitner.
Froissart's Late Fifteenth Century Illustrated Edition. In British Museum. Harl. MS. 4379.
    ,,   Chronicles.

Gay. Glossaire Archéologique.
Gurlitt. Deutsche Turniere, etc. Dresden. 1889.

Hall's Chronicles.
Harleian MSS.
    ,,   Miscellany.
Hefner's Tractenbuch.
Hewitt's Ancient Armour and Weapons.
Histoire Des Ducs de Bourgogne. Barante.
    ,,   de Bretagne.
Hohenzollern Jahrbücher.
Holinshed's Chronicles.

Jusserand. Les Sports.
Juvenal Des Ursin. Histoire de Charles VI.

La Colombière. Théâtre d'Hon and de Chevalerie.
Lacroix. Military and Religious Life in the Middle Ages and Renaissance.
Leber. Collection des Traités, etc.
Leland's Collectanea.
Lingard's History of England to the Accession of William and Mary.
Livre Des Faicts Jean Le Maingre, Maréschal de France, Dit Boucicaut.
Lombarde. Perambulations of Kent.

MSS. in Herald's College, London.
Mémoires. Olivier De La Marche.
    ,,   Philippe De Comines.

Memoires. Le Bon Chevalier Seigneur De Bayart (Bayard).

    „   Le Sire de Heynin. Société des Bibliophiles Belges. Mons. 1842.

Ménestrier. Traité des Tournois, Justs, Carrousels, etc. Lyons. 1669.

Meyrick. A Critical Enquiry into Antient Armor. 1824.

Montesquieu. Esprit de lois. 28th Book.

Nouvelle Collection Des Mémoires pour servir A L'Histoire De France.

Nugae Antiquae. Park. 1769.

Œuvres du Roi René. Angers. 1845. Edited by M. Paulin-Paris.

Origines Des Chevaliers, Armoiries et Heravx. Par Claude Favchet.

Pisan, Christine de. Le Livre Des Fais et Bonnes Meurs Du Sage Roy Charles.

Pluvinal, De. Maneige Royal.

Pollock and Maitland. History of English Law.

Roll of Purchases for the Tournament at Windsor Park in 1278. MS. in the Record Office.

Romances. Roman de Rou.

    „   Richard Cœur de Lion.

    „   Sir Ferumbras.

    „   Du Roy Miliadus.

    „   D'Alexandre.

    „   Pétit Jehan de Saintré. Par Antoine de la Sale. 1459.

    „   Of Three King's Sons. *Circa* 1500. Harl. MS. 326, fol. 113.

Rous' Life of the Earl of Warwick. Cott. MS., Julius, E. IV.

Rymer's Foedera.

Sächsischen Kurfürsten Turnierbücher. Erich Haenel.

Sainte Maria, Honoré de. Des Ordres de Chevalerie.

Schwenk, Hans. Wappenmeisterbuch, picturing the Jousts of Duke William of Bavaria.

Spelman's Glossary.

St. Denys, La moine de. Histoire de Charles VI.

St. Palaye. Mémoires sur L'Ancienne Chevalerie.

Statuta de Armis or Statutum Armorum in Torniamentis. Bodleian Library.

Stothard's Effigies.

Strutt's Sports and Pastimes of the English People.

    „   Horda Angel-cynnan.

    „   Regal Antiquities.

Tapestry, The, at Valenciennes.

Testamenta Vetusta.

Theuerdank.

Tourney Book of the Pole Zuganoviez Stanislaus. At Dresden.

Tourney Books. Of the Electors of Saxony. At Dresden.

Tourney Books. Johanns des Beständigen

    „   „   Johan Frederiks des Groszmüthiges.

    „   „   August.

    „   „   That at Veste Coburg.

Traicte de la forme et Devis d'ung Tournoi (The Tourney Book of King René d'Anjou).

Traité de Tournois. Par Louis de Bruges.

Triumph of Maximilian.

Turnierbuch in the possession of the Prince of Hohenzollern-Sigmaringen.

Turnierbuch of Duke Henry of Braunschweig-Luneburg.

Vetusta Monumenta. Vol. I. Published by the Society of Antiquaries, London.

Viollet-le-Duc. Dictionnaire Raisonné du Mobilier Français.

Weisskönig.

Zeitschrift für Historische Waffenkunde. Dresden.

THE TOURNAMENT

CHAPTER I

IT is impossible to trace the beginnings of these martial exercises, mention of which first appears in history in chronicles of the eleventh century; but they doubtless grew out of earlier forms of the rough games and sports engaged in by the noble youth of the period as practice for actual warfare.

Du Cange in his *Glossarium*, under the heading "Torneamentum," cites Roger de Hoveden, who defines tournaments as being military exercises carried out in a spirit of comradeship, being practice for war and a display of personal prowess.[1] Their chief distinction from other exercises of a kindred nature lies in the fact that they were actual contests on horse-back, carried out within certain limitations, of many cavaliers who divided themselves into contending troops or parties, which fought against each other like opposing armies.

Mention of rules for observance in the conducting of these martial games is made by more than one chronicler of the period as having been framed in the year 1066, by a French Seigneur, Geoffroi de Preuilli of Anjou, and it is stated that he had invented them and even been killed in one of them;[2] and the very names "*tourneamentum*" and "*tournoi*" would imply a French origin. These designations would seem to have been derived from "*tournier*," to wheel round; though Claude Fauchet, writing in the last quarter of the sixteenth century,[3] expresses the opinion that the word "*tournoi*" came about from the cavaliers running *par tour*, that is by turns at the quintain: "*fut premièrement appellé Tournoy*

---

[1] " *Militaria exercitia, quae nullo interveniente odio, sed pro solo exercitio, atque ostentatione virium.*"

[2] " *Torneamentorum repertorum Gaufridum II, Dominum Pruliaci (de Pruilli) in Andibus agnoscit Chronicon Turonense; Anno* 1066. *Gaufridus de Pruliaco, qui Torneamenta invenit, apud Andegavum occiditur.*" Quoted by Du Cange.

[3] *Les Origines des Chevaliers, etc., p.* 9.

pource que les Cheualiers ŷ coururent par tour; rompans premièrement leur bois et lances contre vne Quintaine. . . ."

Military games of a similar nature are often stated to have been practised in Germany earlier than this, and Favine in *Theatre of Honour and Knighthood*[1] prints a list of rules and ordinances for observance at a "tournament" to be held at Magdeburg, as having been issued by the Emperor of Germany Henry I, surnamed the Fowler, 876–936, a century and a half earlier than the date of the promulgation of the rules of Pruilli. The German text, however, bears the impress of a later period than early in the tenth century, and this view is expressed by Claude Fauchet, who gives the rules, which are curious enough for insertion here; and he mentions the authority from which Favine drew his statement.[2]

" *Sebastien Munster au troisiesme liure de sa Geografie, certifie que Henry premier de ce nom viuant enuiron l'an VCCCCXXXVI fit publier vn Tournoy, pour tenir en la ville de Magdebourg qui est en Saxe, lequel fut le premier, & tenu l'an VCCCCXXXVIII. Le mesme Munster recite douze articles de loix de Tournoy :—*

1. *Qui fera quelque chose contre la Foy.*
2. *Qui aura fait quelque chose contre le sacré Empire, et la Cesarce Majesté.*
3. *Qui aura trahy son Seigneur, ou sans cause iceluy delaisse fuyant en vne bataille : tué, ou meurdry ces compagnons.*
4. *Qui aura outragé fille, ou femme, de fait ou de parolles.*
5. *Qui aura falcifié vn seel, ou fait vn faux serment. Qui aura esté declaré infame, & tenu pour tel.*
6. *Qui en repost (c'est secrettement & en cachette) aura meurdry sa femme. Qui d'aide ou de conseil, aura cósenty la mort de son Seigneur.*
7. *Qui aura pillé les Eglises, femmes vefues, ou orphelins : ou retenu ce qui leur appartenoit.*
8. *Qui ayant esté offensé par aucun, ne le poursuit par guerre, ou en Iustice : ains secrettement & par feu ou rapines. Qui gaste les bledz & vignes dont le public est substanté.*
9. *Qui mettra nouuelles impositions sans le sceu de l'Empereur : ou ie croy qu'il entéd parler d'vn Seigneur qui surchargera sa terre.*
10. *Qui aura cómis adultere, ou rauy vierges & pucelles.*
11. *Qui fait marchandise pour reuendre.*
12. *Qui ne pourra prouuer sa race de quatre grands beres, soit battu & chassé du Tournoy."*

Jousts and Tournaments were classed under the heading of *Hastiludia* or spear-play: as also was the behourd or buhurt, *Bohordicum* in Mediæval Latin,[3] a military exercise of a similar nature; though in what respect it differed from the joust or tournament is nowhere stated. That it was an exercise with lance and shield is clearly shown in a passage in *Concilium Albiense*.[4]

---

[1] *Published at Paris in* 1619 : *p.* 460.   [2] *L'Origines, Liv.* 1, p. 10.
[3] *Bohordicum, nostris Bohourt vel Behourt, Hastiludii species, vel certe quodvis hastiludii genus.* Lambertus Ardensis. Cited by Du Cange.
[4] 11, cap. 16. Cited by Du Cange. *Trepidare quoque quod vulgariter Biordare dicitur, cum scuto et lancea aliquis Clericus publice non attentet.*

That the behourd was practised continuously for long after the introduction of the joust and tournament is known by the fact of the issue of royal edicts for the prohibition of these exercises, as late as the reign of King Edward I.[1]

The origin of the joust does not appear to be less ancient than that of the tourney itself,[2] which it gradually almost supplanted ; and it may have been suggested by the quintain. William of Malmesbury thus defines it :—Justa, jouste. *Monomachia ludicra, hastiludium singulare*.[3] The Bayeux tapestry shows a kind of combat with spears.

The terms "tourney" and "joust" are often confounded with each other, but they are sharply different, the former being a battle in miniature, an armed contest of courtesy on horseback, troop against troop ; while the other is a single combat of mounted cavaliers, run with lances in the lists ; though jousting was by no means confined to these enclosures ; indeed, such contests were sometimes run in the open street or square of a town. Jousts were often included with the tourney, though frequently held independently ; and as the lance was the weapon of the former so was the sword greatly that of the latter. The lance was to be directed at the body only, otherwise it was considered foul play. The joust more especially was run in honour of ladies. These martial games were much practised in all the countries of chivalry.

The chroniclers are vague in their definitions of the Round Table game, the *Tabula Rotunda*, or as Matthew Paris calls it *"Mensa Rotunda."*[4] He expressly distinguishes it from the tournament, though in what respect it differs from it he does not enlighten us. He describes a *tabula rotunda*, held at the Abbey of Wallenden in the year 1252, which was attended by a great number of cavaliers, both English and foreign, and states that on the fourth day of the meeting a knight named Arnold de Montigney was pierced in the throat by a lance "*which had not been blunted as it ought to have been.*" The lance-head remained in the wound and death soon followed. We see from this incident that already in the middle of the thirteenth century it was customary to joust with blunted or rebated lances ! In 1279 (8 Ed. I) a Round Table was held by Roger Earl of Mortimer, at his castle of Kenilworth, which is thus described in

---

[1] *Ad turniandum et Burdiandum.* *Ne quis . . . turneare, Burdeare, justas facere, seu alia jacta armorum exercere praeusumat.* *Budeare apud Rymer* (tom 5, p. 223).
[2] The *Mêlée*.
[3] Cited by Du Cange.
[4] *Tabula, seu Mensa Rotunda, Decursionis, aut hastiludii species.*

Historia Prioratus de Wigmore[1]:—"He (Mortimer) invited a hundred knights and as many ladies to an hastilude at Kenilworth, which he celebrated for three days at a vast expense. Then he began the round table; and the golden lion, the prize for the triumphant knight, was awarded to him." Dugdale states that the reason for the institution itself was to assert the principle of equality and to avoid questions of precedence among the knights.

In some "Observations on the Institution of the Most Noble Order of the Garter," printed in *Archæologia* of the year 1846,[2] it is stated that in 1343, King Edward III in imitation of King Arthur, the traditional founder of British Chivalry, bent on reviving the fabled glories of a by-gone age, determined to hold a Round Table at Windsor on the 19th of January, 1344. The intended meeting was proclaimed by heralds of the king, in France, Scotland, Burgundy, Hainault, Flanders, Brabant, and in the German Empire, offering safe-conducts to all foreign knights and esquires wishful to take part in it.[3] King Edward fixed the number of the tenans at forty, enrolling the bravest in the land; and he appointed that a "Feast" should be kept from year to year at Windsor on every following St. George's Day. Walsingham, writing about half a century after Froissart, states that in 1344 the King began to build a house in Windsor Park, which should be called the "Round Table"; that it was circular in form, and 200 feet in diameter. It is also stated that a circular table, made of wood, was constructed at Windsor sometime before 1356; and that the Prior of Merton was paid L26-13-4 for 52 oaks, taken from his woods near Reading, for the material.[4] Walsingham relates that Philip of France, jealous of the fame of our king, had a table made on the Windsor model.

Matthew of Westminster chronicles that a round table was held in 1352, which had a fatal ending.

There is an actual round table of ancient provenance hanging on the eastern wall of the hall of the royal palace at Winchester, the reputed "painted table of Arthur," and there are some remarks concerning it in the Winchester volume of the Archæological Institute, 1846, telling all that is known concerning it. The hall itself may have been standing in the reign of Henry III; and in the sixteenth century, and probably long before, a round table was an appendage to it; but as to the approximate

---

[1] Cited by Du Cange.   [2] Vol. XXXI, 104.
[3] Rot. Patent, 17 Edw. III, p. 2, m. 2.   [4] Issue Roll of the Exchequer, Mich. 30, Edw. III.

date of its make there is no reliable evidence. The earliest historic reference to the table is by Hardyng, late in the reign of Henry VI or early in that of Edward IV, who alludes to it as "hanging yet" at Winchester; and Paulus Jovius tells us that the table was shown to the emperor Charles V in 1520, when it had been newly painted for the "last" time, but that the marginal names had been restored unskilfully. In the reign of Henry VIII a sum of *L66-16-11* was expended in repairing the "*aula regis infra castrum de Wynchestre, et le Round tabyll ibidem*." John Lesley, bishop of Ross, said that he saw the table not long before 1578, and that the names of the knights were inscribed on its circumference; and a Spanish writer, who was present at the marriage of Philip and Mary, thus describes the painting on the table:—

"*Lors du mariage de Philip II. avec la reine Marie, on montrait encore à Hunscrit la table ronde fabriquée par Merlin: elle se composait de 25 compartemens teintés en blank et en vert, lesquels se terminaient en pointe au milieu, et allaient s'elargissant jusqu'à la circonférence, et dans chaque division étaient écrits le nom du cavalier et celui du roi. L'un de ces compartemens appelé place de Judas, ou siége périlleux, restait toujours vide.*"

The forms of the lettering and general decoration of the table point to a date in the reign of Henry VII or early in that of Henry VIII, but this, of course, only applies to the painted enrichment. Whatever may be the date of this table and its painting, they are both undoubtedly of considerable antiquity, probably from five to six centuries old.

The *fête d'armes* held by Boucicaut at St. Ingelbert in 1389 (which is described in Chapter III), is called in the account of the meeting a "table-ronde"; and the text would imply that the holding of a round table meant a *hastilude* at which the challengers or tenans kept open house to all comers, as well as meeting them in combat in the lists; and the institution is thus coupled with the banquet. The passage runs:—

"*Ainsi feit là son appareil moult grandement et très-honnorablement messire Boucicaut, et feit faire provisions de très-bon vins, et de tous vivres largement, et à plain, et de tout ce qu'il convient si plantureusement comme 'pour tenir table rond à tout venans' tout le dict temps durant, et tout aux propres despens de Boucicaut.*" [1]

[1] *Le Livre Des Faicts Du Mareschal De Boucicaut*, Chap. XVII.

The same lavish hospitality was extended here as at Kenilworth in 1279, and at Windsor in 1344.

It is clear from various records that the tenans at a round table of the thirteenth and fourteenth centuries sometimes fought under the names of King Arthur's knights, indeed, "Sir Galehos" appears among the names of the knights inscribed on the actual round table at Winchester; and they also sometimes adopted the names of other legendary heroes, for at a round table held at Valenciennes in 1344, at which the prize was a peacock, victory was achieved by a band of cavaliers which fought under the names of King Alexander's knights.[1] The accounts given of King Edward's tournament at Windsor, and that of the later Boucicaut's *pas d'armes*, both of which are called round tables, may be said to define sufficiently what a "Round Table" of the fourteenth century really was; and we fail to find any material difference from other meetings of the kind and period.

Favine in *Theatre of Honour and Knighthood*[2] refers to "*Hastiludia Rotunda*" as being practice for cavaliers "to sit well their horses, to keepe themselues fast in their saddles and stirrups. For, if any man fell, and his Horse upon him, at these encounterings with their lances, lightly worse did befall him before he could any way get forth of the Preasse. But others came to heauior fortune, their liues expyring in the place, being trod and trampled on by others"—but all this would apply to the ordinary *mêlée*. This form of tourney was much in favour during the thirteenth and fourteenth centuries, but we hear no more of round tables after that.

The Quintain (*quintana*) and Running at the Ring (*Ringelrennen, Corso all' Annello*) were closely allied with the joust, and were practised in preparation for it; the chief objects for attainment in the former being a correct aim, to remain steady in the saddle after impact with the figure, and deftly to get rid of the stump of the broken lance. The quintain was a more ancient game than the joust, and indeed, not improbably, it gave rise to it; and being free from the risk of personal danger, was a sport and pastime of the people. The game assumed many forms, though it was chiefly a means of practice with the lance, sword, baston and battle-axe, indulged in by the young aspirants for knighthood as well as by the citizens and yeomanry. The original quintain was merely a post set up, against which the strokes were directed or against a shield hanging

---

[1] Menestrier, *Chavalrie ancienne*, Chap. 6. Cited by Hewitt.   [2] Page 492.

from it, with the same object in view. Later, the post developed into a human figure, usually fashioned as a Turk or Saracen, who held a wooden sword in his hand. The objective of the lance was the space between the eyes; and the figure was placed on a pivot, and so constructed that a misdirected stroke, that is a hit too much on one side or the other, would cause it to spin round with great velocity, dealing the tyro a smart blow with the sword. Another form was a bag of sand, from which the clumsy operator was apt to receive a buffet as it swung round or to have the contents expended over his horse and person; and there were other similar varieties of the game. The water quintain was practised from a boat, rapidly propelled by rowers; while the player stood at the bow, his lance couched and directed towards a shield, hung from a post standing in the water. The quintain continued to be a popular game right through the seventeenth century, and could be played on foot as well as on horseback. A picture of a quintain is given on a miniature in the *Chroniques de Charlemagne*, in the Burgundian Library at Brussels, and is reproduced by Lacroix in *Military and Religious Life in the Middle Ages and Renaissance*.

Running or Tilting at the Ring was merely a later form of the quintain. An upright shaft or post was holed at intervals for the reception of a rounded bar, socketed into it at right-angles, from which hung the ring placed on a level with the player's eye; and the horseman, couching his lance, rode towards it at full gallop with the object of transfixing it. When fairly hit the ring became detached by the action of side springs and remained on the head of the lance. Pluvinal gives particulars of the game as practised at the beginning of the seventeenth century; it was much in vogue at the court of Louis XIV. For running at the ring the lance was much shorter than that employed in jousting, its length was 10 ft. 7 in. and weight 7 lbs. There is a specimen at Dresden, tipped with a cone to hold the ring when hit, and there is naturally no vamplate. It will be realised what excellent practice these sports afforded for the joust and tourney. Both games are described in Strutt's *Sports and Pastimes*. MS., Ashmole 837, fol. 185, furnishes an instance of the game :—

" These persons here vnderwrytten / beinge one the kinges parte the playntyff / And the other wt therle of Rutland defendant / dyd Run at ye Rynge 111j course every man / at wch tyme none toke the Ryng but only Mr hayward / and Mr Constable beinge wt the defendant / whome are apoynted when yt shall please his grace/ for them to Rune agayne/ he wch shall take the Ring furst shall have the prysse /

wt the kynges matie

the lord marques of Northampton
therle of Worcester
therle of wormewood
the lord admyrall
the lord lyle
the lord Strange
Sr thomas Wroughton
Mr Barnaby
Mr throughmorton
harry nevell
Sr harry gates
Sr harry Sydney
Mr Chetewood
Mr phylpott

wt therle of Rutland

the lord Fyzewater
the lord hastynges
the lord chevers (? Chandos)
Sr Ambrows Dudley
Sr jorge hayward
Mr norrys
Sr William Stafford
Sr Anthony Sturley
Mr Pownynge
Mr Clement paston
Sr William Cobham
Mr Constable
Mr payne (?prynne)
Mr. warcope

This beinge done came VI one ether partye to the tourney whose names are hereafter named

The Kynges syd

therle of worcester
the lord lysseley
Mr harry nevell
Mr Sydney
Sr thomas wroughton
Sr harry gates

Therle of Rutland

lord Fyzewater
Sr Ambrows Dudley
Sr George hayward
MR pownynges
Mr paston
Mr payne (? prynne)."

Probably written by Sir Gilbert Dethick, Garter King of Arms.

Judicial Combats are also properly classed under the general heading of the Tournament, and these duels, on foot and on horseback, were fought greatly subject to its rules and regulations. An account of this singular institution follows after the tournament proper.

CHAPTER II

JOUSTS of Peace, *Hastiludia pacifica*, were those of sport, military exercises and courtesy ; while Jousts of War, *Joûtes à Outrance*, or as Froissart calls them " *Justes Mortelles et à Champ*," were combats to the death, though subjected to the intervention of the umpire at any stage, by the casting of his bâton, by which a serious wounding or death was often prevented. The term " *à outrance*," however, was used not infrequently in *Chapitres d'Armes* or articles of combat where no fatal ending was in contemplation ; they were encounters of courtesy in fact, though contests in which battle-axes, sharp swords and pointed lances were employed.

The chroniclers of the joust and tournament of the earlier centuries exhibit a lack of technical knowledge, and the terms they employ are often mixed and conflicting ; and, indeed, this confusion continues throughout later centuries also, to an extent making any exact definition of terms extremely difficult.

Whatever information we possess regarding tournaments of the twelfth and thirteenth centuries is greatly derived from the Mediæval Latin chronicles of the Anglo-Norman monks ; but the material they furnish requires to be used with discretion, owing to the frequent unhappy blending of fact and legend, a lack of professional knowledge, and a way of reporting things of half a century or more ago in harmony with the environment of the time of writing. Among the chroniclers of the tournament of the period we are immediately dealing with, are William of Malmesbury, whose *History of the Kings of England* finishes at the year 1142 ; Wace, who wrote the *Roman de Rou*, on Rollo and the succeeding Dukes of Normandy, in 1160 ; William of Newbury, 1197 ; Roger of Hoveden, 1201.[1] William Fitzstephen was an eye-witness of the events he relates ; the prolific and illuminating Matthew Paris, 1259 ; Robert of Gloucester, who died in 1290 ; and Matthew of Westminster, 1307.

[1] He began to write the *Annals* just after the death of Henry II, in 1189. They begin with the year 732 and end in 1201 ; and form not only a chronicle of England, but include also the history of many other countries.

Much information concerning the body armour of the twelfth and thirteenth centuries has been derived from seals, and particularly from those of the kings of England; also from illuminations in chronicles, representations on tapestry and carvings in ivory. Military effigies and brasses have also proved of immense value, for they enable us to fill in many of the gaps left in the recitals of chroniclers, and afford precise information as to the knightly equipment for battle, as far as least as the presence of the surcoat will permit. We have, indeed, been favoured among the nations in the preservation of so many of these monuments. There are but few brasses of the thirteenth century existing, though effigies are very numerous. Sad it is that so many of these priceless memorials have been lost or thoughtlessly mutilated; but their very important bearing upon history was but faintly recognised much before the nineteenth century began. Many of them had been thrown on the rubbish heap to make way for some trivial and often mischievous alteration, or lost when some of our finest churches were spoilt by what is so often miscalled restoration; and many even of the effigies left to us have been exposed to a process of tinkering by thoughtless hands. Not a detail is missing on many of those monuments that remain, and even colours are indicated.

William of Newbury states that tournaments first appear in England in the troubled reign of King Stephen, 1135-1154; and that they were introduced from France by the Norman nobles is clear from the expressions employed by Matthew Paris concerning them, viz.: " Conflictus Gallicus " and " batailles francaises." Lombarde[1] states that " the kings of this realm before King Stephen, would not suffer it to be frequented within their land; so that, such as for exercise in that feate in armes, were driven to passe over the seas, and to performe in some different place in a foreigne countrie: but afterwards King Stephen in his time allowed it."[2] It was the Norman knights who introduced the employment and couching of the lance in England. Of that age we have the remarkable description of the martial sports of London by William Fitzstephen. He tells us " that every Sunday in Lent, immediately after dinner it was customary for great crowds of Londoners, mounted on war-horses, well trained to perform the necessary turnings and evolutions, to ride into the fields in distinct bands, armed " *hastilibus ferro dempto*," with shields and headless lances; where they exhibited representations of battle, and went

---

[1] *Perambulation of Kent*, fol 448.   [2] Cited in *Horda*.

through a variety of warlike exercises : at the same time many of the young noblemen who had not received the honour of knighthood, came from the King's court, and from the houses of the great barons, to make a trial of their skill in arms ; the hope of victory animating their minds. The youth being divided into opposite companies, encountered one another ; in one place they fled, and others pursued, without being able to overtake them ; in another place one of the bands overtook and overturned the other."

Robert of Gloucester, in his *Chronicle* in verse, which ends shortly before the accession of King Edward I, writes concerning William Rufus :—

"Stalwarde he was & hardy & god knyght, thorn al thyng
In batayle & in 'tornemnes' er than he were Kyng." [1]

but this of course has not the value of contemporary history.

The knight-errant of the twelfth century and even later often spent the evening of his days as an anchorite, undergoing many self-imposed penances, fastings and flagellations in expiation of many acts of violence and even oppression of his active career.

The tournaments of the twelfth and thirteenth centuries were characterized by all the romantic fire of knight-errantry, though they were often rough and disorderly, and not infrequently degenerated into real battles or free fights, in which many of the combatants were seriously injured or killed. At the meeting held at Neuss, near Cologne, in 1240, sixty of the combatants are stated to have been killed. In England an Earl of Salisbury died from his hurts ; his grandson, Sir William Montague, was killed when jousting with his own father ; and many prominent knights and nobles were so injured in the tourney that they never regained their health. Tournaments generally tended to become milder as rules, regulations and limitations were enacted for their government ; but it was not before the reign of King Edward I that they were brought under any regular disciplined system of control.

After the reign of King Stephen these martial exercises often came under the ban of both church and state, the former even going to the length of excommunication and the refusal of Christian burial to the fallen. Pope Gregory issued a bull against them in 1228, and there were other bulls.[2] King Henry II discouraged them and issued edicts against them ; and we are told by William of Newbury that many young

---

[1] Cited by Strutt in *Horda Angel-cynnan*, p. 92   [2] *Rymer Foed.*, 301.

cavaliers travelled from England to enjoy their favourite pastime in other lands, especially France. Tournaments were revived in England, says Jocelin of Brakelond,[1] after the return of the heroic Richard from the Holy Land, who granted licences for holding them ; and from this time forward unlicensed tourneying was treated as an offence against the crown. Roger de Hoveden writes in *Annals*, under the year 1194 (in translation) :— " King Richard ordered tournaments to be held in England, which he confirmed by charter ; but that all wishing to tourney should pay for the privilege according to rank—viz., an earl, 20 marks of silver ; a baron, 10 marks ; a knight, holding land, 4 marks ; and any who were landless, 2 marks ; and no knight was permitted to enter any lists without first having paid his fee." The charter of this grant was delivered into the custody of William, Earl of Salisbury ; and Hubert Fitz-Walter, the king's chief-justice, appointed his brother, Theobald Fitz-Walter, to be collector.

Hoc ett Breve, Dni Regis Ricardi I. missum Dno Cantuariensi, de concessione Torneamentorum in Anglia.

Heac est forma Pacis fervandae a Torneatoribus (Harl MS. 237).[2]

Tournaments became controlled by royal ordinances, and any infraction of the rules laid down was punishable with the forfeiture of horse and armour, imprisonment and other penalties ; though at times the regulations would seem to have been very loosely interpreted or entirely disregarded. This assumption of control by the state had been brought about by various causes quite apart from the frequently disorderly nature of the meetings, and the large number of casualties involved ; though these were the ostensible reasons often given for the interdiction of all unauthorized gatherings of the kind. Much, however, depended on the character and temperament of the reigning monarch, and the condition of order or otherwise prevailing in the country at the time. At tournaments, whether held by royal licence or not, the combatants were divided into two camps or parties ; and they gathered together large concourses of spectators, who were too apt to become strong and eager partisans, as we see at the football games of to-day ; the unpopular side being sometimes assailed with volleys of stones, some discharged from slings. These meetings were thus frequently looked upon with disfavour by the powers that be, and were either entirely prohibited, or licences were refused in troublous times ; for the

---

[1] *Chronica Jocelini de Brakelonda, de rebus gestis Samsonis Abbatis Monasterii Sancti Edmundi.*
[2] See Appendix B.

assemblage of so many influential knights and powerful barons with their feudatories, coming from all parts of the kingdom, constituted a danger to the state in affording opportunities for cabals, sedition and other disorders, and, indeed, tumults frequently occurred. Tournaments were very popular in France during the reign of Philip Augustus; and Père Daniel relates an incident of that reign affording a striking example of the large gatherings that assembled. An unexpected attack having been made on the town of Alençon, the king was enabled to enrol a sufficient force at a tournament being held in the neighbourhood at the time to repel it. Jousting was not much practised in France at that time or during the thirteenth century, the cavaliers of that country preferring the *mêlée*.

In the year 1196 King Philip Augustus " sent vnto King Richard, requiring him to appoint fiue champions, and he would appoint other fiue for his part, which might fight in listes, for triall of all matters in controusee betwixt them, so to avoid the shedding of more guiltlesse bloud. King Richard accepted the offer, with the proviso that either King might be of the number, that is the French King one of the fiue vpon the French part; and King Richard one of the fiue vpon the English part. But this condition would not be granted."[1]

In the year 1250 " was a great tornie and iusts holden at Brackley, when the earle of Gloucester (contrarie to his accustomed manner) fauoured the part of the strangers, whereby they prevailed. In so much that William de Valance handled one Sir William de Odingesselles verie roughlie, the same Sir William being a right worthy knight."[2]

In 1251 King Henry III forbad the holding of a round table[3] and many examples of such prohibitions are given in *Foedera*. Yet, meetings of the kind were often held in England in spite of them, for the young cavaliers, imbued with the chivalrous spirit of the age, declined being balked of their favourite pastime and were willing to run some risks for its gratification. In the reign of Henry III the king admonishes his subjects "to offend not by tourneying," and, " by the advice of parliament enacted, that all who (without leave) should keep a tournament, should forfeit their estates, and their children to be disinherited."[4] As late as the reign of King Edward II an edict was issued against the

---

[1] Trivet. Cited by Holinshed. II, 263.   [2] Holinshed II, 418.
[3] Ashmolean MS. 860, 88. See Appendix A for catalogue of the Ashmolean MSS. relating to the tourney.   [4] *Horda Angel-cynnan* II, 91.

practice, the ordinance running " *Turneare, burdeare, justas facere, aventuras quaerere* "[1] Prohibitions against tournaments were issued in the years 1220, 1234, 1255 and 1299. In normal times, however, they were often encouraged by the crown, and were presided over, and even taken part in, by kings and princes. Matthew of Westminster states that it was customary for newly made knights to pass over to the Continent to show their mettle by feats of arms ; and that King Henry III knighted eighty gentlemen on one occasion, who all went abroad, accompanied by Prince Edward, to take part in tournaments.

In the early days of tournaments there were only five authorized lists (*champs clos*) in England, and they were all south of the Trent. At a later period these enclosures were usually placed in the neighbourhood of a large town where there was a hall spacious enough for the banquet and the dance ; the size of the lists being regulated by the number of cavaliers expected to take part. Those of the twelfth century were open at the sides, a barrier standing at each end ; later they were made quadrangular in shape, longer than broad by one-fourth. They were enclosed by a double row of palisading, high enough to make it impossible for a horse to leap over ; the space between the rows affording a place of refuge for the varlets (*ephebi*) and attendants. The *rôle* of the varlets was to rush in and steady their masters in the saddle, when swaying after their careers ; and, when unhorsed, to extricate and drag them, as opportunity offered, out of the press or from among the horse's hoofs in the *mêlée* ; for they were unable to help themselves in their heavy armour. This duty was both difficult and dangerous, but they had to manage as best they could. Openings were left at either end of the lists for entrance and exit, and movable barriers were provided for closing them when required. A thick covering of sand was strewn on the ground, or it was well mulched with tanning refuse so as to provide a soft bed for breaking the force of the fall of a cavalier when unseated. The lists were gaily decorated with tapestry, bunting and heraldic devices ; a tribune for the umpire or judge, and benches for the spectators, were provided ; as well as special galleries for the ladies, which were often adorned with gold and silver embroideries. Two pavilions were pitched for the use of the leaders, which were removed before the commencement of the tourney. The scene presented by a tournament must have been brilliant in the extreme ; and the element of danger involved

[1] Foedera III, 982.

would add greatly to the interest and excitement of the spectators. Permament lists were often surrounded by a ditch or moat. The marshals of the lists, kings of arms, heralds and pursuivants-at-arms were stationed within the enclosure to note the various incidents taking place among the combatants ; and it was the duty of the first-named to see that the rules of chivalry and general regulations were strictly observed. Trumpets announced the entry of each competitor, who was followed into the lists by his esquires ; and flourishes of music were heard at intervals to animate the combatants, and to mark special feats of gallantry. Each knight usually bore on his person some token of his lady-love, which was disposed on his helmet, lance or shield. The armour and horses of the vanquished fell as spoil to the victors, unless ransomed by payment in money ; this, however, was the case only in contests of courtesy. The jousting at a tournament usually ended with " *le coup ou la lance des Dames*," a homage to the fair sex joyfully rendered.

We have seen that blunted lances were in use in 1252, but we have not found any record of the coronal, a lance-head formed like a flattened crown (whence the name), before very early in the fourteenth century, when it appears on a picture in a MS. in the British Museum.[1] Cavaliers frequently successful in the tourney enriched themselves by the forfeiture of the horses and armour of the vanquished.

The routine of an early tournament is described in Codex 69 of the Harleian MS.[2] It is first proclaimed over a wide area ; and on assemblage the cavaliers, mounted on horseback, are divided into two parties or squadrons, the challengers and the challenged. Each troop usually varied in number from twelve to twenty, and was headed by its own leader ; the weapons were pointless swords with rebated edges. The two bodies then take up positions at opposite ends of the lists ; the onset is sounded, "*Lasseir les aler*," and they engage in combat until the signal is given to cease fighting. Various perquisites fall to the superintending Norroy King at Arms, and he and the heralds are paid their expenses and six crowns of " nail money " for affixing the cote-armour of the two leaders in front of their pavilions. An illustration on a MS. of the thirteenth century in the royal library[3] is reproduced in *Sports and Pastimes*. It pictures the entry on horseback of the two baron-leaders into the lists, wearing chain-mail and pointed bascinets,

[1] No. 14, E. III.   [2] See Appendix B.   [3] No. 14, E. III.

and with their horses trapped ; they bear no weapons. The King of Arms, in civil dress, is standing between them holding their banners, one in each hand. Trumpeters are seen in the background.

The presence of ladies graced the tournament, and they were treated with great deference : the names and deeds of the successful champions were submitted to them, and it was they who awarded and presented the prizes. The days of combat usually closed with the banquet and the dance. The tourney from the first was confined to men of noble birth, though this rule was not so strictly enforced in England as in Germany and France, where all not of the privileged class were strictly excluded.

The first mention we have found of prizes at tournaments is in 1279, when, at the Round Table held at Kenilworth in that year, the prize (a golden lion) was awarded to Sir Roger Mortimer ; but they do not seem to have become general until much later.

Henry III, on his marriage with Eleanor of Provence, in 1236, held a tournament for eight successive days ; and according to Matthew Paris, there was one at Northampton in 1247, and another at Nebridge in 1248.

The tournaments held during the reign of Richard I were frequently interdicted by the Church owing to the brutal character of many of them; and Jocelin of Brackelond tells the story of a number of knights who held one between Thetford and Bury St. Edmunds, in spite of the fiat of the abbot. Another took place soon after, which had also been prohibited ; and all who had taken part in it were excommunicated. Matthew Paris describes a tournament held at Rochester in 1251, at which foreigners contended with English knights. There was great bitterness at the time between some of the nationalities owing to very rough treatment that had been experienced by some English knights abroad; and all rules and regulations were thrown to the winds at Rochester, the proceedings degenerating there into a free fight. The English set upon the foreigners with staves, beating them severely, and chased them into the town, to which they fled for refuge. Another instance of this kind may be cited in an account given by Matthew of Westminster of a case in 1253, when the Earl of Gloucester and a companion took part in a tournament abroad, at which they were so roughly handled as to require fomentations and baths before they were in a condition to return to England. Trivet relates a further striking example in a case, lawless and brutal in its character, which received the name in history "*La petite Bataille de Chalôns*." Edward I, King of England, was travelling through France in the year 1274 on his way home from the Holy Land to take possession of the crown, when he was invited by the Count de Chalôns to take part in a tournament to be held in the open, near the town of Chalôns, with a certain number of his followers. At an early stage of the contest the Count, a knight of unusual strength, forcing his way through the *mêlée* attacked the King with great vigour and impetuosity ; and casting away his weapons threw his arms around King Edward's neck, hoping to unhorse him. The King, however, being a tall and powerful man kept his saddle, and at the moment of the greatest pressure cut fiercely at his adversary, dragged him from his horse and threw him heavily to the ground. The exasperation of the French cavaliers on seeing their leader fall was very great, and for a time a real battle ensued, in which the outside followers of both sides took an active part, the English using their terrible bows : but some degree of order having been at length restored the count surrendered to the King and acknowledged him to be the victor. After this tournament laying hands on an opponent was strictly forbidden. Thomas of Walsingham also gives a spirited account of this meeting, which runs on similar lines.[1]

At Whitsuntide in the year 1256 great jousting was held at Blei, when the Lord Edward, afterwards King Edward I, "first began to shew proofs of his chiualrie." In one of these encounters "William de Longspee was so brused that he could never after recover his former strength."[2]

"In the ninth year of King Edward's reign, the feast of the round table was kept at Warwike with great and sumptuous triumph."[3]

The Round Table assembled at Kenilworth by Sir Roger Mortimer has been already referred to in the section devoted to the Tabula Rotunda, and Hardyng in his *Chronicle*[4] thus pictures it :

> " And in the yere a thousand was full then
> Two hundred also sixty and nynetene,[5]
> When Sir Roger Mortimer so began
> At Kelyngworth, the round table as was sene,
> Of a thousand Knygts for dicipline,
> Of young menne, after he could devise
> Of Turnementes, and justes to exercise.

---

[1] *Historia Anglicana*, 1272–1422.　　　[2] Holinshed, II, 438.　　　[3] *Ibid*. II, 484.
[4] Chap. 155, fol. 161.　　　[5] *Anno* 1279.

" A Thousand Ladies, excellyng in beautee
He had also there, in tentes high above
The justes, that thei might well and clerely see
Who justed beste, there for their Lady Love
For whole beautie, it should the Knightes move
In armes so eche other to revie
To get a fame in play of Chivalry."

Hardyng died about the year 1465, nearly two centuries after the events he narrates.

The lance, or glaive as it is often called, of the eleventh and twelfth centuries[1] was quite straight and smooth ; a vamplate was added in the fourteenth, small at first but larger later, for the protection of the right arm. The lance for jousting was made of soft wood, so as to splinter easily.

A manuscript in the Record Office, transferred from the Tower about 1855, entitled *Emptiones facte per manum Adinetti Cissoris et visu Albini & Roberti de Dorset contra Torniamentum de Parco de Windsore, nono die Julii anno Sexto* (a Roll of Purchases made for the tournament held at Windsor Park in the year 1278), is copied in *Archæologia* of the year 1814.[2] This document is of rare value in giving particulars of the equipment of the cavaliers engaged in tournaments of the last quarter of the thirteenth century, besides mentioning other matters of interest. Thirty-eight cavaliers took part in the tournament at Windsor Park, twelve of the highest rank being styled *digniores*. Among these were the Earls of Cornwall, Gloucester, Warren, Lincoln, Pembroke and Richmond ;[3] and there were several foreign knights present. Many of the cavaliers whose names appear on the roll had been with King Edward in the Holy Land. Both arms and armour[4] were provided for the occasion for all the cavaliers taking part. Thirty-seven of the outfits ranged in cost from 7s. to 25s. each ; that for the Earl of Lincoln, however, was much higher than any of the others, being 33s. 4d. The equipments must thus have differed widely in quality and embellishment. The armours were of leather gilt, each suit consisting of a coat-of-fence (being a " quiretta "[5] of leather), brassards of buckram, a surcoat (the material for the majority of these garments being carda,[6] but those for the four earls were of cindon silk),

---

[1] The Bayeux tapestry shows one of the eleventh century.   [2] XVII, 297.
[3] John de Britannia.   [4] *Hernesium de Armis.*
[5] Cuirass.   [6] A kind of cloth.

a pair of ailettes, of leather and carda,[1] two crests (one for the man, the other for the horse), a shield of wood heraldically ensigned, a helm of leather, and a sword of whale-bone and parchment, silvered over. The shields of wood cost 5d. each, without emblazonment; the swords 7d. each, and 25s. was paid for silvering the blades, and 3s. 6d. for gilding the hilts. The helmets for the "*digniores*" were gilded at an expense of 12s., the others silvered. Each helmet cost 2s., and the ailettes 8d. the pair. Eight hundred little bells (*grelots*) were provided, to be used in necklets for the horses; sixteen skins for making bridles; twelve dozen silken cords for tying on the ailettes;[2] and seventy-six calf-skins for making crests. The cuirasses and helmets were made by Milo, the currier; and the cost of carriage for the whole of the sets from London was 3s. The sum total for all these outfits provided in England was £80 11s. 8d.; but some other purchases were made in France, and in the list are items for saddles and horse-furniture. There is no mention of lances, and many of the items scheduled are only open to conjecture. Sir Roger de Trumpington, whose effigy lies in Trumpington Church, Cambridgeshire, was among those taking part in the tournament. If one can imagine this passage of arms, its participants armed with swords of whalebone and parchment, with their arm-defences of buckram, it does not seem a very dangerous affair, though a rough enough sport.

There is another document of about the same period of the highest importance, viz. the *Statuta de Armis*, or *Statutum Armorum in Torniamentis*. This was drawn out at the request of the earls and barons of England and by the king's command, and affords much information as to the equipment for the tourney late in the thirteenth century, the usages to be observed, and the regulations as to the heralds, esquires, and varlets. There are several copies extant, one of which, and that perhaps the most reliable, may be seen in the Bodleian Library. Part of the text is reproduced by Hewitt in his invaluable work on

---

[1] Ailettes first appear in the second half of the thirteenth century and continued in fashion for about sixty years. They assume various forms, and were worn upright at the outsides of the shoulders, attached by laces. On brasses they appear at the backs of the shoulders, but this is probably for the reason that the artists found some practical difficulty in picturing them so as to appear as they were really worn. It is not clear whether these singular pieces were intended for defence or to be used as planes for the ensignment of heraldic devices; it is certain, however, that they could afford but little protection against a stroke from a sword or a battle-axe.

[2] Aiguillettes, or laces, later termed arming points, played an important part in the arming of a man, and were freely employed in fastening certain parts of his armour together. These points were also an important item in civil dress, and were usually of cord, silk, or leather.

ancient armour,[1] and the document is referred to in *Archæologia* of the year 1814.[2] These statutes provide that :—

No " conte," baron or other chevalier shall henceforth be attended by more than three armed esquires, who shall all bear the cognizance of their master.

No knight or esquire taking part in any tournament shall bear a pointed sword or dagger, a staff or baston, but only a broadsword for tourneying. All should be armed with " mustilers ; "[3] " quisers ; "[4] " espaulers ; "[5] and " bacyn,"[6] and no more.

If any " conte," baron or other chevalier break any of the rules of the tourney, he shall, with the assent and command of the Seigneurs, Sire Edward, fiz le Rey ; Sire Eumond, frère le Rey ; Sire William de Valence ; Sire Gilbt de Clare ; and Cunto Nichole,[7] lose horse and armour and be imprisoned at the discretion of the said court of honour, and all disputes shall be referred to it for settlement.

Any esquire to a knight breaking the regulations in any way should lose horse and armour and be imprisoned for three years ; and none was allowed to raise up a fallen knight but his own appointed esquire, bearing his device. Spectators were prohibited the wearing of armour or the carrying of arms. Etc.

May we see in the comparative mildness of these rules, and the control exercised by the court of honour, some results of King Edward's own dangerous experiences at the Chalôns tournament.

It is an interesting fact that the effigies of two of the members of this distinguished committee have been preserved, viz. : those of Edmund Crouchback, whose sword-belt is enriched with heraldic bearings ; and William de Valance. Both are in Westminster Abbey. The figure of the former wears the coif or hood of mail ; the body is covered by a surcoat with long sleeves and reaching nearly to the ankles ; but poleynes or knee-kops can be discerned. In the case of the other effigy the surcoat is sleeveless and shorter than the other, reaching down to just over the knees. Poleynes are present, but there are no coudes. A concave triangular shield hangs by the belt. Chain mail ; quilted stuffs,

---

[1] I, 366.   [2] XVII, 298.   [3] Probably a coat-of-fence.
[4] Cuisses.   [5] Shoulder-pieces.   [6] Bascinet.
[7] Edward, the King's son ; Edmund, the King's brother ; William de Valance, Earl of Pembroke ; Gilbert de Clare ; and the Earl of Lincoln. These five noblemen constituted a court of honour, a committee in fact for the control of the tourney. William de Valence died in 1296, so the document must date before that year.

often reinforced with rings or studs of iron, bone or horn ; ordinarily dressed leather and *cuir bouilli*, which is leather boiled or beaten—were all quite capable of resisting an ordinary sword-stroke or lance-thrust.

An effigy of the twelfth century in the Temple Church, London, that of Geoffrey de Mandeville, Earl of Essex, dating in the year 1144, in the reign of Stephen, exhibits the knight completely encased in mail, wearing a coif of mail of the same fabric, and over it is the tall cylindrical, flat-topped helm. It was found, however, that certain vital and more exposed parts of the body required further protection, for the mail, far from presenting a glancing surface towards the strokes and thrusts from weapons of attack rather afforded them a lodgment. The mail therefore became gradually reinforced over the most vulnerable places with pieces of leather or plates of iron until a full panoply of metal plating had been attained, a process which had not been quite completed before the first decade of the fifteenth century. The course of transition can best be followed by a study of brasses and effigies. The Crouchback and de Valence effigies show us that but little progress in the direction of plate armour had been made up to the end of the thirteenth century, though after that time the transition became rapid.

The usual knightly panoply was a coif of mail and beneath it a cap of cloth, worn in battle with or sometimes without a surmounting helm ; the tunic ; the gambeson or pourpoint, of quilted cloth ; the hauberk, of chain-mail ; the chaussons, which covered the upper part of the leg ; the chausses, the lower ; and the surcoat.

Chain-mail is probably a fabric of Eastern origin, consisting of forged iron rings, each ring interlinked with four others. This web must have been somewhat of a rarity even as late as the eleventh century, and, indeed, until the process of wire-drawing had been invented, owing to the laborious and costly nature of its manufacture. Each ring required to be cut from a long strip of wire, hammered-out from the solid, then interlinked, riveted, forged or butted together. The Romans employed chain-mail, as shown by the compressed masses which have been found, but whether it was interlinked in the manner just described is doubtful. Hauberks of quilted stuffs, reinforced with rings or studs of iron, bone or horn, were much in use; and so were those of ordinarily dressed leather; or of *cuir-bouilli*, which is leather prepared by boiling and beating. All these defences were quite capable of resisting an ordinary sword-stroke or lance-thrust.

The arming of the horse with a bard of chain-mail or its substitutes did not take place before the third quarter of the thirteenth century ; the trapper came into use somewhat earlier, though probably not painted or embroidered with heraldic bearings before the reign of Edward I.

CHAPTER III

THE fourteenth century was eminently a period of transition and development in arms, armour, jousts, tournaments, and, indeed, in everything that related to warfare. During its course chain-mail harness had been gradually replaced by iron plate, bit by bit ; a process hardly completed at the end. It was a century of almost incessant fighting among the nations, in the East as well as in the West ; and the knightly armour of the period in its advancing stages lies open as a book before us, in a study of our effigies and brasses.

An epoch-making detonating force had come into operation, which inaugurated a new era in the art of war. In its early days ordnance was greatly inferior in destructive power to most of the mechanical engines of the period, but by the end of the century it had developed to an extent which produced a revolution in the relative resources at command for attack and defence ; and the old chivalry became at length second in importance to the infantry arm.

Contemporary information regarding the jousts and tournaments of the earlier part of the fourteenth century is sparse ; they are described in the *Romances of Richard Cœur de Lion, Sir Ferumbras*, and others, which teem with improbabilities though still of the greatest value ; and there is a pictorial representation in *Roman du roy Meliadus* of " *Une Mêlée de Tornois*."[1] This romance, probably written about the middle of the century, contains several pictorial examples of jousts and tournaments, and a wealth of coloured and gilded drawings on military subjects generally ; while others are figured in the Froissart plates[2] Hefner's *Tratchten* and Carter's *Painting and Sculpture*. It is to Froissart that we are immeasurably most indebted for information regarding these martial games, more especially those of the second half of the fourteenth century, and his recitals contain much invaluable detail, which

---

[1] British Musium. MS. Addl. 12, 2228, fol. 181.
[2] The illustrated Frossart in the British Museum, Harl. MS. 4379, was produced late in the fifteenth century.

had been industriously collected from heralds, pursuivants, kings-of-arms and other officials at the tourney. Froissart was born about the year 1337, and he began to gather the material for his history when about twenty years of age, viz. eleven years after the battle of Crecy. *The Chronicles* commence with the coronation of Edward III, in 1337, and with the accession of Philip of Valois to the crown of France, and they close about the end of the century with the death of Richard II of England. At the beginning of his career Froissart was closely associated with the English court as a poet and historian, acting, indeed, as clerk to the closet to Queen Philippa, after which he entered the Church, becoming later canon of Chimay. His fine personal gifts soon placed him in excellent and confidential relations with many prominent and influential personages, both of France and England, able to give him reliable information for his history. His industry was remarkable, his style of writing both original and luminous, and his facts and narrations, though often marshalled with some confusion, are most reliable, so far at least as we can judge now. He was no extreme partisan, but tried, as he often says, whenever possible to hear both sides to a question. The weak place in his history is his dates and the lack of them. Sainte-Palaye says of him: " *Froissart, qui a mieux réussi qu'acun de nos historiens à peindre les mœurs de son siècle,* . . .

Royal jousts were often held in celebration of the coronations and weddings of princes ; and such were usually proclaimed in advance in in other countries of chivalry, so as to afford opportunities for the attendance of foreign cavaliers anxious to distinguish themselves ; and these were provided with safe-conducts by the crown.

In 1302 "Tournies, iustes, barriers, and other warlike exercises, which yovng lords and gentlemen had appointed to exercise for their pastime in diuerse parts of the realme, were forbidden by the kings proclamations sent downe to be published by the shirifs in euerie countie abroad in the realme : the teste of the writ was from Westminster the sixteenth of Julie."[1]

A tournament was proclaimed by the King of Bohemia and the Earl of Hainault, to be held at Condé in 1327, just after the coronation of Edward III ; and Sir John de Hainault, who had been present at the ceremony, left England to attend this tourney, accompanied by fifteen English knights, who intended taking part.[2]

[1] Holinshed, II, 536.   [2] Froissart (Johnes'), I, Chap. XLV.

Holinshed states that in September, 1330, the King (Ed. III) held jousts in Cheapside, when he with twelve challengers answered all comers. The meeting continued over three days, and no serious accidents took place.

A joust of the same year is figured in *Codex Balduini Trevirencis*. The cavaliers are seen jousting with lances tipped with coronals and with flat triangular shields, heraldically ensigned: they wear ample surcoats and the horses are trapped in cloth. The heaumes bear fan crests, the saddles are without supports; and the object in contemplation is the splintering of lances and unhorsing.

"Great iustes was kept by King Edward at the toune of Dunstable in 1341, with other counterfeited feats of warre, at the request of diuerse yovng lords and gentlemen, whereat both the king and queene were present, with the more part of the lords and ladies of the land."[1]

King Edward held a tournament in London in the middle of August, 1342; and had sent heralds into Flanders, Brabant and France to proclaim it. Froissart states that the eldest son of Viscount Beaumont[2] was killed at this tournament. Other chroniclers date this passage of arms in 1343.

To cry a tourney—"Cy sensuyt la façon des criz de Tournois et des Joustes. *Cy peut on à prendre à crier et à publier pour ceulx qui en seront dignes,*" etc. Ashmolean MS., No. 764, 31, 43.[3] On the reverse of the last leaf is a picture of a Joust, wherein two combatants on horseback, bearing their crests, are fighting with lances within the lists.

The Round Table held at Windsor on St. George's Day in 1344 has been referred to in the section devoted to the *Tabula Rotunda*. These hastiludes and jousts are mentioned by Froissart, who tells us that they were characterized by great splendour. The Queen was attended on the occasion by three hundred ladies, richly attired; while the King had a great array of earls and barons in his train. The "feast" was noble, with all good cheer and jousting, and lasted over fifteen days. Holinshed's account, under the year 1344, is as follows:—"Moreouer, about the beginning of the eighteenth yeare (?) of his reigne, King Edward held a solemne feast at his castell of Windsore, where betwixt Candlemasse and Lent, was atchiued manie martiall feasts, and iusts, and tornaments, and diuerse other the like warlike pastimes, at which were present manie

---

[1] Holinshed, II, 623.   [2] There were no viscounts in England then.   [3] Appendix A.

strangers of other lands, and in the end thereof, he deuised the order of the garter, and after established it, as it is to this daie. There are six and twentie companions or confrers of this felowship of that order, being called knights of the blew garter, and as one dieth or is depriued, an other is admitted into his place. The K. of England is euer chiefe of this order. They weare a blew robe or mantell, and a garter about their left leg, richlie wrought with gold and pretious stones, hauing this inscription in French vpon it, Honi soit qui mal y pense, Shame come to him who euill thinketh. This order is dedicated to S. George, as chéefe patrone of men of warre, and therefor euerie yeare doo the knights of the order kéepe solmne his feast, with manie noble ceremonies at the castell of Windsore, where King Edward founded a colledge of canons."[1]

Shortly after this round table the King issued letters patent for hastiludes and jousts to be held annually at Lincoln, over which the Earl of Derby was nominated as Captain by the King, the office to be retained by the earl during life-time, but after his death to become elective.

The "Feast of the Round Table" was again held at Windsor in 1345, and within a few years of it jousts took place at Northampton, Dunstable, Canterbury, Bury, Reading and Eltham, the exact years of which do not appear in the wardrobe accounts which have been preserved. In July, 1346, King Edward invaded France, and did not return to London until October, 1347, his home-coming being celebrated by jousts, tournaments, masques and other festivities.

A manuscript covering the expenses of the great wardrobe of Edward III from December, 1345, to January, 1349, now in the Public Record Office, is printed in *Archæologia* for the year 1846.[2] Some of the items scheduled cover robes for the person, which were delivered to certain of the knights taking part in a "round table" held by the King at Lichfield in 1348 or 1349, more probably the former year; viz. for the King's person and eleven knights of his chamber, these being Sir Walter Manny, John de L'Isle, Hugo Courtenay, John Gray, Robert de Ferrers, Richard de la Vache, Philip de Spencer, Roger de Beauchamp, Miles de Stapleton, Ralph de Ferrers and Robert de Mauley. To each of these knights two yards of blue cloth for coats and "three quarters and half a yard" of white cloth for hoods[3] was delivered.

---

[1] Holinshed, II, 628.

[2] Vol. XXXI, 26, in connection with "Observations on the Institution of the Order of the Garter," a paper by Sir Nicholas Harris Nicolas, G.C.M.G.

[3] The use of white hoods had its origin in an ancient custom of the town of Ghent (Froissart, V, XX).

Similar cloth was also issued to some of the other knights. The challengers, or *tenans*, of the round table consisted of the king and seventeen of his knights; their opponents, the *venans*, comprised fourteen knights, with the Earl of Lancaster at their head. An entry in the wardrobe accounts shows that King Edward wore a harness bearing the arms of Sir Thomas Bradeston on the occasion. Any further particulars of this round table, beyond the details of the robes for the banquet, are lacking. This tournament was celebrated with great pomp and magnificence.

A spirited verse from Chaucer's " Knight's Tale " follows :—[1]

> " The heraudes lefte hir prikyng up and doun ;
> Now ryngen trompes loude and clarioun ;
> Ther is namoore to seyn, but west and est
> In goon the speres ful sadly in arrest ;
> In gooth the sharpe spore into the syde.
> Ther seen men who kan juste and who kan ryde ;
> Ther shyveren shaftes upon sheeldes thikke ;
> He feeleth thurgh the herte-spoon the prikke.
> Up spryngen speres twenty foot on highte ;
> Out gooth the swerdes as the silver brighte ;
> The helmes they to-hewen and to-shrede,
> Out brest the blood with stierne stremes rede ;
> With myghty maces the bones they to-breste.
> He, thurgh the thikkeste of the throng gan threste,
> Ther, stomblen steedes stronge, and doun gooth al ;
> He, rolleth under foot as dooth a bal."

We see in the *Romance of Perceforest* how the ladies at a tournament tore off pieces of their apparel to be used as tokens or favours by their devoted knights, to an extent leaving them in a condition of dishabille. A knight often wore " a kerchief of pleasance " on his helmet, a token from his lady-love.

In 1358 " Roiall iustes were holden in Smithfield, at which were present the Kings of England, France and Scotland . . . of which the more part of the strangers were as their prisoners."[2]

" Moreouer, this year (1359) in the Rogation weeke was solemne iusts enterprised at London, for the maior and his foure and twentie brethern as challengers did appoint to ansuer all commers, in whose name and steed the King with his foure sonnes, Edward, Lionell, John and Edmund, and ninetéene other great lords ; in secret manner came and held the field with honor, to the great pleasure of the citizens that beheld the same."[3]

[1] A text by Alfred W. Pollard. 1898.   [2] Holinshed, II, 669.   [3] *Ibid.* II, 671.

" Moreouer this yeare (1362) the fiue first daies of Maie, were kept roiall iusts in Smithfield by London, the king and queene being present, with a great multitude of ladies and gentlemen of both the realms of England and France."[1]

Much detailed information concerning the jousting of the fourteenth century has fortunately been preserved in the records of the wars in France, some examples of which follow.

At the time when the siege of Tournay was raised by means of a truce, a tournament was held at Mons, at which Sir Gerard de Verchin, Seneschal of Hainault, was mortally wounded.[2]

Froissart states[3] that a combat took place before the walls of the town of Rennes in 1357, then being besieged by the English forces, between *a young knight-bachelor*,[4] Bertrand du Guesclin, and an English cavalier, Sir Nicholas Dagworth. The articles of combat provided for three courses with the lance, three strokes with the battle-axe and three thrusts with the dagger. These were all duly delivered, the knights bearing themselves right gallantly, without hurt to either of them. The fight was viewed with extreme interest by both armies.

So far Froissart. But there is some doubt whether it was Sir Nicholas Dagworth who was one of the principals in this duel; for in the *Histoire de Bretagne* it is stated that it was William de Blanchbourg, brother of the Governor of Fougerai, who was Sir Bertrand's opponent on the occasion, and that he was wounded and unhorsed. It is more probable, however, that both duels were fought, though the last-named combat was not likely to have taken place under the walls of Rennes, for both cavaliers were Frenchmen.

There is a singularly beautiful brass in the pavement of the south chapel of Blickling Church, Norfolk, in memory of Sir Nicholas Dagworth, who was a man of importance in the reigns of kings Edward III and Richard II. He lived until the year 1401,[5] and his will appears in *Testamenta Vetusta*. The brass is given in the Boutell Collection. It affords an excellent example of the armour prevailing at the end of the fourteenth century, when the evolution from chain-mail to full plate-armour had been almost completed. The helmet is the pointed bascinet, with the camail, the latter with an ornamental bordering coming over the top of the jupon. The cyclas, which has an

---

[1] Holinshed, II, 677.   [2] Froissart, I, 249.   [3] II, 374.   [4] The italics are ours.
[5] A Sir Thomas Dagworth was slain in France in 1350 (Holinshed, II, 651).

enriched fringing, hides the body-armour from view, and the knightly belt is elaborately decorated; the pouldrons are articulated. The gauntlets, with short cuffs, have gads over the fingers for use in the *mêlée*, and they show an imitation of finger-nails, and the solerets are freely articulated. The knight's head rests on his great helm, which has a mantling; and a wreath, surmounted by the crest, a griffin. The armour is enriched with chasing. The Arms—Erm, on a fesse, gu., three bezants : impaling Rosale, Cu., a fesse between six martlet's or.

The armour of the Black Prince in the Chapel of the Holy Trinity, at Canterbury Cathedral, affords an excellent illustration of the degree of progress reached in the last quarter of the fourteenth century. The process of evolution from chain-mail to plate is here almost completed, there being only small pieces of the former at the skirt, arms and insteps of the solerets. The Prince died in 1376, and the date of his effigy is somewhat later.

During a skirmish at Toury, in France, shortly before the death of King Charles V, in 1380, an esquire of Beauce, named Gauvain Micaille, enquired through an herald if any English gentleman would be willing to try a feat of arms with him—a joust of three courses, and the exchange of three blows with the battle-axe and of three thrusts with the dagger. The challenge was accepted by an English esquire, named Joachim Cator. The Frenchman received a severe wound in the thigh in the jousting, which was in contravention of the rules of the tourney; but the Englishman pleaded that it was an accident solely due to the restiveness of his horse; and this explanation was accepted by the umpire.[1]

An interesting tournament took place at Cambray in 1385 on the marriage of the Count d'Ostrevant to the daughter of Duke Philip of Burgundy. The ceremony was followed by a banquet at which the King of France was present as well as the Duke. The tournament was held in the market-place of the town, and forty knights took part, the King tilting with a knight of Hainault. The prize was a clasp of precious stones, taken from off the bosom of the Duchess of Burgundy; it was won by a knight of Hainault, Sir John Destrenne, and was formally presented by the Admiral of France and Sir Guy de la Trimouille.[2]

The number of courses run in jousting and the blows and strokes exchanged with battle-axes, swords and daggers at a meeting like that

---

[1] Froissart, V, Chap. XXXVIII. [2] Froissart (Johnes') VI, 378.

just described was usually three each; but they tended to increase as the century advanced, and five got to be a common number, and later as many as ten or even twelve. In the duel between Sir Thomas Harpenden and Messire Jean des Barres, at Montereau sur Yonne in 1387, they numbered " *cinq lances à cheval, cinq coups d'épée, cinq coups de dague et cinq coups de hache.*" The first four courses of the jousts were run with equal fortune, but in the fifth Sir Thomas was unhorsed and lay senseless on the ground; he revived, however, after a time, and all the strokes and blows were duly exchanged without further hurt to either knight. The King of France was present on the occasion.[1]

About this time, when the war between France and England was in full progress, there was much jousting with pointed lances between the knights and esquires of the two nations; safe-conducts being issued by the commanders on either side.

A meeting was arranged to take place near Nantes, under the auspices of the Constable of France and the Earl of Buckingham. The first encounter was a combat on foot, with sharp spears, in which one of the cavaliers was slightly wounded; the pair then ran three courses with the lance without further mishap. Next Sir John Ambreticourt of Hainault and Sir Tristram de la Jaille of Poitou advanced from the ranks and jousted three courses, without hurt. A duel followed between Edward Beauchamp, son of Sir Robert Beauchamp, and the bastard Clarius de Savoye. Clarius was much the stronger man of the two, and Beauchamp was unhorsed. The bastard then offered to fight another English champion, and an esquire named Jannequin Finchly came forward in answer to the call; the combat with swords and lances was very violent, but neither of the parties was hurt. Another encounter took place between John de Châtelmorant and Jannequin Clinton, in which the Englishman was unhorsed. Finally Châtelmorant fought with Sir William Farrington, the former receiving a dangerous wound in the thigh, for which the Englishman was greatly blamed, as being an infraction of the rules of the tourney; but an accident was pleaded as in the case of the duel between Gauvain Micaille and Joachim Cator. At this meeting the honours lay with the Frenchmen.[2]

Somewhat later a combat *à outrance*[3] took place at Chateau Josselin, near Vannes, between John Boucmel, a Frenchman, and Nicholas Clifford, in which Boucmel was struck on the upper part of the breast-

---

[1] Froissart, II, 756.   [2] *Ibid.* (Johnes') V, Chap. XLVII.   [3] Meaning here with pointed lances.

plate by his opponent's lance, which, glancing off, entered his neck through the camail and severed the jugular vein, killing him instantly.[1] A plate of Froissart's represents this duel as a combat on foot with long lances, taking place in a small quadrangular enclosure.

Juvenal des Ursins states[2] that at the marriage of Charles VI, of France, with Isabel (Isabeau) of Bavaria, 1385, jousts and grand fêtes took place in its honour. Sir Peter Courtenay came to France at the time with the object of accomplishing a feat of arms with the Seigneur de la Tremouille. The King's consent to the duel had been obtained, and the day and place were fixed for its accomplishment. The knights appeared in the lists on the day appointed in order to fulfil their engagement in presence of the King, who, however, at the last moment, owing to some remonstrances, forbade the combat: but a duel did take place at the time between an English knight and the Seigneur de Clery, in which the Englishman was wounded and unhorsed. This joust had been brought to the notice of the Duke of Burgundy, who said that the offence committed by a Frenchman in jousting with an enemy without the consent of his sovereign was worthy of death; his Majesty, however, at length pardoned the offender.

Froissart describes a realistic tournament, held at Paris during the wedding festivities, as between the Saracens under Saladin, and the Crusaders, led by Richard Cœur de Lion.

The feat of arms between Sir John Holland and Sir Reginald de Roye, a French chevalier of distinction, held at the town of Entença, before the King and Queen of Portugal and the Duke and Duchess of Lancaster, presents features of its own. The French knight sent an invitation to the Englishman entreating him to joust with him three courses with the lance, and to exchange the same number of strokes with the battle-axe, sword and dagger, for the love of his lady. The challenge was promptly accepted, and an answer returned by the herald, together with a safe-conduct for the Frenchman and his company. Sir Reginald arrived in due time at Entença, handsomely accompanied by six score knights and esquires. The meeting was held in a spacious close in the town, the ground well strewn with sand; and galleries had been erected for the accommodation of the royal and ducal parties, with other spectators. The jousting was to be with sharp lances, to be followed by a contest with sharp and well-tempered battle-axes, swords and daggers. The

---

[1] Froissart, V, XLVIII.   [2] *Histoire de Charles VI*, p. 368.

champions were well mounted and rode into the lists in full armour, taking up positions for their careers at either end of the lists, with the distance of a bow-shot between them. The signal for the onset having been sounded, the knights charged each other at the gallop, and Sir Reginald struck the bars of his opponent's visor so stoutly that his lance splintered on impact. Sir John Holland also struck the visor of his adversary well and fairly, but the helmet of the Frenchman, instead of having been securely laced to his body-armour as was usual, was only held by a single thong, and of course slipped off, leaving the knight bare-headed and Sir John's lance unbroken. The jousters then returned to their stations, and charged each other as before, and again the same thing happened, owing to the same cause. The English who were present regarded the unusual loose fastening of the helmet as a trick, but the umpire, the Duke of Lancaster, ruled that it was admissible for Sir John Holland to have employed the same artifice had he chosen to do so, and that therefore he could not decide against the French knight.[1] After the stipulated three courses with the lance had been run, the knights fought three rounds each with battle-axes swords and daggers, without either receiving a scratch. The French chevalier was adjudged to have had the advantage, though both had done well.[2]

In 1389 a deed of arms was performed at Bordeaux before the Duke of Lancaster, between five Englishmen and five Frenchmen : three courses with the lance, three courses with swords, and the same number with battle-axes. None was wounded, but one of the English knights killed the horse of a Frenchman with his lance, which greatly angered the Duke, who replaced the loss with one of his own chargers.[3]

The most prominent and accomplished jouster of his day was the Chevalier Jean Le Maingre, called De Boucicaut, Mareschal of France 1368–1421, and his *Mémoires*,[4] by an unknown author, contain descriptions of some of his exploits in the tilt-yard. One of these recitals[5] follows :—During the three years' truce between France and England, when King Charles VI was at Montpellier,[6] the French Seigneurs De Boucicaut, de Sampi and de Roye challenged all comers, being foreign knights and esquires, to joust five courses with lances, pointed or blunted, at their pleasure, at St. Ingelbert,[7] a place near

---

[1] This loose fastening of the helmet was a custom prevailing in Spain and Portugal.
[2] Froissart, VIII, Chap. XXXI.   [3] *Ibid.* IX, 336.   [4] *Le Livre des Faicts du Mareschal De Boucicaut.*
[5] Chap. XVII.   [6] About 1389.   [7] St. Inglevert.

Calais ; the *pas d'armes* (or the " *table-ronde*," as it is called in the *Chapitres d'Armes*, or articles of combat) to continue for thirty days. A great elm stood before the pavilions of the challengers, and hanging from its branches were two shields of wood, one of them plated with iron, " *l'un de paix, l'autre de guerre*," so that each venant on arriving at the rendezvous could signify his pleasure as to whether he elected to fight with pointed or rebated lances by striking with a wand the shield for peace or that for war. The arms and devices of the three tenans were painted above the two shields, so that each venant might be able to select his adversary among them, and a note blown on a horn proclaimed his choice. Each venant was to furnish the king-of-arms with his name and titles, and to bring another cavalier with him as his sponsor. The lists were richly decorated, the challengers handsomely apparelled ; and lavish hospitality was dispensed in a pavilion specially pitched for the purpose. Any arms, armour, or other requisites of which the venans might stand in need, were freely provided, the motto everywhere displayed being " Ce que vouldrez." The chronicle goes on to state that on the first day of the jousting, Jean de Holland, Earl of Huntingdon, half-brother to King Richard, signified his intention of jousting with Boucicaut. Both lances were fairly splintered in the first encounter, the second and third being fought with equal fortune ; but in the fourth the horse of the English knight fell with its rider, who was severely injured, his antagonist only retaining his seat by the prompt support of his varlets. Boucicaut then retired to his pavilion, but was not allowed to remain resting for long, for other English cavaliers desired to joust with him, and he disposed of two other knights the same day. While he was engaged in combat day after day, his fellow tenans were not idle, and the thirty days stipulated in the *Chapitres d'Armes* ran their course. Among other cavaliers from England taking part were Earl Marschal, the knights de Beaumont, Thomas de Perci, de Clifford and Courtenay, besides Sir John d'Ambreticourt and many Spanish and German cavaliers. Boucicaut is said to have gone through the whole thirty days of jousting without a scratch.

The rôle of the tenans at a *pas d'armes* was no sinecure, and for three knights to have held the *pas* for thirty days against all comers, as in this case, must have been an arduous undertaking ; and very dangerous also, more especially as much of the jousting was with pointed lances. No. XI of Froissart's plates professes to depict one of the jousts of this *pas d'armes*; but it pictures one at the tilt, so that the drawing is obviously of a later date than that of the Inglevert meeting, and was, in fact, executed in the reign of Edward IV, when the tilt was in common use. Froissart[1] gives a long and circumstantial account of this meeting, and states that it was very richly appointed. King Charles of France was present incognito, and had subscribed very handsomely towards the heavy expenses incurred.

Monkish chronicles, written in times not contemporaneous with the events they describe, are usually unreliable in being coloured with the circumstances of a later age ; and any illuminations or woodcuts accompanying them are apt to reflect the times in which they were executed, rather than those they are represented to portray, for the artist fills in his picture with the details of the scenes before him. However, with the accumulated knowledge we now possess, we are enabled to correct some of the mistakes, from a chronological point of view.

A royal tournament was held in London by King Richard II, immediately after the Michaelmas of the year 1390, in honour of Queen Isabella; and heralds were sent to proclaim it throughout England, Scotland, Hainault, Germany, Flanders and France. Sixty knights were to joust with rebated lances, as tenans, for two successive days, the Sunday and Monday, against all comers ; and the Tuesday following was set apart for the esquires. The jousting was to be followed by banquets, dances and sumptuous fêtes and entertainments of various kinds. The prizes for the Sunday were as follows :—A rich crown of gold for the best lance among the venans ; and, for the most successful among the tenans, a very rich golden clasp. Those for the Monday are not stated ; but for the Tuesday, the esquires' day, they were a handsome charger, fully accoutred, and a falcon, for the best lances of the venans and tenans, respectively. The ladies were to act as judges and to present them. The Sunday's jousting was called the feast of the challengers. At three p.m. the procession started from the Tower of London. Sixty barded chargers, an esquire mounted on each, advanced at a foot's pace ; then sixty ladies of rank richly apparelled and mounted on palfreys, rode in single file, each leading a knight, in full armour, by a silver chain. The procession thus formed proceeded along the streets of London, down Cheapside to Smithfield, attended by minstrels and trumpeters. The King and Queen, with their suites, accompanied by some of the great

---

[1] X, Chap. XI.

barons, had gone earlier to Smithfield, and there awaited the arrival of the procession and the knights from abroad. Their Majesties were lodged in the Bishop's palace, and there the banquets and dances were to be held. Many foreign knights and esquires attended, and among them Sir William of Hainault (Count d'Ostrevant)[1] and the Count de St. Pol.

On the arrival of the procession at Smithfield the knights mounted their horses and prepared for jousting, which began soon after. The prize for the best lance of the venans on the Sunday, the first day of jousting, was awarded by the ladies to the Count de St. Pol; and that for the most skilful knight among the tenans, to the Earl of Huntingdon.[2] The King led the tenans on the Monday; and the prize for the best lance of the venans was awarded to the Count d'Ostrevant; that for the most successful of their opponents to Sir Hugh Spencer. The esquires jousted on the Tuesday, after which there was a banquet, and dancing was continued until daybreak. There was jousting on the Wednesday for knights and esquires indiscriminately; and on Thursday and Friday fêtes, masques and banquets, after which the royal party left for Windsor.[3]

Caxton refers to these royal jousts in the following terms:—

" All of the King's hous were of one sute, theyr cotys, theyr armys, theyr sheldes and theyr trappours were embrowdred all with whyte hertis, with crownes of gold about their necks, and cheynes of gold hangyng thereon; whiche hertys were the King's leverey, that he gaf to lordes, ladyes, knyghtes, & squyers, to know his houshold peple from other; then four and twenty ladyes comynge to the justys, ladde[4] four and twenty lordes with chynes of gold, and alle in the same sute of hertes as is afore sayd, from the Tour on horsback thrurgh the cyte of London into Smythfeld." The narrative of this tournament by Holinshed[5] is far from being so picturesque as that of Froissart, and it differs in some particulars from it. He says there were twenty-four ladies, not sixty, mounted on palfreys; and that the prizes for the first day were awarded to the Comte de St. Pol and the Earl of Huntingdon; and on the Monday to the Earl of Ostravant and Sir Hugh Spencer.

King Richard proclaimed another grand tournament to be held at Windsor in one of the closing years of his reign; the tenans or challengers to be forty knights and forty esquires, clothed in green. The

[1] He was great-nephew of Queen Philippa of Hainault.
[2] Sir John Holland, afterwards Duke of Exeter.   [3] Froissart, X, XXI.
[4] Led.   [5] Chronicles, II, 810.

Queen was present, but very few of the barons attended, owing to the great unpopularity and arbitrary actions of the King,[1] whose reign had begun under the happiest auspices, but the manifest defects in his character brought his career to a sorrowful ending.

There was a kind of tourney called the *Espinette* held at Lille, in honour of a relic preserved there, which, though obscure, would seem to have been but an ordinary joust with which certain annual ceremonies were connected. Hewitt[2] quotes the *Chronicle of Flanders* concerning a celebration in the year 1339 :—"Jehan Bernier went to joust at the *Espinette*, taking with him four damsels, namely, the wife of Seigneur Jehan Biensemé, the wife of Symon du Gardin, the wife of Monseigneur Amoury de la Vingne, and mademoiselle his own wife. And the said Jehan Bernier was led into the lists by two of the aforesaid damsels by two golden cords, the other two carrying each a lance. And the King of the *Espinette* this year was Pierre de Courtray, who bore Sable, three golden Eagles with two heads and red beaks and feet." M. Leber gives some account of the *fête de l'épinette* in the *Collection des traités*.

The vamplate, *avant-plate*, placed on the shaft of the lance, for the protection of the right hand and arm, first appears in the fourteenth century ; and so does the lance-rest on the breastplate. An ordinance of the thirteenth century orders the lance to be blunted for the tourney ; but in the fourteenth it was ordered to be tipped with a coronal, the short points of which were just sufficient to catch on to the armour without being capable of piercing it. The helmet of the fourteenth century was the pointed bascinet, with the camail or hood of mail worn over the top of the cyclas. The great heaume used early in the fourteenth century differs little from that of the end of the thirteenth ; later it assumed the form of a cylinder, surmounted by a truncated cone. It was usually of iron, though sometimes of leather, either ordinary or of *cuir-bouilli*. The fan crest, doubtless adopted from a classic prototype, came into vogue in the last quarter of the thirteenth century, though it is represented on the seal of King Richard I.

Crests were made of various materials. Those for the cavaliers taking part in the tournament at Windsor Park, in 1278, were of calf-skin, one for the man and another for the horse, as shown in the Roll of Purchases; that of the Black Prince, at Canterbury,[3] was of cloth. They were attached to the helm by means of a thin iron bar. Crests were usually

---

[1] Froissart, XII, 104.   [2] *Ancient Armour and Weapons*, II, 340.   [3] Died 1376.

affixed to the great helm, which was worn over the bascinet; though there are instances of their being used alone on the smaller head-piece.

The heraldic crest does not appear before towards the close of the thirteenth century; a notable instance may be cited in the case of the remarkable effigy of Sir John de Botiler, in St. Bride's Church, Glamorganshire, which dates about the year 1300. The helmet of this monument is the cervellière, which is a visor-less, saucer or shallow basin-shaped head-piece, going over the hood of mail; and the crest is embossed on its front. Crests were not generally worn before about the end of the first quarter of the fourteenth century, after which period they develop from comparative simplicity into fantastic and even ridiculous conceptions.

A strange fancy was the cap-of-maintenance, the placing of a cap of velvet or other material on the helm, surmounted by the family crest; and in the second half of the century or a little later the orle or wreath and mantling or lambrequin are added.

The shield of the century was of the triangular kite or heater-shaped form.

In 1390 "John de Hastings earle of Pembroke, as he was practising to learne to ioust, thrugh mishap was striken about the priuie parts, by a knight called Sir John S. John, that ran against him, so as his inner parts being perished, death presentlie followed."[1]

In 1398 the Earl of Crawford, of Scotland, jousted *à outrance*, i.e. with sharp lances, with Lord Wells of England at London Bridge, the 23rd April, being the feast day of St. George. An attaint was made in the first course, and both champions kept their seats. The Earl sat so steadfast in his saddle under the shock that the by-standers cried out that he was locked to his seat, on hearing which he jumped off his horse and then vaulted back into his saddle again with such agility as greatly to astonish the people. In the second course they met again as before without either being hurt; but in the third Lord Wells "was borne out of the saddle and sore hurt with a grieuous fall."

Not long after a duel on horseback took place in Scotland between Sir Robert Morley, an Englishman, and Sir Archibald Edmounston, and afterwards with another Scot Hugh Wallace, and the first-named was the victor in both cases; but he was at length overcome by one Hugh Traill, at Berwick, and died shortly after from chagrin.[2]

[1] Holinshed, II, 800.   [2] *Ibid*. V, 443.

CHAPTER IV

THE fifteenth century marks a very distinct epoch in the history of the tourney, which became milder and less dangerous to life and limb ; and during its course a stricter observance than hitherto of the rules, regulations and limitations prescribed were progressively more strictly enforced, and their infringement subjected the offenders to severe and sometimes degrading penalties. An oath to observe the rules of chivalry was administered to all cavaliers taking part in the tournament.

Body-armour had proved inadequate to resist the then weapons of attack, and at the commencement of the century, or perhaps a couple of decades earlier, the armour-smith was especially directing his attention towards the strengthening of the knightly harness. The chief seat of the industry for the greater part of the century was at Milan, at which city armour was forged of such strength as to be capable of resisting thrusts with the lance and strokes from the terrible battle-axe, sword and mace practically without fracture ; and one meets with references in English and other records to orders being sent to Milan for harnesses of proof, a civil garment being forwarded to indicate the stature and build of the person, since ill-fitting suits would be apt to chafe the wearers. But, while the best and most costly harnesses came from Italy, less expensive equipments were imported into England from Germany ; for " *ostling* " (Easterling) armour is sometimes mentioned in English articles of combat, and it was probably obtained through the agency of the Hanseatic Confederation from their London depôt, the Steelyard, then situated in what is now Lower Thames Street, London. The cost of carriage also would be much less from Germany.

The great armour-smiths of Milan at the period immediately under review were members of the Missaglia Negroli family, which, like many others, carried on their craft for several generations. The Germans have always been wont to borrow the inventions and processes of other nations, and then often to cheapen them ; and so it was with body-armour. They gradually succeeded, under the personal inspiration and direction of the Emperor Maximilian, in transferring the bulk of that industry, even in the best harnesses, to German soil, until at length cities like Nuremberg and Augsburg became the chief seats of the manufacture; and indeed the bulk of the armours preserved to us of the later "Gothic" and "Maximilian" styles are of German make. That Maximilian engaged armour-smiths from Italy is seen by a contract made in 1494[1] with the Milan armourers Gabrielle and Francesco de Merate, to erect and equip for him a smithy in the town of Arbois, in Burgundy, to forge there a certain number of harnesses at fixed prices. The armour worn by Maximilian I at Worms, in 1495, in a combat on foot with the Burgundian, Claude de Vaudrey, bears the stamp "m,e,r," surmounted by a crown, the Milan mark of these smiths, who came next in celebrity to the Missaglias.

Many ameliorations were conceived in the fifteenth century with a view to further minimizing the risk of serious accidents, and one of the most far-reaching and important was the application of the tilt in jousting. Many injuries had befallen the riders in the tourney by the collision of their horses, sometimes by accident, at others by design, and the idea of the tilt was conceived greatly with a view towards obviating this danger. The tilt, or *toile*, was at first a rope hung with cloth, stretched along the middle of the lists, but later it became a barrier of planks, along which the tilters charged in opposite directions, their bridle-arms towards it, their lances held in rest in their right hands on the tilt side of the horse's neck, striking the polished, glancing surface of their adversary's armour at an angle. The tilt had the advantge of lending a fixed direction to the jousters in their careers, though they often failed to touch each other. With the danger of these collisions removed, the knight ran his course with but little risk.

Jousting in the open with pointed lances was, however, continued by a hardier type of jousters until long after the introduction of the tilt; and here the saddle was without cantle, so as to offer no impediment to unhorsing; and a cushion or mattress, stuffed with straw, was placed over the chests of the horses, to act as a buffer in case of collision. A rough game it was for a cavalier to be unseated and thrown to the ground in his heavy armour, sometimes carrying a weight of two

---

[1] Referred to by Wendelin Boeheim in *Meister der Waffenschmeidekunst*, Chap. LVII.

hundred pounds ; though his fall was broken by the ground of the lists being covered with thickly strewn sand or mulched with refuse from the tan-yard. This form was much practised in Germany, though strange to say but little harm would seem to have been experienced by the champions in their falls, greatly owing to the extensive padding of their harnesses. Other important departures in the direction of comparative safety were the designing of special forms of armour for the tilt-yard, and the introduction of additional or reinforcing pieces, for doubly protecting those parts of the body on which the brunt of the attack fell, viz. mainly on the left side. They first appear in England in the reign of Edward IV. " William Lord Bergavenny bequeathed to his son the best sword and harness for justs of peace and that which belong to war."

The vamplate of this century was much enlarged, for the protection of the lance-arm ; and the steels of the saddles lent great protection to the bodies of the jousters below the breast. The effect of all this was to encase those taking part in the tourney in an almost impenetrable shell, from which they could barely see or do more than couch and aim their lances.

Armour for the lists became sharply divided from that employed for " hoasting " purposes, as harnesses for the field were called, though in what country the change had its origin, whether in Burgundy, Italy or Germany, is uncertain. It was in use in Burgundy in the year 1443, for we read in the account given in *Mémoires D'Olivier De La Marche*,[1] that during the time the necessary preparations were being made for the tournament held at L'Arbre de Charlemagne, Dijon, in that year, the young cavaliers practised jousting before the duke "*et là furent faictes une jouste à selles plattes et en harnois de joûte.*"

Harnesses for the lists assume different forms in Germany from those in Italy. In the first-named country in the case of the armour for jousting in the open, so to speak, the breastplate was flattened on the right side for better couching and aiming the lance, which was supported by a *Rasthaken* or queue behind, as well as by a lance-rest in front, while in Italy the cuirass continued rounded in form. The lance-rest (*Rüsthaken*) assumed various forms, though usually that of a curved bracket. Reinforcing pieces were employed in all courses.

There is another variety of armour which was used in *Scharfrennen*,[2]

---

[1] Chap. VIII, p. 380.   [2] Running with sharp lances.

but it, with the others, will be particularly described and illustrated later on. Jousting at the tilt prevailed greatly in England, though abroad many other varieties were practised as well. Jousting lances were often painted or ornamented with party-coloured puffs of cloth along their length. Lance-heads assumed various forms, examples of which may be seen in several of the German museums and in the Tower of London. Illustrations are given by Boeheim.[1] The shafts varied in form, weight and thickness for the different courses.

The armour for combats on foot was made very strong and heavy, and so padded with under-clothing as to cause faintings and even deaths in hot weather. Foot-fighting was rendered much safer by the introduction of "barriers," over which the champions fought, but they do not appear much before the sixteenth century.

The physical strain on those taking part in a tournament must have been great, and the combatants weary at the end of a long day; nevertheless they joined the ladies in the evening, when the successful competitors received the prizes from their hands; and after the banquet came the dance.

The century saw the mingling of the tourney with the pageant; the *mêlée* had been much supplanted by the joust, which demanded more individual skill, for in the throng and confusion of the *mêlée* the element of chance helped certain of the combatants to a distinction beyond their real deserts; while in the joust, which was a contest between two champions only, each had to stand or fall solely on his own merits.

A favourite form of the tourney of the fifteenth century was the *Kolbenturnier* or baston course, which differed essentially from all the others in that no personal injury was intended in the contest, the object being to batter off the crest which decorated the helm of an adversary; and it was thus purely a game or trial of skill. The weapon employed was a *Kolben*, a heavy polygonally-cut baston or mace of hard wood, about 80 cm. in length. The *Kolben* swells out along its shaft to an obtuse point, has a round pommel, short grip, and a rondel-guard of iron. There is an illustration of this weapon in the *Tourney-book of René d'Anjou*. The helm, a huge, globose form of bascinet, was latticed over the face with strong iron bars, and screwed to the cuirass back and front; it was thickly lined inside and roomy enough to prevent

[1] *Waffenkunde*, p. 551.

any injury which might be caused by the heavy blows exchanged. It was covered outside with leather and painted with various devices. A fine example of this type of helm is at Dresden, and Boeheim in *Waffenkunde*,[1] figures one of them in the Collection Mayerfisch at Sigmaringen. The saddle was the high one, known as the *Sattel im hohen Zeug;* an example, of the second half of the fifteenth century, is in the Germanische National Museum at Nuremburg. The *Kolbenturnier* ceased being run about the end of the first quarter of the sixteenth century. It was at first practised on foot, and doubtless grew out of the Judicial combats with the baston of the lower classes. Boeheim in *Waffenkunde*[2] illustrates Duke Georg of Bayern-Zandshut, at Heidelberg, armed for a *Kolbenturnier* in 1482: from Hans Burgmaior's *Turnierbuch*, in possession of the Prince of Hohenzollern-Sigmaringen.

The crests of the fifteenth century are most fanciful and fantastic, such as a crowned unicorn or the tail of a fox; many examples may be seen in the tourney-book of King René, the Beauchamp pageants, the German tourney books, and other works of the kind; and René describes their construction very fully. They are fragile and made greatly of the same materials as those of the century preceding, though oftener of *cuir-bouilli*, which substance was more substantial and enduring. The tapestry at Valenciennes, which pictures a *mêlée* of the fifteenth century, shows numerous fragments of crests lying on the ground under the hoofs of the horses. The knights prized their crests greatly; and they were often buried with them. They were fixed in position by an iron bar or brooch; an example of the latter may be seen at the Musée d'Artillerie, Paris. Sometimes the horse was also provided with a crest, as in the tournament at Windsor Park in 1278.

The hours during which *fêtes d'armes* took place show that the lists were frequently artificially lighted, and, indeed, torches and flambeaux are sometimes mentioned.

Tournaments held at the royal and princely courts of the countries of chivalry were strictly games, the hosts often challenging their guests to trials of skill; and some correspondence preserved of the fifteenth and sixteenth centuries, between German princes, shows what a great part these martial sports played in the routine of their daily lives; second only, if even that, to the chase. Kurfürst Albrecht von Brandenburg, writing to a friend in the last quarter of the century, says:—"*Wir sind*

[1] Fig. 612.   [2] Fig. 615.

yor mit gots hilff die fordersten im Turnier gewesen und gedenkens aber zu bleiben.[1] Maximilian, writing, at the age of nineteen, to Sigmund Pruschenk, remarks:—"*Ich hab das pest gethan, wann ich hab VIII stechholz zerstossen.*"[2]

Much depended on the docility and training of the chargers, which were often ridden blindfolded, and they were sometimes influenced by a spirit of combat like their riders. The bodies of the horses were padded and covered by the trapper, which fell down almost to the ground, considerably hampering their motions ; a mattress of straw, crescent-formed, protected their chests ;[3] their ears were sometimes stopped with wool or oakum ; the head and tail frequently decorated with feathers ; and the animals advanced towards each other at a hand-gallop. The rowel-spurs had long necks. Each variety of joust had its own special type of saddle, devised with the object of making unhorsing either difficult or easy as the case might be. These saddles will be described in their order. Each prince or man of rank and fortune kept a considerable number of horses continually in practice ; and the correspondence of the times reveals many requests for their loan.

It was at the courts of Aix and Burgundy where for long the tourney was much fostered ; and at both it may be said to have been reduced almost to a science. At the first-named court it was much a matter of amusement, emulation and relaxation ; while in the latter, then the most brilliant in Europe, it was greatly the policy of the sovereign to encourage tournaments and fêtes of all kinds. They kept the leaders of the armies and the chevaliers generally in close touch with the head of the state and the country, besides providing gladiatorial spectacles for the duke's somewhat restless and discontented subjects, who were often smarting under heavy imposts to provide him with the means for constant schemes of aggression and a profuse display, and who were frequently in a state of revolt. After the tragic death of Charles the Bold, the jousting traditions of the court of Burgundy passed over to that of Maximilian of Austria, who would seem to have made successful jousting one of the great objects of his life.

There is perhaps necessarily a certain degree of monotony and repetition in the narrations of the chroniclers of the joust and tourney,

---

[1] With God's help we are foremost in the tourney, and intend to continue so. (*Zeitschrift für historische Waffenkunde*, II, 66.)

[2] I have done my best when I have broken eight lances. (Boeheim's *Waffenkunde*, p. 554.)

[3] One is figured by King René ; another by Boeheim.

but they convey collectively a much clearer idea of these encounters than a mere bald statement of the leading facts could do, and they reflect the chivalrous spirit of the times in the incessant craving of the young cavaliers for notoriety and distinction in the tilt-yard. Many examples of jousts and *pas d'armes* of the fifteenth century are given in the *Chronique de Monstrelet*, the *Mémoires de la Marche*, and *Chastelain's Cronique Jacques de Lalain*. The *Chronicle of Euguerrand de Monstrelet*, with its somewhat irregular continuations by de Couci and others, commences where that of Froissart leaves off, viz. in the year 1400; and it has the advantage of being for the most part contemporaneous in regard to the events it narrates. Monstrelet's style of writing is less sprightly and more monotonous than that of Froissart; but he gives dates to his recitals, which, however, leave much to be desired on the score of accuracy. The names of personages and even towns given in the *Chronicles* are most perplexing, being frequently so distorted as to make identification an impossibility. Like Froissart, Monstrelet does not confine himself to the events of the period under review in France and Burgundy, but deals also with those of other countries in relation to them. The *Chronicles*, which really amount to a history, afford a good insight into the subject of the jousts and tourneys of the times; and Monstrelet states that his information was carefully collected from heralds, kings-of-arms and other officials of the lists. Monstrelet was born about 1390 and died in 1453.

The Bibliothèque de Bourgogne in the National Library at Brussels possesses many illuminations of the reign of Philip the Good and Charles the Bold; and there are also several in the Paris Collection and particularly in the *Armorial de la Toison d'Or*.

An Ashmolean MS., No. 1116, ff. 137b-86, gives the names and arms of the sovereigns and knights of the Order of the Golden Fleece (Toison d'Or) from its institution in 1429 to the twenty-third festival of the Order, which was held by Philip II, King of Spain, 12 Aug. 1559; it gives historical accounts of the celebration of the feasts. The MS., which is in French, is beautifully written, with the arms tricked. Other MSS. in the same Collection, 139-66, 167-75b, of the year 1431, give the statutes and ordinances of the Order.

Appendix A furnishes an abstract of all the Ashmolean MSS. relating to the tourney, for reference by our readers.

The Mémoires D'Olivier De La Marche teem with spirited descriptions of numerous *fêtes d'armes* held at the Burgundian court during the reign of Duke Philippe le Bon, which are full of detail ; and several of them bear the impress of having been written by an actual eye-witness, with ample opportunities for getting information, and with a sufficiency of technical knowledge for placing the scope and minutiæ of the encounters accurately and vividly before us. They also afford invaluable details of the costumes of the period, giving minute particulars of the dresses, and all matters connected with the lists. The Seigneur de la Marche was a Burgundian, born about 1425 ; he was appointed a page to his master the Duke in 1447, and was dubbed chevalier after the battle of Montlehéry. He distinguished himself before Ghent in 1452, was appointed a commissionary to the forces in 1456, was made a prisoner at Nancy in 1476, and died in 1502. The Mémoires cover a period of about fifty-three years, and form a very valuable contribution to the history of the tourney. They were first published in 1562.[1] Jean de Féore, Seigneur de St. Remy, describes some of the *pas d'armes* of the century ; and the *Traité de Tournois*, by Louis de Bruges, written in the reign of Charles VIII, of France, deals with others of a later period. The Beauchamp Peageants[2] afford some excellent illustrations of jousts and combats on foot and on horseback. They are reproduced in the *History of the Life and Acts of Richard Beauchamp, Earl of Warwick*, by John Rouse, the Warwickshire antiquary and historian, who died on the 14th of February, 1491, the seventh year of Henry VII. Earl Richard was born in 1381 and died in 1439. Hefner's plates, Nos. 109 and 138, also picture jousts and tourneys of this period.

The Romance of Petit Jehan de Saintré,[3] written in 1459, by Antoine de la Sale, contains fifteen large and fine illustrations of jousts, combats on foot, etc., which, as far as we can judge, fairly represent such knightly encounters of the period. Hewitt[4] mentions the equipments and colours, as shown on fol. 39 : "*Near Knight.*—Armour, iron-colour ; feet, black ; crest, red flower with gold leaves ; saddle, bridle, and stirrup-leather, red ; trapper, blue, marked with darker blue and lined with white fur. *Far Knight.*—Armour and feet as before ; crest, gold with red feathers ; saddle, buff ; trapper, dark with black markings ; bells, gold. Chanfreins both ridged and spiked, gold ; the rest iron. The barrier is red and marked with a deeper red. It will be observed

---

[1] The edition used here is that among *Collection Des Mémoires pour servir A L'Histoire De France.*
[2] Cotton. MS., Julius, E. IV.　　[3] Cotton. MS., Nero, D. IX.　　[4] *Ancient Armour*, III, 509.

that, except the helm, the whole armour differs in nothing from the usual war suit." The *Mémoires of the Sire de Haynin*[1] afford some interesting details in connection with *pas d'armes*.

The rules of the tourney promulgated by René d'Anjou, King of Naples, Sicily and Jerusalem, and Duke of Lorraine, in *Tournois du Roi René*, are most important. They contain many restrictions in the use of weapons, and all tend towards restraining the violence and disorder which had hitherto prevailed, and towards rendering these warlike games less dangerous ; and they inculcate a spirit of chivalry, thus doing away greatly with much of the brutality of the former age. René thought lances too cumbersome for the tourney, and considered the proper weapons to be rebated swords and maces. The famous duel between the dukes of Brittany and Bourbon is described. But little jousting took place at Aix, the *mêlée* being preferred. There are several splendid manuscrips of the King's writings extant, four of them at Paris, illuminated by the King himself, and they go into the minutest details of all which concern the tourney as practised at Aix.

"The Ordinaunce, statutes and rules made by John Lord Typtoft, Erle of Worcester, Counstable of England by the Kinges commaundment, at Windsor the 29 of May ao sixto Edwardi quarti (1466), to be observed and kepte in all manner of Justes of pees royall with in this realme of England."[2]

There are several copies of the rules extant. The version here given, in an abridged form, is taken from the *Antiquarian Repertory*. It was copied from a MS. M. 61 in the Herald's College.[3]

Another copy may be seen in *Nugae Antiquae*, by Park, which is referred to in *Archæologia*, for the year 1813.[4] They are also printed in Dr. Meyrick's *Critical Essay on Antient Armor*, III, 179-86, with valuable notes from the MS. M. 6, in the Herald's College.

These rules run :—

"Firste, whoso breaketh most speares, as they ought to be broken, shall have the price.
Item, whoso hitteth thre tymes in the heaulme, shall have the price.
Item, whoso meteth two tymes coronoll to coronoll, shall have the price.
Item, whoso beareth a man downe with stroke of speare, shall have the price.

For the price.
Firste, whoso beareth a man downe owte of the saddell, or putteth him to earthe, horse and man, shall have the price, before him that striketh coronoll to coronoll two times.

---

[1] Société de Bibliophiles Belges. Mons. 1842.
[2] Ashmolean MS. 148–9. See Appendices A and B.   [3] Marked I, 26   [4] Vol. XVII, p. 290.

Item, he that striketh coronoll to coronoll two tymes, shall have the price before him that strike the sight thre tymes.

Item, he that striketh the sight thre tymes, shall have the price before him that breake the moste speares.

Item, yf there be any man that fortunetly in this wise shalbe deemed he bode longest in the feeld heaulmed, and ranne the fairest course, and gave the greatest strokes, helpinge himself best with his speare."

How prices shalbe loste.

First. Whosoe striketh a horse, shall not have the price.

Second. Whosoe striketh a mannes backe, turned or disarmed of his speare, shall have no price.

Third. Who hitteth the toyle, or tilte 3 times, shall have no price.

Fourth. Whosoe unhelmes himselfe 2 times, shall have no price, without his horse faile him.

How speares shall be allowed.

First. Whoso breaketh a speare betweene the saddle, and the charnell of the helme, shall be allowed one.

Whoso breaketh a speare from the charnell vpwards, shall be allowed one.

Whoso breaketh and putteth his aduersary downe, and out of the saddle, or disarmeth him in such wise, as he may not runne the next course after, shall be allowed three speares broken.

How Speares broken be disallowed.

First. Who breaketh a speare on the sadle, shall be disallowed for a speare broken.

Second. Who hitts the tilt or toile once, shall be disallowed for 2 speares broken.

Third. Whosoe hitts the tilt twice shal be for the two times abated, for 3 speares broken.

Fourth. Whosoe breaketh a speare within a foot of the crownall (coronal), shall be judged as no speare broken, but a good attaynte."

A few short rules follow for the *mêlée* and barriers.

There is much confusion in the nomenclature employed by chroniclers in their descriptions of these chivalric war-games, and the terms " *tournois*," " tourney," " joustes " or " *joûtes* " and " *pas d'armes*," are often confounded with each other, all or any being sometimes, used in a general sense to cover various forms of jousting and the tourney : and such meetings often received the general appellation of *fêtes d'armes*. In a contemporary recital of the meeting in 1559, at which Henry II of France received his fatal wound, the terms " *joûtes*," " *tournois* " and *pas d'armes* are all employed to express the proceedings as a whole. The term " tourney " is very frequently used to denote the *mêlée*.

A *pas d'armes* or passage of arms usually covered a variety of martial exercises. It was open to all comers, being knights and esquires qualified to take part, who were invited by proclamation to attend. The field was held by a certain number of challengers, called " *les tenans*," or holders of the *pas ;* while the attacking cavaliers were known as " *les venans*," or comers, who came to try and wrest the *pas* from them. A *pas d'armes* was also an imitation of an operation of war, a *Scharmützel*, in the attack and defence of a supposed position of strength, such as a pasteboard bridge-head, a castle of wood or the assumed gate to a town ; the contest being waged with all the ardour of real warfare, though tempered by certain rules, pretences and limitations. The term *pas d'armes* is comprehensive, for besides jousting and strokes with the sword, etc., such meetings often included combats on foot ; and, after the middle of the fifteenth century, contests on horseback with the baston or mace ; and they often concluded with the tourney proper or *mêlée*, troop against troop.

In the *Antiquarian Repertory*[1] is the following account of a *pas d'armes* held about the end of the fifteenth century :—

"The king assigns to four maidens of his court the umpireship of the castle called 'Loyall'; for the attack and defence of which they are to arrange as they may collectively decide upon. The castle is a mock fortress, representing one which had been subjected to a remarkable siege in history. The ladies confide its guard and custody to a captain and fifteen cavaliers to defend the 'pas' against all comers. A unicorn is placed within the lists, the four legs of which support as many shields, coloured white, red, yellow and blue respectively. The first shield signifies the opening jousts at the tilt, to be run in 'hoasting' armour, with double or reinforcing pieces ; the second shield denotes that in the tourney which follows the jousting twelve strokes with the sword are to be exchanged ; the third a combat on foot at barriers, the same number of strokes with one-handed swords ; the fourth, the defence and assault of the castle, with swords, shields and morris-pikes. The points and edges of all the weapons employed in the four sections to be rebated, only the foyne[2] excepted. Any cavalier, except the leader of either side, if taken prisoner, may be ransomed with three yards of satin, but captains must pay the cost of thirteen yards for their freedom. The *pas d'armes* to continue from the 27th November to New Year's Day. The hours, after the first day, from one in the afternoon to seven in the evening."[3]

Other clauses in the *Chapitres d'Armes* are :—

"Item. Yt shalbe lawfull for the assaulters to devise all manner of engynes for the wynenge of the said castell ; engyn or tole to breake the ground or howse with all only excepted.

Item. None do meddell with fier neyther within or without but to fire their gunnes.

Item. If any man be disarmed, he maye withdrawne him-selfe if he will ; but once past the barres, he may not com agayne into the torney for that daye. Also there shall no man have his servant within the barres with any peace of harnois, for no man shalbe within the said barres but such as shalbe assigned by the king's grace.

Item. Who shall beste demeane him-selfe at thee same arte of armes, shall have a sword, garnished, to the valew of three hundred crownes or under.

Item. If any man strike a horse with his speare, he shalbe put out of the torny withowt any favour ; and if any slaye an horse, he shall paye to the owner of the said horse an hundred crownes in recompence ; also yt is not to be thought that any man will slaye an horse willingly ; for if he do it, it shall be to his great dishonor.

---

[1] Vol. I, 146.   [2] The estoc.
[3] The lists must thus have been artificially lighted.

Item.   He that uses a close gauntlet (a locking or forbiden gauntlet) shall win no prize.[1]
Item.   He that his sword falleth owt of his hand, shal win no prize."

The gaining of prizes in jousting was settled as a rule by a counting of points, for and against, and they were usually :—

Breaking a lance fairly on the body of an adversary, below the helmet, 1 point ; above the breast, 2 points ; unhorsing, 3 points. Points would be lost by striking the saddle or the tilt. A lance should be splintered more than a foot above the head.

The long wars between France and England had engendered much hatred and bitterness between the nations, and frequent combats in the lists, *à outrance*, continued to take place between the respective cavaliers, many of which fights were characterized by great violence and ruthlessness. Matters at length got to such a pass that in the year 1409 the French King issued an ordinance against all such combats between cavaliers of the two nations.[2] Certain combats, however, continued to take place under royal licence.

In the year 1400 by advice of the Earl of Huntingdon, "solemne iusts were to be enterprised between him and 20 on his part, and the earle of Salisburie and 20 with him, at Oxford." This was a conspiracy for the assassination of King Henry IV, but the plot miscarried.[3]

In the year 1400 Michel d'Oris, an esquire of Arragon, sent to Calais, by a pursuivant-at-arms, a challenge to a deed of arms, addressed to the Cavaliers of England, in the following terms :—

"Au nom de Dieu, et de la benoite vierge Marie, de saint Michel et de saint George, je, Michel d'Oris, pour mon nom exhausser, sachant certainement la renommée des prouesses de chevalerie d'Angleterre, ai, au jour de la date de ces présentes, pris un tronçon de gréve à porter à ma jambe jusqu'à tant qu'on chevalier du dit royaume d'Angleterre m'aura délivré à faire les armes qui s'ensuivent. Premièrement, d'entrer en place à pied, et d'être armé chacun ainsi que bon lui semblera, et d'avoir chacun sa dague et son épée sur son corps, en quelque lieu qu'il lui plaira, ayant chacun une hache, dont je baillerai la longueur. Et sera le nombre des coups de tous les bâtons et armes ensuivant : c'est à savoir : de la hache, dix coups sans reprendre. Et quand ces dix coups seront parfaits et que le juge dira : Ho! nous férirons dix coups d'épée sans reprendre ni partier l'un de l'autre, et sans changer harnois. Et quand le juge aura dit : Ho! nous viendrons aux dagues et férirons dix coups sur main. Et si aucun de nous perdoit ou laissoit cheoir un de ses bâtons, l'autre pourra faire son plaisir du bâton, qu'il tiendra jusqu'à ce que le juge ai dit : Ho! Et les armes à pied accomplies, nous monterons à cheval ; et sera armé du corps chacun ainsi qu'il lui plaira, et aura deux chapeaux de fer paraux, lesquels je liverai ; et choisra mon dit compagnon lequel qu'il lui plaira des deux chapeaux : et aura chacun tel gorgerin qu'il lui plaira, et avec ce, je baillerai deux selles, dont mon dit compagnon

[1] The locking gauntlet is in the form of a closed hand, the fingers being made to fasten on the weapon held, the object being to prevent it being struck out of the hand by an adversary. Examples may be seen in the Tower of London, and there is one which belonged to Sir Henry Lee in the Armourer's Hall, London.
[2] *Histoire Des Ducs De Bourgogne*, II, 262.   [3] Holinshed, III, 10 ; and Hall, 16.

aura le choix. Et outre plus, aurons deux lances d'une longueur; desquelles lances nous férirons vingt coups sans reprendre, à cheval, sur main; et pourrons férir par devant et par derrière, depuis le faux du corps en amont. Et icelles armes de lances faites et accomplies, ferons les armes qui s'ensuivent: C'est a savoir, s'il advenoit que l'un ou l'autre ne fût blessé, nous serons tenus après, en icelle journée même et au second jour après, férir de coups de lance à course de chevaux à trois rangs, tant que l'un ou l'autre cherra par terre ou soit blessé, si qu'il n'en puisse plus faire. Et que chacun s'arme à sa volonté le corps et la tête. Et les targes soient de nerfs ou de cornes, sans ce qu'elles soient de fer ni d'acier, ni qu'il y ait aucune maîtrise. Et courrons les dites lances atout les selles que les dits chevaux auront, faisant les dites armes à cheval: et chacun liera et mettra ses étriers à sa volonté, sans faire nulle maîtrise. Et pour y ajouter plus grande foi et fermeté, je Michel d'Oris, ai scellé cette lettre du sceau de mes armes: laquelle lettre fut faite et écrite à Paris le vendredi vingtième jour d'Août l'an 1400." [1]

This letter is given in full, for it affords much first-hand information in a concrete form of the procedure of a combat of the period as well as the manner of such cartels.

The letter states that the Spaniard had attached to his leg "*un tronçon de gréve*," being a piece of a greave (armour for the shin), presumably of iron, causing him pain and inconvenience, which he had vowed to continue wearing until delivered from it by a combat with a gentleman of England. To this end he had sent his cartel to Calais, proclaiming his wish for such an encounter, laying down very precise conditions for a fight at which ten strokes with the axe, ten with the sword, and the same number of thrusts with the dagger were to be exchanged; to be followed by twenty courses with lances, on horseback. The pursuivant duly delivered the letter at Calais, where it was seen by Sir John Prendergast, who accepted the challenge in his own person, on behalf of the chivalry of England, subject, of course, to the permission of his sovereign to the duel being obtained. No reply being forthcoming from the Spaniard within a reasonable time, Sir John sent him a letter, stating that the time and place for the combat had been arranged, and an umpire appointed. There being still no reply, another letter followed demanding an answer, and at length one arrived, with excuses for the delay and complaining that Sir John had broken the treaty in an umpire having been chosen without the name having been first submitted to him; though showing no burning desire to have the matter arranged to his own satisfaction. The correspondence continued over four years and came to nothing after all; but for how long the Spaniard continued wearing the piece of greave pricking his leg history does not tell.

In the year 1402 the Sire de Harpedenne, Seneschal de Saintonge,

---

[1] *Chroniques De Monstrelet*, Liv. I, Chap. II.

having heard that certain English knights desired to perform a deed of arms for the love of their ladies, suggested to the Duke of Orleans that six gentlemen of his household should challenge a like number of English cavaliers to a combat *à outrance*. The duke agreeing, the invitation was duly sent and promptly accepted, the fight to take place near Bordeaux on the 19th May, 1402. Much pressure was brought to bear on the duke to induce him to withdraw his sanction, on the ground that such a combat would tend to increase the bitterness between the nations which already prevailed; but he continued to encourage the scheme, and even went to Saint Denis to pray for the success of his countrymen. Arnault Guilhem, Sire de Barbazan, a chevalier of repute, undertook the leadership of the French contingent.

The Sire de Harpedenne and the Earl of Rutland were appointed umpires of the fight; and on the arrival of the French chevaliers at the place of combat they heard Mass, and the Sire de Barbazan addressed them on the justice of their cause, animating them to deeds of valour for their country's sake; while the Englishmen thought more of a good meal before fighting. According to the French account of the fight, the Englishmen had conceived a stratagem for two of their number, by preconcerted action, suddenly to assail one of the French cavaliers, with the object of reducing their number to five, as against the English six; but the plan failed, and it was one of the Englishmen that was killed, thus turning the tables.[1] This gave a preponderance to the Frenchmen, but the fight continued long, obstinate and bloody, resulting in the victory of the French.[2]

In the same year Louis, Duke of Orleans, sent a challenge to Henry IV, King of England, proposing a combat between them with lances, battle-axes, swords and daggers, the fight to continue until one of them surrendered, which the king declined, on the ground that he could only fight with his equal.

In 1403 a deed of arms, *à outrance*, was performed at Valentia, four Spanish cavaliers against four Frenchmen, the King of Arragon acting as umpire; and the articles of combat provided for a fight on foot with axes, swords and daggers. The Seneschal of Hainault led the French, and the Seigneur de Sainte Coulombe, a member of the king's household, the Spaniards. Highly decorated lists had been erected for

---

[1] Such plans made beforehand would seem to have been quite common, but they usually miscarried.
[2] *Histoire Des Ducs De Bourgogne*, I, p. 185.

the occasion, and the king took his seat on the tribune, expressing the hope that the fight might not take place ; but the parties urged that great expense had been incurred, and that the French cavaliers had come from a distance at heavy charges in answer to the challenge. The king yielded to these arguments, and gave the signal for the onset. A gallant fight with axes ensued, during which one of the Spaniards seized a Frenchman by the leg and was preparing to stab him with his dagger when the king cast his bâton, putting an end to the conflict, to the great chagrin of both sides.[1]

Plate XI in *Horda Angel-Cynnan* " shewes how atte coronacion of quene Jane[2] erle Richarde kepte juste for the quene's part ageynst all commers, when he so notably and so knyghtly behaved himself, as redounded to his noble fame and perpetuall worship." Sir Richard was then twenty-two years old. The illustration shows a joust at the tilt, run with lances tipped with coronals, the earl's crest being the bear and ragged staff. The armour and general aspect of the picture point to the period when the Memoir was written rather than to the actual date of the joust. The tilt is of four planks, and appears to be nearly six feet in height. The royal party is seated in a balcony overlooking the lists, and there are raised galleries for the officials and better-class spectators, and seats on the level of the lists for the general public.

Plate XX. Sir Pandolf Malatesta sent a challenge to Earl Richard, first to joust, and " then go togedres with axes ; after which armyng swerdes ;[3] and last with sharp daggers." The jousting finished, " they went to gedres with axes, and if the lord Calcot hadde not the sonner cried peas, Sir Pandolf sore wounded on the left shoulder hadde been utterly slayn on the felde."[4] The illustration pictures the combat on foot with *becs de faucon*, weapons more picks than axes. The helmets are armets, the earl's crest his well-known cognizance, and he wears a tabard-shaped surcoat. The equipment is not contemporaneous with the time of the duel, but rather that of the date of the Memoir. The plate in *Horda* is reproduced on our Plate I. The copy from the MS. is not quite correct in the delineation of the weapon wielded by the earl, owing to a blur on the original.

Plate XXVIII pictures a combat on horseback, with rebated swords.

Plate XXXV shows Earl Richard jousting at the tilt incognito. He wears a " volant-piece."

[1] *Chronique de Monstrelet*, I, Chap. XIV.   [2] Queen of Henry IV, married in 1403.
[3] Kuriss-swords.   [4] Cott. MS., Julius E. IV.

PLATE I

COMBAT ON FOOT BETWEEN SIR RICHARD BEAUCHAMP AND SIR PANDOLF MALATESTA

THE TAPESTRY AT VALENCIENNES

Plate XXXVI. The earl is jousting at the tilt. " The erle smote up the visar (of his adversary) thries, and brake his besauges and other harneys."

Plate XXXVII pictures the earl jousting with his face exposed.

Plate XL " shewes howe a mighty duke chalenged erle Richard for his lady sake, and he justyng slewe the duke," the lance going through his body. This joust is with sharp lances in the open. The duke wears a jousting shield, and the earl a " volant-piece."

In 1415 three Portuguese cavaliers fought the same number of Frenchmen, at St. Ouen, near Paris, in presence of the King of France. The combat was a severe one, resulting at length in the discomfiture of the Portuguese, who succumbed to the Frenchmen. The manner of this surrender so disgusted the authorities and spectators that the defeated party was forcibly expelled the lists.[1]

In 1420 there were several curious subterranean combats, between French and English cavaliers, at Montereau, that town being then besieged by the troops of the Dauphin. The English had laid mines extensively under the walls ; and it was in these excavations that the fights took place, by the light of the flambeaux and torches. The first who fought on the French side was Louis Juvenal des Ursins, a valiant esquire, son of the advocate-general, who was dubbed a chevalier on the occasion. The King of England and Duke of Burgundy were present, and wished to break a lance together, from which, however, they were dissuaded. The Sire de Barbazan jousted with the king, at first without knowing who he was, but as soon as he became aware that it was his Majesty, he respectfully retired from the contest. Everything passed with great courtesy between the members of the two nations, and the king gave great praise to the cavaliers engaged.[2]

In the seventh year of Henry V "triumphant iusts and turneis, in the whiche, Erle of Arundell, and the Bastard of Sent Polle by the iudgment of the Ladies, won the price and got the honor."[3]

A combat on horseback and on foot took place at Arras in 1425,[4] between the Sires de Sainte-Treille and Lionel de Vendôme, the Duke of Burgundy acting as umpire. On the first day the chevaliers ran six courses with the lance, and de Vendôme was slightly wounded in the

[1] *Chronique de Monstrelet*, I, Chap. XIV. [2] *Histoire Des Ducs De Bourgogne*, I, 412.
[3] Hall, 162. A MS. in the Harleian Collection gives "La Statute d'Armes de Turnoys par le Parlement d'Angleterre," *Temp*. Henry V. See Appendix A. [4] Monstrelet says 1423.

head. The day following they fought on foot with axes of the *bec de faucon* type, and de Vendôme attacked his adversary with great impetuosity, but all his strokes were parried. Sainte-Treille then delivered several blows on the visor of his opponent, forcing it open, leaving the face exposed; then hooking his axe in the opening wounded de Vendôme slightly in the face with his gauntlet, perceiving which the duke cast his bâton. A joust followed between the Sire de Champremi and the Bastard of Rosbeque, the latter piercing the armour of his adversary with his lance, on which the duke's bâton fell.[1]

The *bec de faucon* or *bec de corbin* was a weapon with a curved beak-like spike or pick, as its name implies, sometimes with a blade at the opposite side, at others with a narrow *mail* or mallet, with four short points, somewhat like those on the coronal to a lance, though sharper: in both varieties there is usually a long spike at the head and a point at the foot; strictly speaking, however, a weapon with a blade can hardly be termed a *bec de faucon*. An illustration is given in " Barriers and Foot Combats," a paper by Viscount Dillon,[2] of a weapon of this kind belonging to Captain Hutton, which has a beak or pick on one side, and opposite to it a *mail* or mallet of four points and a spike at the head. There is another example at the Musée d'Artillerie, Paris, with a very pronounced beak, but neither *mail* nor spear. It is stated in Lord Dillon's paper that in the duel between Merlo and de Charny, at Arras in 1435, before the fighting began, an objection was lodged by Charny's friends against the Spaniard using a *bec de faucon*, axes being stipulated for in the *Chapitres d'Armes*. It was contended that the weapon was not an axe at all; but after some discussion the objection was not pressed. The weapon, which is a terrible one, does not seem to have been much used in Germany.

In 1428 a grand tournament was held at Brussels. The Duke of Burgundy attended and was magnificently entertained and feasted by his cousin, Duke Philip of Brabant, and the City of Brussels. The Lady of Gezebêque awarded the prizes. The dukes announced their intention of jousting together, but were dissuaded from doing so by the kings-of-arms, for fear of accidents. Many cavaliers took part, before a great concourse of nobles, ladies, and the general public. The prize for the most successful combatant in the first day's fighting was awarded to a

---

[1] *Histoire Des Ducs De Bourgogne*, I, p. 435. Monstrelet, in Liv. II, Chap. VIII, gives a somewhat different account. [2] *Arch. Journ.*, LXI, Plate I, Fig. 2.

gentleman of Brabant named Linquart. On the morrow and following days there was great jousting, and the Duke of Brabant and the Seigneur de Mamines were adjudged to be the best lances, and the prizes were awarded to them. This *fête d'armes* was distinguished by great splendour, and banquets, dances, masquerades and other mummeries continued for several days.[1]

In 1430 a combat took place in the great market place at Arras, between five French and a like number of Burgundian cavaliers, under the umpireship of the Duke of Burgundy, for the breaking of a certain number of lances. The French contingent consisted of the Seigneurs Théode de Valeperghe, Pothon de Sainte-Treille, Philibert d'Abrecy, Guillaume de Bes and L'Estendard de Nully; that of the Burgundians of Simon de Lalain, the Seigneurs de Charny, Jean de Vaulde, Nicolle and Philibert de Menton. The combat was to continue over five days. Lists were prepared, "*garnie d'aisselles, afin que les chevaux ne ce puissent recontrer l'un l'autre,*" and here we have an example of a joust at the tilt.

On the first day de Lalain jousted with de Valeperghe, when the latter, with his horse, was thrown violently to the ground. Jousts followed over the second, third, fourth and fifth days, in which many lances were broken. In the third course run between de Charny and d'Abrecy, the visor of the latter's "armet" was pierced by his opponent's lance, causing a very serious wound in the face; and on the last day the same thing happened to de Nully, in jousting with Philibert de Menton, The injured knights were removed to their lodgings, and left behind in charge of the surgeons; both subsequently recovered from their wounds. On the conclusion of the *fête d'armes*, the honours lay with the Burgundians, and the duke loaded the Frenchmen with handsome presents.[2]

In 1435 there was a passage at arms at Arras, held under the umpireship of Duke Philip of Burgundy; and seated on the bench near him were the dukes of Bourbon and Cueldres, with other noblemen of distinction. The parties to the duel were Messire Juan de Merlo, a chevalier banneret of Spain, and Pierre de Beauffrement, Sire de Charny, a banneret of Burgundy, knight of the Toison d'Or, and one of the most noted jousters of his day. The articles of combat provided for a joust of three courses, and then a combat on foot, with axes, swords and daggers, to be continued until one of the twain was placed *hors de combat*, though, as always, subject to the fiat of the judge. The Spaniard first entered the lists attended by four noble cavaliers, who had been specially attached

---

[1] *Chronique de Monstrelet*, Liv. II, Chap. LIV. [2] *Ibid.* Liv. II, Chap. LXXXI.

to his person by the orders of the duke. De Charny followed, attended by the Comtes d'Étampes, de Saint Pol and de Ligny ; and with them was the Earl of Suffolk, who carried the lances to be used on the occasion. The champions ran the three courses with the lance, without mishap to either beyond a slight fracture to the armet of the Spaniard. This ended the contest for the first day ; and on the morrow the combat on foot took place. It began with the knights hurling lances at each other, the weapon of the Spaniard striking the Burgundian on the arm, causing a slight wound, notwithstanding which the fight continued with axes. The combatants displayed much skill and gallantry with their weapons, without much advantage to either knight, when quite unexpectedly the duke cast his bâton, putting an end to the fight. The Spaniard protested most energetically to the duke at the combat being brought to so premature an end, urging that he had travelled a long way in order to achieve this feat of arms, and had been put to a vast expense. The duke appeased him, however, by praising his gallantry, and ordered a handsome present in money to be paid to him to cover his outlay. This duel is remarkable as furnishing an early instance of fighting with the visor up. To set against the danger of having part of the face exposed, it gave great advantage in the way of vision, in clearness as well as in radius. The visor was a mark so often aimed at, and was in its nature very vulnerable.[1]

In the twentieth year of King Henry VI a French Chevalier named Louis de Bueille challenged Rafe Chalons, an esquire of England, to a feat of arms ; and the King of France was present at the meeting. The Englishman ran the Frenchman through the body and killed him.[2]

Sir John Astley fought on foot with the Chevalier Philip Boyle of Arragon at Smithfield in the year 1442, King Henry VI acting as umpire. An illustration in the MS. in the possession of Lord Hastings pictures quadrangular lists of open railings showing the openings and the bars for closing them. They are of a kind usually erected for combats of this nature. King Henry sits in the tribune ; and within the lists, besides the principals, is a herald-at-arms and a guard of four, armed with battle-axes, for keeping the ring. The combatants wear bascinets ; bases ; solerets, *à la Poulaine ;* and tabard-shaped surcoats, on which the respective arms of the parties are embroidered. Boyle's axe has a flook or *bec de faucon* and an axe blade ; that of Astley's a blade and a three-pronged mail or mell. The MS. does not state the issue of the fight.

[1] *Histoire Des Ducs De Bourgogne*, I, p. 339.　　　　[2] Holinshed, III, 214.

CHAPTER V

A NOTABLE *pas d'armes* was held at L'Arbre de Charlemagne, near Dijon, in the year 1443,[1] presided over by Duke Philippe le Bon, which was proclaimed in most of the European countries of Christendom. The account of this meeting has a great historical value, owing not only to its reference to the tilt, additional pieces, and special forms of armour, but also to the amount of detail it presents. It is given here in a much abridged form.

Thirteen noble Burgundians of distinction, headed by Pierre de Bauffremont, Chevalier, Seigneur de Charny, held the *pas* for six weeks against all comers. De la Marche remarks that during the time necessary for erecting the lists and making the general arrangements for the meeting the young cavaliers practised various forms of jousting before the duke " *et là furent faictes une jouste à selles plattes, et en harnois de ioûte.*" He graphically pictures the general arrangements for this *pas d'armes*, the profuse hospitality extended to all comers, the construction and decoration of the lists, the dresses and equipments of the officials, pages, combatants, etc. He describes the lists for jousting as follows, making clear mention of the tilt :—" *et au milieu d'icelle lice fut la toille mise, pour la conduitte des chevaux, et pour servir à la course des hommes d'armes, comme il est de coustume en tel cas.*" " *Celle lice fut de bonne hauteur et grandeur : et, aux deux bouts de ladicte lice, furent faictes deux marches : qui se montoyent à degrés, faits de ce bonne grandeur, que l'on pouvoit aider à l'hommes d'armes, tout à cheval, pour l'armer aiser, ou desarmer, selon le cas : et hors de ladicte lice, du costé de Digeon, aux jours qu'il besoing faisoit, avoit une grande tente, haute et spacieuse, tendue, pour aider et soulager le venant de dehors, si mestier en avoit.*" There was another enclosure for combats on foot.

During the duration of the *pas* two shields were hung suspended in the lists : one, painted black, besprinkled with gilded tear-drops ; the other, violet, *semé*, with tear-drops in black. Each venant who, through

---

[1] *Mémoirs de la Marche*, Liv. I, Chaps. VIII and IX.

a pursuivant, placed a gage, such as a sword or spur, below the first-named shield, signified his election to engage on horseback one of the tenans or defenders of the *pas*, and to run twelve courses, "*à la toille*," that is along the tilt, with sharp or rebated lances at his pleasure ; and should either of the jousters be unhorsed he was to present his adversary with a diamond of whatever value he pleased. The venant who placed his gage below the violet shield, with tear-drops in black, elected a combat on foot, consisting of fifteen strokes with the axe or estoc ;[1] but should he place gages below both shields, his challenge applied to a joust at the tilt and a foot encounter as well. The duke took his seat on the 11th July, 1443, holding a white wand or bâton in his hand as judge, which when cast down put an end to a fight at any stage, the officials at once separating the combatants. We describe briefly a few of the encounters. The first contest lay between the leader of the tenans, the Seigneur de Charny, and a Spanish cavalier of mark, Pietre-Vasque de Suavedra. The chevalier venant having placed gages below both shields, the combat was to be on foot, to be followed by another on horseback ; and on the opening day the champions entered the enclosure for foot contests at 9 o'clock in the morning. The choice of weapons, as between axes and *épées d'armes*,[2] lay with the chevalier venant, who chose axes. Eight men-at-arms in complete armour, bearing white wands, ranged themselves in the enclosure, to keep the ring and to separate the combatants when necessary. The duke gave the signal and the combat began. Suavedra had taken off his visor, while Charny fought with his visor down. The stipulated fifteen strokes having been exchanged, without bodily injury to either party, the combatants were separated and left the lists.

On the 13th day of the same month the jousting between the same cavaliers took place. The Spaniard first entered the lists with his following, his horse trapped in blue and white silk, and presented himself before the judge. De Charny followed in like manner, the trapper of his charger being of cloth of gold ; he was attended both by his esquires and by five pages on horseback, sumptuously attired in blue and violet satin. The onset having been sounded, the champions charged, each splintering his lance on the body of his antagonist in the centre of the lists ; in their second career both lances glanced off, and so on until the number of courses had been run. Challengers continued

---

[1] A short thrusting sword.   [2] A stout foining sword.

to come forward, and each combat is recorded by the chronicler in its turn.

On the 8th of August a joust took place between an Italian, Jacques de Visque, Comte de St. Martin, and the Chevalier Guillame de Vaudrey, "*qui couroit de droit et du long de la toile.*" In the first course St. Martin was struck on the visor of his helmet by the lance of his opponent, the fastening being broken; in the fourth he was wounded severely in the lance-arm, the lance-head remaining in the wound, and the expressions of regret at the occurrence were so general as to show that serious injuries in such encounters had become comparatively rare. This mounted contest was followed by a combat on foot between Anthoine de Vaudrey and Jehan de Compays, Seigneur de Torain. The venant chose *estocs*, and a smart fight ensued, without personal injury to either chevalier, though their armour was much battered and torn.

The chronicler continues his narrations of the various combats which followed during the remaining days provided for in the *Chapitres d'Armes*, throughout the course of which the defenders of the *pas* held it against all comers with conspicuous honour and distinction. The tenans of the *pas d'armes* made an offering to the Virgin of the two shields of L'Arbre de Charlemagne, which were hung suspended in the Church of Nôtre Dame at Dijon.

While de la Marche devotes his narration more to the fighting and spectacular aspects of the meeting, Monstrelet deals with the challenges and *chapitres d'armes*.

THE CHALLENGES

"In honour of our Lord, and his most glorious mother, of my Lady Sainte Anne, and of my lord St George, I, Pierre de Bauffremont, lord of Chargny, of Monliet and of Montfort, knight, councellor and chamberlain, to the most high, most puissant and excellent prince the Duke of Burgundy, make known to all princes, barons, knights and esquires, without reproach, with the exception of those of the kingdom of France and of the countries in alliance, or subjects to my said sovereign lord, that for the augmentation and extension of the most noble profession and exercise of arms, my will and intention is, in conjunction with twelve knights, esquires and gentlemen, of four quarterings, whose names follow:—Thibault, lord of Rougemont and Mussy; Messire William Breremont, lord of Sees and of Sauvegon; William de Brenne, lord of Mombis and of Gilly; John, lord of Valengen; John, lord of Rap and of Tirecourt; William de Champdivers, lord of Chivigny; John de Chiron, lord of Rancheinères; Antony de Vaudray, lord of Aille; William de Vaudray, lord of Collaon; James de Challant, lord of Ainvilie; Messire Amé, lord of Espirey; and John de Chavigny,—to guard and defend a *pas d'armes*, situated on the great road leading from Dijon towards Auxonne, at the end of the causeway from the said town of Dijon, at a great tree called the Hermit's Tree in the form and manner following.

" In the first place, two shields, (one black besprinkled with tears of gold,—the other violet, having tears of sable), shall be suspended on the tree of the Hermit, and all those who shall, by a king at arms or pursuivant, touch the first shield, shall be bounden to perform twelve courses on horseback with me, or with one of my aforesaid knights or esquires, with blunted lances.—Item, if either of the champions, during their twelve courses, be unhorsed by a direct blow with the lance on his armour, such person, thus unhorsed, shall present to his adversary a diamond of whatever value he please.—Item, the champions may arm themselves according to their pleasure, *double or single*,[1] but without any wicked intentions, having their rest similar to the usual custom in war.—Item, each person shall make provision of lances—but the rondelle, which lies on the hands, shall be only four fingers broad, and no more.[2] Item, the lances shall be all of similar length, from the point to the rest.—Item, for the accomplishment of these feats of arms on horseback, I will supply all who may come without lances, precisely like to my own and to those of my companions.—Item, these deeds of arms on horseback shall be performed *à la toille*, which shall be six feet high."

Chapitres d'Armes.

" Those princes, barons, knights and esquires, of the rank before mentioned, who shall rather take their pleasure in performing feats of arms on foot, shall touch the violet shield, and shall perform fifteen strokes with battle-axes or swords, as may be most agreeable to them.

" Item, if, during these courses, any champion shall touch the ground with his hand or knees, he shall be bounden to present his adversary with a ruby of whatever value he please.—Item, each champion *shall be armed with the accustomed armour for combating in lists*.[3]—Item, should any person be unprovided with battle-axe or sword, I will furnish him with the same, similar to my own or to those of my companions. These axes and swords are not to have anything extraordinary in their make, but such as are usual in these kinds of combats.

" Item, he that shall have engaged himself to fight with me, or either of us, and shall throw the other to the ground, the person so thrown shall be obliged to surrender himself a prisoner whithersoever the conqueror shall order him.—Item, the person thus made prisoner shall pay for his immediate ransom, to whomsoever the conqueror shall direct, any sum above five hundred crowns.

" Item, foreigners need not seek for particulars from me, or from my companions, for they will find persons ready to deliver such at the usual hours and places.—Item, no stranger will be permitted to enter the lists with me or with any one of my companions, for more than one course at arms, namely, once on horseback and once on foot—and no one can require more of any of us during the present undertaking.

" Item, the aforesaid feats of arms, on horseback and on foot, shall be performed on the following days : those on horseback on Mondays, Tuesdays and Wednesdays ; those on foot, Thursdays, Fridays and Saturdays.

" Item, this pas d'armes shall commence on the first day of July in the year 1443, and shall last forty days, exclusive of feast-days and Sundays, and the feasts commanded to be kept by the court of Rome.

" Item, no prince, baron, knight or esquire, shall pass within a quarter of a league of the spot assigned for these combats without entering the lists and taking part, or otherwise leaving as pledges his sword or spurs, according to his pleasure.

" Item, for the accomplishment of these feats of arms, as well on horseback as on foot, according to the articles above specified, I have most humbly supplicated and entreated my aforesaid sovereign lord, that he would grant me his licence and permission to perform them, which he has most benignantly assented to. He has likewise most graciously appointed, as judge of

---

[1] " Double ou single." *Chroniques de Monstrelet*, Liv. II, 835. This would imply an option to use reinforcing pieces or not ; for some of the foreign cavaliers might not be provided with them at this time.

[2] The Vamplate.   [3] The italics are ours.

the lists, that puissant prince and my most redoubted lord, the count of Nevers and of Rethel —and in his absence, the lord marshal, count of Fribourg and of Neufchâtel.

"Item, in order that this my intention of performing these deeds of arms in the manner before specified may be more fully declared, I have fixed my seal to these presents, and signed them with my own hand, this 8th day of March, in the year 1442.

"Item, all noble foreigners shall have sure and loyal pass-ports from my aforesaid sovereign lord, or in his absence from his marshal."

On such occasions a proclamation was made against outsiders giving signals to any combatant.

The following documents occur among the Harleian MSS. :—

Le Declaracon du Pas a l'Arbre D'Or.

i.e. How the Lady L'Isle sent her Knight with a Rich Tree of Gold, for him to Sett near Brughes, and there to Challenge the Nobles of the Duke of Burgundies Court both to the Justs, & to the Tourney: the Articles whereof do follow. Dated July . . . A.D. 68, i.e. 1468.

Petition & Articles of the Justs-Royall to be held at Wesminster, by 4 Gentlemen Challenging all comers (upon the Creation of Henry second Sonne to King Henry VII).

To Run 6 Courses with Speares.
To Tourney 18 Strokes with Swords.

Petition of 4 Gentlemen to K. Henry VII to be received into His Royal Army purposed for Fraunce ; but first that he would Authorise their Challenge of all Comers to the Tilt, in any Realme or Place where the King shall be, for one year & a day longer.

Challenge of 6 Noble Persons to hold a Justs-Royall & Tourney at Westminster, for the Pleasure of the King, The Queene, and the Princess the Kings Eldest Daughter, where the 6 Challengers and Six Answerers shall together Run against each other with Spears on Horseback ; and after the Course Passed, to fight with Swords till the King Commaund them to Cease.

Relation (in French) of the Battel of Justs held in the city of Tours, between Jelcan (or Jehan?) Chalons, a Native of the Kingdom of England, & Loys de Beul who took the part of King Charles of France. A.D. 1446, wherein Loys de Beul was Killed.

Le Challenge Philip de Bouton, Natif de Pais Burgoigne, premier Esquire a Monsser le Conte de Charollois : qui ait Charge & Esleve Emprise de un Fleurer Penser a tacher a son Bras dextre, lequelle il portra ouverte jusque autant que il defendra au Royaulme d'Angleterre, en la Campagnie de son Seigneur Monsieur le Bastard le Burgoigne, comme a la Roche. Dat. 1. may. 1467.

The Relation made by Garter King of Arms to K. Edward IV. concerning the Arrival of 3 Knights of the K. of Hungaries Court, named Uladislaus of Bodna, Fredericus of Waredma, & Lancelagus of Trefulwane, who desired to performe some Feats of Arms with the English Gentlemen. With their Instuctions given to the said Garter touching his Declaration of their Desires, and the Articles of the Jousts and Tourney.[1]

Lacroix in *Military and Religious Life in the Middle Ages and Renaissance*, gives a picture of a king-of-arms proclaming a tournament ; copied from a miniature in King René's tourney-book.

During the meeting of the Chapter of the Toison d'Or, at Ghent in 1445, duels were fought between the Chevalier Jehan de Boniface (Jean de Bonifazio), an Italian, and a Burgundian cavalier, Jacques de Lalain, the latter then a young man of twenty-four years, who later achieved great celebrity as a combatant in the lists. Duke Philip of Burgundy acted as umpire, and was supported on the tribune by the Duke of Orleans ; and immediately before the fight began Lalain was dubbed a chevalier.

Lists had been prepared, and after the usual preliminaries were over a combat on foot between the parties took place, followed by many courses at the tilt.

The combatants entered the lists for the fight on foot, each bearing a heavy sword in the right hand and in the left a *hache d'armes* ; a smaller sword was attached to the belt, and small rectangular shields were carried on the left arms. Lalain fought with part of his face exposed, half of his visor having been removed. The parties took up their positions some distance from each other, and the fight began by Boniface hurling his spear at Lalain, who parried it. The latter cast his sword at his opponent, but without effect ; then each threw his shield at the other's legs with a view of causing him to stumble, and the fight at close quarters with axes began. After some hard blows had been exchanged Boniface dropped his axe, and Lalain struck at his visor, in which his axe struck until the point broke. Boniface then siezed the Burgundian's weapon and drew his dagger, hoping to stab his opponent in the face, but Lalain with admirable *sang-froid* beat down that weapon, and striking the visor of his opponent, slightly penetrated one of the apertures with his axe. Boniface then drew his sword and struck savagely at Lalain ; at which stage of the combat the duke's bâton fell.

The jousting was accomplished later on, with varying fortune, though without special features. It was at the tilt, " *et au milieu de la lice avoit une toille, pour conduire les chevaux, pour les courses de lances, qu'ils devoyent accomplir.*"

---

[1] See Appendix B.

The armour of de Lalain was provided with reinforcing pieces : "*Messire Jacques de Lalain estoit armé de plusieures rondelles, l'une sur la main, l'autre sur le coude du bras de la bride, et l'autre tenant au gardebras, a maniére d'escu,*" but they were detached before the jousting, Boniface being without them.[1] The different chroniclers of such combats differ more or less in many details.

The position and dignity of an esquire is defined in Ashmolean MS. 162a :[2] "The definition of an Esquire and the severall sortes of them according to the customs and usage of England. *An esquire called in Latine armiger.* . . ."[3]

Another of these MSS., 158ab, defines the duties and emoluments of a king-at-arms.—The office of a Kinge at Armes. "Fyrst as nyghe as he canne he shall take knowledge and kepe recorde of creastes cognissances and auntient used wordes," etc.[4]

The principal additional or reinforcing pieces, *pièces d'avantage*, are :—the grand-guard or main-guard, which is in two plates, the volante-piece and the body portion, and these, though sometimes separate, are usually riveted together. The former is adapted to the contour of the helmet, to which it is firmly attached ; while the latter, fixed to the breastplate, conforms to the curves of the neck, fits round the left side of the chest and left shoulder, and is flanged over the right shoulder to protect the weak place at the armpit on that side. The whole thus forms a double defence for that portion of the body against which an attack was mainly directed. The term "volante-piece," as applied to the face piece of the grand-guard, is, however, of doubtful authority. It is sometimes referred to in English chronicles, though without stating what it really is. Meyrick employs it in the sense above referred to, but Lord Dillon[5] inclines to the opinion that the term properly belongs to the two extra plates over the forehead attachable to some helmets, and I am sure he is right. These plates are present on jousting salades, and are called *Stirnplatten* or *Stirndoppolstuck* (forehead-plates) by the Germans. However this may be it is convenient to apply the term generally in use unless quite assured of its incorrectness. The elbow-guard or pas-guard is a reinforcement for the left elbow-

---

[1] *Mémoires de la Marche*, I, Chap. XVI; and *Histoire Des Ducs De Bourgogne*, II, 63.
[2] See Appendix A.
[3] Sainte-Palaye in *Mémoires sur L'Ancienne Chevalerie*, Vol. I, 15, defines and describes the different grades and sorts of esquires.
[4] MS. 506. Rights due att the Tournay. "Firste the Kinge of Armes . . ." See Appendix A.
[5] *Arch Journ.*, XLVI, 135.

joint, fastened by a pin. The manifer, or mainfere, *main de fer*, *steife henze*, or miton-gauntlet is the stiff, heavy jousting gauntlet for the bridle hand and forearm ; the name " manifer " is given by Meyrick to the crinet, absurdly connecting the word with the mane of the horse. The polder-miton or *épaule de mouton*, is a piece for the defence of the right forearm and bend, which is further protected by the vamplate of the lance. In the course with sharp lances, called *Scharfrennen* by the Germans, a dilge or jousting-cuisse is employed, strapped to the saddle ; and there was an armlet for the right lower-arm, used in that and some other courses The jousting-shields differ in form in the various courses : they will be described in their order.

Catalogue No. 383 of the Wallace Collection, London, comprises a small set of additional pieces, which from the subject and character of enrichment (chevrons with minute pomegranates and scrolls, etched and gilt) would appear to have belonged to a suit of armour in the possession of the Duke of Northumberland, at Alnwick Castle, which was acquired in Italy by Duke Algernon, about the year 1840 ; and it has been freely and excellently restored.

When arming, the additional pieces were screwed on one after the other, the jousting-shield being adjusted last. This process completed, the jouster was almost immune from injury and was left almost an automaton, with little power of initiative beyond aiming his lance, and that with difficulty.

Jacques de Lalain sent a challenge to a feat of arms in the year 1448 to James, brother to Earl Douglas ; the fight to take place in Edinburgh in the same year. He stated the conditions of combat proposed, for a foot encounter, *à outrance*, with spear, battle-axe, sword and dagger, which conditions were accepted by Douglas, with the reservation, at the instance of the King of Scotland, that no lance-casting should be allowed. The Burgundian party consisted of Jacques and his uncle Simon de Lalain, and a Messire de Mériadacq : while a Scottish trio, the brothers Douglas and a Lord de Haguet, arranged to fight them : the King to act as umpire. After some initial misunderstanding the knights fought paired against one another as follows :—Haguet against Simon de Lalain, Jacques against James Douglas, and Mériadacq against the other Douglas. The chronicler describes the course of the encounter, going into much detail, from which one would imagine that there was deadly peril to life and limb, but no serious hurt was sustained by any of the combatants; that fact being that the armour of proof enclosed each of the fighters in an almost impregnable fortress. La Marche was not present at this fight, but got his information from hearsay. Two out of the Burgundian trio were Chevaliers (Knights), the third combatant an Escuyer (Esquire), and it is interesting to note the difference in costume between the two grades. Matthieu de Couci gives it in the following terms[1]:—Chevaliers "furent revêtus de longues robes de velours noir, fourrées de martes zibelines fort riches"; quant au troisième qui étoit seulement Escuyer, "il en avoit une seulement de satin noir fourrée comme les autres." King René says the stuff of an esquire's costume at his court should be "drap de damas," and it would appear generally that an esquire could wear either satin or damask, but the chevalier must be clad in velvet. Further regulations were made in 1486, when cloth of gold and cloth of silver came in.

The armour of the fifteenth century up to almost its close is usually termed "Gothic," an incongruous appellation, though one convenient to employ owing to its having been so generally adopted and understood. Beyond a few fragments there is no armour of the first half of the century left to us; and for our knowledge of the knightly body-harness of that period we are mainly indebted to an ample series of monumental effigies and brasses. Though one cannot draw any decided line, it may be said that the process of transition from chain-mail to plate armour had been practically completed at the commencement of the fifteenth century; and the progress made in the directions of elegance, comprehensiveness and strength had been steady and continuous until towards the middle of the century, when we have glorious complete suits of armour spread out before us.

The brass of Sir John Wylcotes, in Great Tew Church, Oxfordshire, dating about 1410, affords an example of the standard of mail, which was a collar worn under a gorget of plate. The figure is without jupon, so that the breastplate and taces are exposed to view, and they are of plate; small motons, oval in form, cover the weak places at the armpits.

The brass in South Kelsey Church, Lincolnshire, dated about a decade later, shows the armour to be much more ornate, having crescent-shaped motons, fan-formed wings to the coudes; taces of six lames and short tuilles; the figure wears a pointed bascinet. The armour on the effigy in Hoveringham Church, Nottinghamshire, believed to have been

---

[1] Hist. de, Ch. VII, p. 568.

ascribed by Stothart to Sir Robert Grushill, is certainly not of the reign of Richard II, 1377–1399, but should rather be dated in that of Henry VI. There are fluted motons over the armpits, of a curved tooth-like form; coudes with elaborate heart-shaped wings; taces of eight narrow lames, with short rectangular tuilles, attached to the bottom rims by straps and buckles. The helmet is still the bascinet. This effigy exhibits an instance of the presence of the collar SS. There is an example of this collar in the Tower of London.[1] It was found in one of the turrets of the White Tower in 1913.[2] It is beyond the province of this work to discuss the probable meaning of these ciphers, which is obscure.

The Gothic armour of the connoisseur is reached in the beautiful effigy of Richard Beauchamp, Earl of Warwick, in St. Mary's Church, Warwick. It is cast in laton, a golden looking blend something between bronze and brass. The earl died in 1439, but the contract for his monument was not given out until fifteen years after, so that the type of armour is later than that of any actual harness worn by the earl. The effigy exhibits body-armour at its very best, as well in dignity of form as in beauty of outline ; and if it was not directly copied from a suit made by Tomaso Missaglai of Milan, the design for it certainly came from Italy. The breastplate exhibits a deep curved groove on either side ; it is shorter than was usual somewhat later, with a large number of taces ; and there are low neck-guards. Mr. Stothart also gives a back view of the figure, showing the armour as completely delineated behind as in front. The effigy is depicted on Plate II, giving both a front view and one in profile.

The great armour-smiths of the fifteenth century were fine artists in steel, and many of their creations preserved are models for all time in elegance of form and excellence of workmanship. One can trace their individuality and idiosyncrasies to an extent making it often possible to attribute their work even when unstamped with their monograms and devices. The Missaglias Negrolis and Piccininos of Milan, the Kolmans of Augsburg, the Seusenhofers of Innsbruck, the Grünewalts and Von Worms of Nuremberg, and many others, carried on their craft from generation to generation.

During the fifteenth century and somewhat later, new modes in armour, as well as in dress, had their birth in Italy ; but they took some time to travel to other countries less advanced in fashion and refinement.

[1] Class XVI, No. 5.　　　[2] The Armouries of the Tower of London, p. 440.

PLATE II

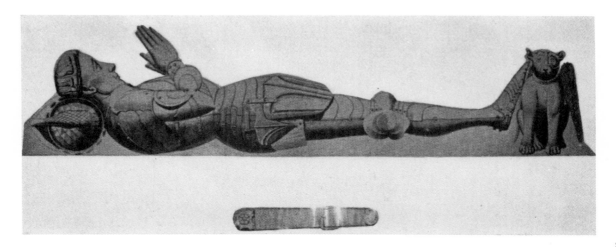

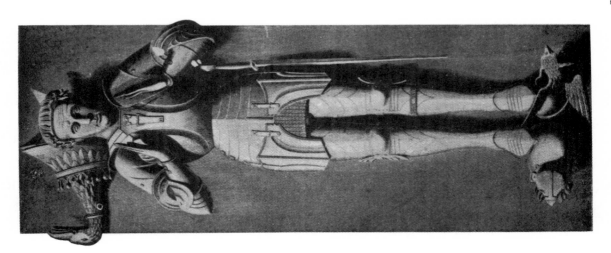

THE BEAUCHAMP EFFIGY

Much artistic skill of the highest order was lavished on the enrichment of armour. Suits were delicately chased, engraved and decorated with repoussé work ; and artists of the highest celebrity were engaged in such work. The trapper of mixed mail and plate appears frequently in this century.

A very important paper, printed in *Archæologia*, LVII, by Viscount Dillon, P.S.A., read in 1899, deals with a MS. Collection of Ordinances of Chivalry of the fifteenth century belonging to Lord Hastings, which contains among other matters :—

> The " Abilment for the Justes of the Pees."
> " To crie a Justus of Pees."
> " The comyng into the felde."
> " To arme a man."

The same manuscript is also commented on by the late Mr. Albert Way in the *Archæological Journal* of 1847.

Two of the illuminations depict jousting at the tilt, and another a combat on foot with axes before King Henry VI. The fight on foot, which took place in 1442, is between John Astley and Philip Boyle of Arragon. The lists, enclosed by an open railing, have at one end a stand for the king, who acted as judge, and four steps lead up to the tribune. On either side of the steps two men-at-arms are posted, holding long-shafted axes, and within the lists a herald is standing watching the fight. The combatants are wearing globose bascinets, which were the usual helmets for foot-fighting. They were roomy enough for plenty of padding against heavy blows from the axe. Boyle is armed with an axe having a blade on one side and a *bec de faucon*, or flook, on the other ; while Astley's weapon has a *mail*, or mallet, with three prongs, in place of the flook.

The terms of Sir Philip Boyle's acceptance of the challenge are given in Lord Dillon's paper.

The first illumination of a joust at the tilt pictures the moment when the tilters have shivered their lances, tipped with coronals of three prongs, on each other's bodies. The tilt is composed of six planks, and appears to be between five and six feet in height. Sir John Astley's crest is seen to be a crowned harpy, with torse and mantling ; his armour, the sort termed " tonlet"; the legs and feet are unarmed, being sufficiently protected by the saddle steels. The horse is trapped and has a chamfron. But little of the person of his adversary can be seen ;

what there is show his crest, three maidens in a corb, and he also is wearing bases. Both riders have tilting helms and shields, and bear poldermitons on their lance-arms. The vamplates are somewhat conical in form.

The other joust pictured is that between Astley and Pierre de Masse, which took place in a street in Paris in the year 1438. It is also at the tilt. The date is an early one for that form of joust, if the drawing be contemporary, which is unlikely. The tilt is composed of four planks, and is rather lower than the other example. The jousters wear no crests on their helms, and they are running with sharp lances. There are no poldermitons worn in this case. This important illumination has suffered much from damp, the central figures more especially.

The articles of combat are given in Lord Dillon's paper.

The "Abilment for the Justus of the Pees," as reproduced from the manuscript belonging to Lord Hastings, is as follows :—

> " A helme well stuffyd wt a Crest of hys de viis.
> A peyre of platus and xxx Gyders.
> A hanscement for the Bode wt slevis.
> A botton wt a tresse in the platis.
> A schelde coverid wt his deviis.
> A Rerebrace wt a rolle of ledyr well stuffid.
> A Maynfere with a ring.
> A rerebrasce a moton.
> A vambrase and a gaynpayne & ij bricketts.
> And ij dosyn tresses. and vj vamplates.
> And xij Grapers. and xij Cornallis & xl Speris.
> And a Armerer wt a hamor and pynsons.
> And naylys wt a byckorne.
> A Goode Cowrscer and row schode wt a softe bytte.
> And a gret halter for the rayne of the brydyll.
> A Sadyll well stuffud.
> and a peyre of jambus.
> and iij dowbill Gyrthis wt dowbill bokollus.
> and a dowbill sengull wt dowbill bokullus.
> and a rayne of ledir hungre teyyd from the
> horse hede un to the gyrthys be twen the forther
> bowse of the horsce for revassyng. A Rennyng paytrell.
> A croper of leder hongre.
> A Trappar for the Courser.
> And ij servantis on horseback well be sayne.
> And vj servantis on fote all in a sute."

This equipment is for a mounted contest, and differs of course materially from that worn in fighting on foot.

The writer of the paper (Lord Dillon) explains such of the terms employed as are not fairly obvious. Viscount Dillon's researches are mainly embodied in a series of valuable contributions to the pages of *Archæologia* and the *Archæological Journal*. Many old records, which had not been seen by such excellent authorities as Meyrick and Hewitt, have been examined and compared since their day, and they throw much light on points and terms which were obscure until recently, and which had been misunderstood by the earlier writers to whom we owe so much.

The " peyre of platus " is the cuirass, consisting of the breast and back plates : the " Gyders," attachments of some kind. The " hansce-ment " is a close-fitting garment, worn beneath the armour. A "botton wt a tresse in the platis," probably also refers to fastenings or attachments of some kind. The " Rerebrace wt a rolle of ledyr well stuffid " is probably a padding protection for the left upper-arm. The " Maynfere with a ring " is the manifer or mainfaire (main de fer), described in this work under the heading of reinforcing pieces. The " rerebrase a moton " is the rerebrace of the right arm, with its small movable plate, the moton or besaguè over the armpit. The " vambrase and gaynpayn and ij brickettss," are the further defences for the right arm and hand. The " ij dosyn tresses " are arming points, laces for attaching various parts of the armour together. The " vamplates," " Grapers," and " Cornallis " are the furniture of the lances, in their order, the conical or circular steel hand-guards, metal rings with points which stick into the wooden blocks in the lance-rests ; the coronals, heads of the lance with blunt points, calculated to catch on to the armour but not to pierce it. The " bycorne " was the anvil. Illustrations of Grapers, later termed *burres*, are rare. They are present on the illumination of the joust at the tilt between John Astley and Pierre de Masse, being shown on a lance standing ready for use when required. They are for distributing the force of the shock on impact over the whole body and especially to lessen the pressure on the wrist ; and are placed towards the lower end of the lance, the space between the graper and the vamplate constituting the grip.

The rest of the " Abilment " applies to horse furniture.

" To crie a Justus of Pees."

We Herrowdys of Armis beryng scheldis of deviis here we yeve in knowlache un to all Gentill men of name and of armus. That ther ben vj Gentilmen of name & of armus. That for the gret desire and worschippe that the sayde.vj.Gentilmen hath taken up pon them to be the.iij.day of May nex comyng be fore the hy & myghtty redowttyd ladys & Gentyll wymmen. in thys hey & most honorabull Court. And in thayre p̃sens the sayde.vj.Gentilmen there to a pere.at.IX.of the belle.be fore noone.and to Juste a yens all comers wt oute.on the sayd day.un to.vj.of the belle at after noon.

And then be the a vise of the sayde ladys & Gentill wymmen to yeve un to the best Juster wt oute A Diamunde of.xl.li.

And un to the nexte the best Jusꝑ a rube of.xx.li. And un to the thyrde well Jusꝑ a sauffer of.x.li. And on the sayde day there beyng offecers of armis schuyng thayre mesure of thayre speris garnyst. That ys Cornall wamplate & grapers all of asyse that they schall.Juste wt. and that the sayde Comers may take the lengthe of the sayde speris wt the a vise of the sayde offecers of armys that schall be in defferant un to all parteys on the sayde day."

The comyng. in to the felde.

The. vj. Gentilmen most com in to the felde un helmyd. and theyre helmes borne be fore tham. & thayre servants on horsbake beryng eyther of tham a spere garniste. yt is the sayde.vj. speris. the wheche the sayde servantis schall ride be fore them in to the felde. & as the sayde. vj.Gentilmen ben come be fore the ladyys & Gentilwīmē. Then schall be sent an harawde of armes up un to the ladys & Gentillwimmen sayyng in this wise. Hey & myghtti redowtyd & ryght worschypfull ladys & Gentylwymmen these.vj.Gentill men ben come in to yowre presens. and recōmaundit ham all un to yowr goode grace in as lowli wyse as they can.besechyng you for to gyffe.un to iij.best Justers wt owte.a Diamownd.& a Rube.& a sauffer.un to them that ye thenk best can deserve hit.

Thenne this message is doon.then the.vj.Gentill men goyth un to the tellws and do on theyr helmes. And when the harrawdis cri a lostell a lostell.then schall all the.vj.Gentill men wt in un helme them.be fore the sayde ladyys.and make theyre abeisans and go hom un to ther loggynges & chaunge them.

Now be com the Gentyll men with oute in to the presens of the ladyys

Then comyth forth a lady.be the a vise of all the ladiis & Gentill wymmen.& yevis the Dyamond unto the beste Juster wt oute.sayyng in this. wise sere these ladiis & Gentill wymmen thank yow.for yowr dysport and yowr gret labur that ye have this day in thayre presens.and the sayde ladiis and Gentill wymmen sayyn the ye have beste Just this day.there fore the sayde ladys & Gentyllwymmen gyff you this Diamunde & sende yow mych worschyp & ioye of yowr lady. Thus schall be doon wt the Rube & the Sauffer.un to the other ij nex the best Justers this don.

Then schall ye harraude of arms stonde up all on hey & schall say with a hey voyce.John hath well Justyd. Rycharde hath Justyd better.& Thomas hath Justyd best of all.

Then schall he to whom the Diamonde ys gyf un to he schall take a lady by the honde & be gynnyth the daunce. and when the ladiis hath dauncyd as longe as hem lykyth then spisys & wyne & drynke And then a voyde.

Another illumination depicts a man in the course of being armed for a combat on foot, his "hanscement" is on his body; the sabatons, greaves and cuisses, adjusted over his lower limbs; the attendant is fitting on the breech of mail; and all the remaining pieces of his equipment are lying on a table ready to be put on in their turn. These consist of the huge, globose bascinet, the cuirass of breast and back pieces, the tonletis, vambrace and rerebrace, a moton for the arm-pit, and a gauntlet. The "griffus" mentioned are the greaves; the "tonletis," the skirt of bases; and the "pensill" is a small banner.

The accompanying text is as follows:——

" How a man schall be armyd at his ese when he schal fighte on foote."

He schal have noo schirte up on him but a dowbelet of ffustean lynyd with satene cutte full of hoolis.the dowbelet muste be strongeli boūdē there the poyntis muste be sette aboute the greet of the arme.and the b ste (sic) before and behynde and the gussetis of mayle muste be sowid un to the dowbelet in the bought of the arme.and undir the arme the armynge poyntis muste be made of fyne twyne suche as men make stryngis for crossebowes and they muste be trussid small and poyntid as poyntis. Also they muste be wexid with cordeweneris coode. and than they woll neythir recche nor breke Also a payre hosyn̄ of stamyn sengill and a peyre of shorte bulwerkis of thynne blanket to put aboute his kneys for chawfynge of his lighernes Also a payre of shone of thikke cordewene and they muste be frette with smal whipcorde thre knottis up on a corde and thre coordis muste be faste sowid un to the hele of the shoo and fyne cordis in the mydill of the soole of the same shoo and that ther be betwene the frettis of the heele and the frettis of the myddill of the shoo the space of thre fyngris.

To arme a man.

ffirst ye muste sette on Sabatones and tye hem up on to the shoo with smale poyntis that wol breke And then griffus & then quisses & the the breche of mayle And thē tonletis. And thē brest And the vambras And the rerebras And then glovys And then hange his daggere upon his right side And then his shorte swerde upon the lyfte side in a round rynge all nakid to pulle it oute lightli And then putte his cote upon his bak And then his basinet pȳnid up on two greet staplis before the breste with a dowbill bokill behynde up on the bak for to make the basinet sitte juste. And then his long swerde in his hande. And then his pensill in his hande peyntid of seynt George or of oure lady to blesse him with as he gooth towarde the felde and in the felde.

A list of various accessaries and necessaries for a fight on foot is given ; such as a tent, the refreshments, "Also a longe swerde shorte swerde and dagger Also a pensell to bere in his hande of his avowrye," also the tools for repairing damaged armour.

The *Pas de la Pélerine*, held by the Seigneur de Haubourdin Bastard de St. Pol, and the feat of arms performed between Jacques de Lalain and an Englishman named Thomas, both took place near St. Omer, before the Duke of Burgundy and the Comte de Charolois, in the year 1446. Jehan, Seigneur de Haubourdin, and six others, calling themselves *pélerins* (pilgrims), were to hold the *pas* for six weeks against all comers. The meeting had been proclaimed in the neighbouring countries; but, owing to national animosities and other causes prevailing at the time, only a single cavalier, and he a German fifty years old, attended from abroad to contest the *pas*. Great preparations had been made : lists prepared and a tribune, built of stone, erected for the judge. Two shields were hung in the lists, one representing Sir Lancelot of the Lake, the other Tristan de Leonnois. The German cavalier touched the shield of Sir Lancelot, and was given leave to do his devoir in accordance with the *chapitres d'armes* drawn up for the occasion. The duke took his seat on the tribune on the day of combat at 9 a.m., and soon afterwards the fight with axes began between the German and the Sire de Haubourdin, who appeared as Sir Lancelot. The German, a tall man-at-arms, though well up in years, was still vigorous, but not very expert at the use of the axe. The number of strokes stipulated in the articles having been exchanged, without injury to either party, the duke cast his bâton. No other foreign venant presented himself, to the great disappointment of all concerned. A knight, Bernard de Bearne, Bastard de Foix, had been on his way to contest the *pas*, but had been struck down with fever and could not be present in time.

In the combat on foot between Jacques de Lalain and the Englishman named Thomas, Lalain fought in light armour, wearing a salade (*sallade de guerre toute ronde*), leaving his face exposed; while the Englishman wore heavy armour, his helmet being a visored bascinet. Lalain was armed with a long-shafted axe, with spikes at the top and bottom, having on one side a *bec de faucon*, or flook, and on the other a mallet (*mail rond*) with three prongs. The Englishman's weapon had an axe-blade on one side, a hammer-head (*long mail*) on the other, and spikes top and bottom; it had also a roundel guard. After several strokes had been exchanged Lalain was wounded on the wrist, in spite of which the fight continued unabated. Thomas then struck some heavy blows at his adversary, who stepped suddenly back, so that the Englishman lost his balance and fell heavily to the ground. This ended the fight.

Bernard de Bearne, Bastard de Foix, on recovering from his attack of fever, presented himself at Bruges, ready to fulfil his engagement at the *Pas de la Pélerine;* but as the time arranged for the course of that meeting had expired, the *chapitres d'armes* prepared for it had ceased to operate. Nevertheless, a combat took place at Bruges with de Haubourdin, and new articles provided that lances were to be cast, and then a fight with axes, until one or the other had lost his weapon. On the day appointed for the duel the Bastard de Foix entered the lists, in full armour, the back of his jupon embroidered with the family arms, with the addition of the bâton of illegitimacy. Having paid his respects to the duke, who acted as umpire, he retired to his pavilion. De Haubourdin came and went in like manner, his jupon bearing the cognizance of Sir Lancelot. The champions then re-entered the lists for battle, both armed with *becs de faucon*, when it was observed that the weapon of de Bearne was garnished with a long, slender spike, calculated for easy penetration between the bars of the visor. De Haubourdin on seeing this had his visor removed, saying that he would save his adversary the trouble of piercing it. The combatants each carried a lance in the right hand, an axe and shield in the left. The fight commenced by the parties hurling their lances at each other; that of de Haubourdin missed his opponent, but de Bearne's weapon struck the shield of his adversary, and glancing off wounded him in the arm. Hurling their shields at each other, the champions then closed, and after some heavy strokes had been delivered the duke's bâton fell.[1]

De La Marche thus describes a feat of arms which took place on foot and on horseback between the Seigneur Philippe de Ternant, a Chevalier de la Toison d'Or, against Galiot de Baltasin, an esquire and chamberlain to the Duke of Milan, in April, 1446.

Lists of strong planks, with a double enceinte, had been erected in a large square in the town of Arras, near the Hostelerie de la Clef. They were spacious in extent, and within them handsome pavilions had been pitched for the use of the combatants, and there were gaily decorated stands for the use of the officials and spectators. On the day appointed Duke Philip of Burgundy took his seat on the tribune on the stand overlooking the lists, and with him were his son, the Comte de Charolois, and his nephew, Adolph de Cléves. On the first day of the fighting the Seigneur de Ternant entered the lists on horseback, armed at all points, accompanied by the Seigneur de Beaujeu and the Comte de Sainct Pol, who acted as his esquires. Dismounting, he paid his respects to his master the duke, after which he retired to his pavilion. His adversary entered the lists soon after in like manner, supported by the Comte d'Étampes, who presented him to the duke. Eight men-at-arms, holding bâtons in their hands, were posted in the lists in order to be ready to separate the combatants when necessary and to carry out the orders of the duke.

The usual preliminaries having been gone through, each knight made the sign of the cross and the first encounter commenced, which was a combat on foot with lances. Baltasin attacked his adversary with such force as to break the point of his lance; while de Ternant holed the bascinet of his opponent. The rule as to following up would seem to have been infringed by Baltasin, for the king of arms now measured

---

[1] *Mémoires D'Olivier De La Marche*, I, chap. XVIII.

the ground with cords and marked the limits of advance and retirement, seven paces each way. New lances were issued, and in the next round both weapons were broken; after which the seven thrusts provided for in the articles were duly and gallantly accomplished. The next fight was with estocs and, after some heavy thrusting, the limits of advance and retreat were again marked, this time five paces each way. On the resumption of the fight, which is described as terrible, Baltasin's helmet was again holed, pieces of armour was shed on both sides and gauntlets broken. Baltasin then struck de Ternant on the lower end of the right pauldron, forcing off the coude, and the combatants assailed each other with such violence that the points of their estocs were broken off and others had to be supplied. At length the eleven thrusts were duly and gallantly performed and the combatants retired to their pavilions.

Then came the fight with hammer-headed axes, the heads having three prongs, *la mail à manière de trois coings à fendre bois, point de poincte de dessous;* and the fifteen strokes provided for were duly accomplished. The champions were then led before the duke, who complimented them on their prowess.

After an interval of a few days the combat on horseback took place. On the chamfron of the Italian's horse was a long spike, which was disallowed by the umpire, and the piece was replaced by another. De Ternant laid his lance in rest, and his sword was at his belt; while the Italian held his lance with the right hand, his sword and the bridle with his left. In the first course De Baltasin evaded impact with the lance, but spurred his charger at de Ternant's horse, apparently with the object of unseating its rider. The Burgundian, however, kept the saddle, and after some further fighting the combat ended without hurt to either party. The action by the Italian was a contravention of one of the laws of the tourney, but it was passed over by the umpire without remark.[1]

The first joust of the Comte de Charolois, afterwards Charles the Bold, then in his eighteenth year, was run in the park at Brussels in 1452. His father, Duke Philip, selected the redoubted champion Jacques de Lalain as the first adversary; and a grand tournament was proclaimed to take place in Brussels soon after. In the trial course the Comte and Lalain charged each other, the former breaking his lance on the shield of his opponent, but Lalain passed without touching him with his lance. The duke was much displeased at this, and ordered that

[1] *Mémoires de la Marche,* I, Chap. XIV.

in the course next following there should be absolute equality between the parties ; and on the signal being given they charged, each knight breaking his lance fairly and well on the other's body. This time it was the duchess who was angry with Lalain, for his dangerous assault on her son. On the day of the tournament at Brussels in the same year the Comte de Charolois played his part manfully and well, and in the evening he was awarded the first prize by the ladies. In the *conte des finances* of 1452 there is an item for 360 livres for his outfit.[1] The tournament had been proclaimed throughout the countries of chivalry, and was held in honour of the eighteenth birthday of the Comte de Charolois, in the Rathhausplatz of the city. Five challengers held the field against all comers. Charles ran in eighteen courses, his adversaries being, Adolph de Cléves, Seigneur de Ravastain ; Wolfart de Borssele ; the Earl of Buchan ; Messire de Vere ; Jean de la Tremoille ; Charles de Ternant ; Jacques de Lalain ; and the Seigneur de Bugnicourt.

The jousting was followed by the quintain, and by a combat on foot. The meeting concluded with the *mêlée*, after which the prizes were presented. It was this *pas d'armes* that was selected for reproducton at Brussels in 1905.

Jousting was now frequently combined with masques, mummeries and pageants. The Duke of Cléves was on a visit to his uncle Philip, Duke of Burgundy, in 1453 ; and a series of fêtes was held at Lille in his honour. During the inaugural banquet a beautiful girl entered the hall bearing a chaplet of flowers, with which she gracefully crowned the duke ; and it seems that this was the sign that the entertainment immediately following would be given by him. This duly began on the morrow, an hour after noon, when a knight of the distinguished order of the swan issued from the palace, fully armed. It was the Duke of Cléves who was to hold a joust in the market-place at Lille that day ; he, the tenant, against all comers, being ready to break a lance with all venans who presented themselves for combat. He was preceded by the figure of a gigantic swan, of the size of a horse ; the bird, on each side of which marched a savage in his war-paint, led the knight along by a chain of gold. The knight was encircled by little angels, and was followed by the duke, who was magnificently dressed. The procession thus formed marched to the lists, where the knight of the swan tilted with the Comte de Charolois, the Comte de St. Pol, Sir Anthony, Bastard

---

[1] Histoire des Ducs De Bourgogne, II, 90.

of Burgundy, and many others. After the jousting was done the duke escorted the ladies to the palace, where a banquet was served. The hall was gorgeously decorated. Facing the upper table a fountain played, and there was a live lion in the hall. After the company had taken their seats a holy friar advanced and addressed the duke, urging him to lead his armies against the infidel; and his grace swore that if the King of France would engage to leave his dominions in peace he was ready to march with his entire forces in defence of Christendom.[1]

A tournament was held on the coronation of King Edward IV, at which the ring and ruby were won by Lord Stanley.

The following account is given in *Mémoires de la Marche*[2] of the *pas d'armes* held by King Edward IV of England in the year 1467, at West Smithfield, in which the Bastard of Burgundy took a leading part. The narration is here much condensed. King Edward had caused lists of unusual magnificence to be prepared for the occasion, and costly galleries were erected at the sides. The stand for the accommodation of the king and his court, his knights and others, was in three stories, a flight of steps leading up to the umpire's tribune. The knights occupied the first story; the esquires, the second; and in the third were posted the royal archers of the guard. The second erection, lower than the other, was occupied by the mayor and aldermen of London, the judges, and other persons in authority: and pavilions, richly decorated, were pitched for the use of the combatants. In due time the king ascended the steps of the tribune, preceded by his sword-bearer, an earl; his majesty was clad in a purple robe and wore the insignia of the order of the garter; and in attendance was a score or more of his coun-sellors. Chairs were provided for the constable and marshal, and the king took his seat on the tribune as judge. The constable's guard of eight men-at-arms then entered the lists and took up their positions, when a knocking was heard at the gate. It was a knight who knocked, and the constable asked to know his purpose. "My name," said the knight, "is Escallis,[3] and I am come to accomplish a deed of arms with the Bastard of Burgundy, and demand entrance into the lists to do my *devoir*." Permission having been accorded, the knight entered the lists in full armour, and was followed by ten or a dozen horses, richly caparisoned, led by pages; and after making his obeisance to the sovereign he retired

---

[1] Monstrelet's *Chronicle*, (Continuation) Johnes' II. Chap. LXIII.   [2] Liv. I, Chap. XXXVII.
[3] Anthony Woodville, Lord Scales, brother to the Queen of England.

to his pavilion. The Bastard of Burgundy then entered the lists in a like manner, accompanied by the Duke of Suffolk, who had been deputed by the king to attend him; and in his train were twelve horses, trapped in cloth of gold and velvet, with the arms of Burgundy and the bâton of illegitimacy embroidered upon them. After paying his compliments to the king he also retired to his pavilion. Both knights re-entered the lists for battle, their lances were handed to them, and they took up positions for their careers. The onset being sounded they placed their lances in rest and charged towards each other, meeting in the centre of the lists, without injury to either party; then drawing their swords they attacked each other with great fury. Lord Scales, spurring up his horse, dashed violently against that of his adversary, the shock of the collision bearing the Burgundian and his charger to the ground, where the Bastard lay with his horse upon him. The officials of the lists raised up the fallen champion, when it was found that he had not sustained any serious injury. The king was annoyed at this incident; Lord Scales, however, pleaded that it was the freshness of his horse which had caused the accident. This put an end to the fighting for the day, and the Bastard retired to his lodgings, where he was afterwards visited by the constable with a message of sympathy and enquiry from the king, and an expression of regret at the accident. "Thank the king," replied the bastard, "and tell him that to-day I have fought with a beast, but to-morrow I will engage a man."

The champions joined in a combat on foot the next day, with spears, axes and daggers, the fight to continue until one or other should be disarmed or borne to the ground. It had been arranged that spears should be cast, but on the king objecting that part of the proceedings was omitted. The fight then began. Lord Scales dealt the Bastard some heavy strokes with his axe, and the Bastard, attacking with great violence, seriously fractured the armour of his adversary, at which stage of the combat the king cast his bâton.

De la Marche was present at the fight.

Other contests took place on the following day; but on intelligence arriving of the death of Duke Philippe le Bon, of Burgundy, the meeting broke up.

Monstrelet states that the lists were 370 feet long by 250 feet broad, and gives a somewhat different account of the mounted combat. He says that the jousting was with pointed lances, and further that the chamfron of the horse of Lord Scales was garnished with a long steel spike, which, being thrust into the mouth of the Bastard's charger, caused the animal such pain that it reared and at length fell, with its rider, the Burgundian, underneath.

Holinshed's version[1] is as follows :—

"The first daie they ran togither diurse courses with sharpe speares, and departed with equall honer. The next day they turneied on horsseback. The lord Scales horsse had on his chafron a long sharpe pike of steele, and as the two champions coped togither, the same horsse (whether through custome or by chance), thrust his pike into the nosethrils of the bastard's horsse ; so that for verie paine he mounted so high, that he fell on the one side with his maister, and the lord Scales rode round about him with his sword in his hand, vntill the King commanded the marshall to helpe vp the bastard, which openlie said ' I cannot hold me by the clouds, for though my horse faileth me, surelie I will not fail my counter-companion.' "

The king would not suffer them to do any more that day. On the morrow the champions fought with pole-axes, when at length the point of the axe wielded by Lord Scales was thrust into the sight of the Bastard's helm with such force that it brought him to his knees, on which the king cast his bâton. The Bastard wished to fight again, but the umpire ruled that should the encounter be continued it could only recommence at the stage reached at the termination of the last combat, with the Bastard on his knees. On hearing this judgment the Bastard relinquished his challenge.

An Ashmolean MS. (111–3b) furnishes the following[2] :—"A demonstracōn by John Writh alias Garter, to King Edward the Fourth, touching three Knyghtes of high Almayn wch came to do arms in England, with the instruccōns by them geven unto the saide Gartr and the articles of their feates and enterprise." The year must have been 1473.

The blending of the tourney with the pageant, mummeries and buffoonery continued to gain ground, and the sumptuous and costly fêtes held at Bruges in 1468, on the occasion of the marriage of Charles of Burgundy with Margaret of York, sister to King Edward IV of England, afford an excellent example of these combinations. All is minutely described at great length by de la Marche.[3] He gives details of the dresses, ceremonial and armour, and full particulars of each joust ; he also names the historic personages taking part. The plot of the leading pageant, if it can be called a plot, is inconsequent, though staged with great splendour and elaboration. There were tableaux of the Twelve Labours of Hercules, and many allegorical representations.

---

[1] *Chronicles*, III, 286.   [2] See Appendix A.   [3] Liv. II, Chap. IV.

Lists were erected in the Grande Place, and just within them stood *l'arbre d'or*, a great fir-tree, the trunk of which was gilded over, and it was this tree which lent its name to the fête. The Bastard of Burgundy and Adolf de Cléves, Seigneur de Ravastain, cousin-german to the duke, assumed the rôle of Chevaliers de L'Arbre d'Or, and they were to hold the *pas* in its defence. The fêtes were arranged to extend over ten days. On the first day the duke took his seat on the tribune, and a " poursuivant-at-armes," clad in the livery of *l'arbre d'or*, handed him a letter from the princess of an unknown isle, in which she proffers her favour to any knight who would deliver a certain giant from captivity, whom she had placed under the guardianship of her dwarf. The dwarf, gaily dressed in crimson and white satin, now entered the arena, leading in the giant by a chain, and, binding him to the golden tree, took up a position on a flight of steps, with a trumpet and sand-glass in his hands. The dwarf then sounded a note on his trumpet, and turned the sand-glass, which was timed for half an hour, at the expiration of which Adolf de Cléves, as Chevalier de L'Arbre d'Or, who was to open the *pas*, knocked at the gate of the lists, and the pursuivant demanded his name and errand. " I am come," said he, " to accomplish the adventure of the giant, and demand admission." The blazon of his arms having been submitted to the judge it was hung suspended on the tree, and the dwarf admitted him. De Ravastain was borne into the lists in a litter, carried on the backs of two black horses, and made a brilliant entrance with his team of drummers and trumpeters on the march ; his robe was of velvet, the colour of leather, trimmed with ermine, and on his head was a cardinal's hat. His handsome charger, richly caparisoned, bore a pair of panniers on his back, between which a court fool was seated, and it followed the litter, led by a varlet. The duchess was seated on her tribune, and the chevalier, throwing away his hat, knelt down before her and set forth the details of the rôle he had assumed, praying for her permission to carry out his plan. This being graciously accorded, he retired to his pavilion to arm him, re-entering the lists on horseback. The dwarf then gave the signal for the jousting, and the venans, sumptuously arrayed and brilliantly attended, were successively disposed of. After they had been dealt with, the dwarf again blew his trumpet and the prize was presented to de Cléves. The cavaliers then jousted each with a *gros planchon blanc*, but without touching each other ; and the first day's proceedings finished with a banquet. Jousts of different kinds, dinners and entertainments continued over each succeeding day of the fêtes. On the sixth day the Bastard of Burgundy had his leg nearly broken ; on the eighth the Sire Philippe de Poictiers was wounded; and on the ninth day Duke Charles jousted with his kinsman, de Ravastain, breaking eight spears to eleven by his opponent. The prize was a *destrier*, richly accoutred, provided with panniers, and in them was an entire jousting equipment of the Bastard of Burgundy. The prize was won by the Sire de Arguel, who had broken thirteen lances on the third day of the fêtes. In keeping account of the splintered lances, the *articles du pas* determine how they shall be broken :—"*car nulles lances ne furent tenues pour rompues, s'il n'y avoit quatre doigts de franc au-dessous du roquet, ou devant la grape.*" The lances for every contest were always carefully measured before being used, so that they were of equal length.

The lists were cleared of the tilt and stands, and the *mêlée* began, there being twenty-five cavaliers on each side. They fought with rebated swords, and with such ardour that all signals to stop were disregarded, and it was only when the duke rode in among them unhelmed, sword in hand, that they could be induced to cease fighting and go and prepare for the banquet which was to follow.

Philip de Commenes was present and tilted with Jerom of Cambrai. The banquet was served on a splendid scale, and the side tables were curiously embellished. On one of the dishes was the figure of a unicorn the size of a horse, with a leopard on his back waving the banner of England in one hand, and holding in the other a *fleur de marguerite*. The unicorn was trapped in silk, on which were embroidered the arms of England. A *fleur de marguerite* was presented to the duke by the hand of a little female dwarf belonging to Marie of Burgundy. The dwarf was dressed as a sheperdess, in cloth of gold, and was mounted on a huge lion, bearing the arms of Burgundy, which opened its mouth by means of springs, and chanted a poem in honour of the beautiful shepherdess. There were many more mechanical contrivances ; and on the last day of the fêtes a whale sixty feet long entered the hall, escorted by two giants. The whale wagged its tail and fins ; its eyes were great mirrors, and when it opened its mouth sirens issued from it, chanting most melodiously. After further conceits the two giants were swallowed by the whale.

A copy of a very quaint manuscript, portions of it written at different times in the reign of Edward IV and up to that of Henry VIII, is given in *Archaeologia* of the year 1846. It describes the marriage ceremony and the pageants, remarking as to the latter :— " the pageantes wear so obscure, that I fere me to writ or speke of them, because all was cuntenaunce and no wordes."

As to the excitement of the *mêlée* and the disregard of the signals and commands to cease fighting, the MS. says :— " the Duke unhelmed hyme, and with a great staffe his person charged pece in paine of deth, and soe wt great labore he droffe the parties asounder."

There was not much tourneying at the court of Burgundy after this, for Duke Charles was too busily and constantly engaged in military enterprises against his neighbours ; and, indeed, his ambitious, predatory and headstrong career was fast drawing to a close, ending, in fact, in 1477 on the fatal field of Nancy. The jousting traditions of his house passed over through his daughter, his only child, to the Austrian and German courts, under Maximilian : and it is to these countries, more especially, to which we must now turn for the history of the tournament in its decline.

In the same year as the fêtes at Bruges, 1468, a joust was held in front of the king's hotel at the Tournelles, Paris ; the challengers against all comers being four gentlemen of the company of the Seneschal of Normandy. John Raquier hastened from Rouen to take part, and he broke five lances with distinction ; then came Marc Senamy and two sons of Sir John Sanguin, who all acquited themselves well, after whom Charles de Louviers, cup-bearer to the king, jousted successfully, and the prize of the day was adjuged to him. After all these encounters the tenans were much bruised, two of them carried their arms in slings and a third was severely wounded in the hand ; so that the honours of the meeting lay with the venans.[1]

" At the marriage of Richard, duke of York, son of Edward IV, with Ann Mowbray, daughter to the duke of Norfolk in 1477, six gentlemen challenged all comers at the *Just Roial*, with *helme* and *shield*, in manner accustomed.

" Secondly, To runne in *Ostling* [2] *harneis* alonge a tilte.

" And thirdly, to strike certaine strokes with swoards and guise of *torney*."[3]

A narrative by an eye-witness of this marriage and " of the grand justing then celebrated" is given in the Ashmolean MS. No. 856,

---

[1] Monstrelet, *Continuation*, Chap. CLXIX.
[2] Easterling.
[3] " Certaine Triumphes," a MS. in Bib. Harl. insig., No. 69. See Appendix B.

94-104,[1] which is at least as curious as the account of the jousting of Anthony Lord Scales with the Bastard of Burgundy. It was published by W. H. B. in the *Excerpta Historica*, in June, 1830.

"In the reign of Henry VII certaine gentlemen who stiled themselves servants of Ladie Maie, in honour of that month, gave a challenge to be performed at Greenwiche ; the articles run thus :—

Imprimis, The fourteenth daie of Maie, shall be redye in the field centaine gentlemen, perteyning to the Ladye Maie, armed for the tilt, in harneis therunto accustomed ; and there to kepe the fielde (in such place as it shall please the kynge to appoint) from 2 of the clocke, til 5 at the afternoone, to run with every commer 8 courses ; and thus the answerers all answered and served, that than if there be any that desireth for their Ladyes sake other 4 courses, it shall be granted, so the hower be not past, if it be then at the queenes pleasure.

"The second day, to shoot Standart Arrowe and fighte, with all commers ; he that shootes the standart furthest to have a prise, and so in like case of the arrows of the flight.

"The third day with swordes rebated (without points or edges) to strike with any commer 8 strokes in way of pleasure ; and four strokes more for any of the commers mistress sake, under the above restrictions, (and the queen's pleasure).

"The fourth day to wrestle all manner of ways.

"The fifth day, armed to fighte on foote, with speares in their hands rebated, and then swordes by their sides for the battle ; and then with speare and sworde to defend their barriers ; that is to say, with spears 8 strokes, whereof two with foyne (thrusts) and 6 strokes ; and that done, to drawe their swordes and strike 8 strokes every man, to his best advantage, with gripe or otherwise ; and four strokes for a lady, under the above restrictions.

"The sixth day to cast the barre on foote, and with the arme both heavie and light."

"At these *tournois* the challenger doth engage to come in *harneis* for the tilt, without targe or brockett, *woalant piece over the head*,[2] rondall over the garde, rest of advantage, fraude, deceit, or other malengine.

"And some time after four gentlemen challenged all commers at Greenwich : To the feate called barriers, with the casting speare, and the targatt and the bastarde sworde.[3] And one cast with the speare hedded with the morn (coronal), and 17 strokes with the sworde, point and edge rebated ; without close or griping one another with handes, upon paine of such punishment, as the judges for the tyme being should thinke requisite."

"The tilts, we find, were performed with long tilting spears, on horseback; and when their lances were broken, they often took to their swords as well as axes" : see the method of challenge in the description of the plates in the life of Earl Warwick, and the manner of performing, Plates 35, 36, & 37, etc.[4]

Caxton, writing in the reign of Edward IV, in his epilogue to *The book of the Order of Chyvalry and Knyghthode*, says :—

"I wold it pleasyd our soverayne Lord that twyes or thryes in a yere, or at least ones, he wold do crye *Justes of pees*, to thende that every knyght shold have hors and haryneys, and also the use and craft of a knyght, and also to torneye one ageynste one, or ij ageynst ij ; and the best to have a prys, a dyamond, or jewel, such as shold please the prynce. Thys shold cause gentylmen to resorte to thauncyent customes of chyvalry, to grate fame and renōmee, and also to be alway redy to serve theyr prynce when he shalbe calle them or have nede."

---

[1] See Appendix A.　　　　[2] The Italics are ours.　　　　[3] Hand and a half sword.
[4] MS. in Bib. Harl. insig., Cod. 69.　See Appendix B.

A superb representation on tapestry of a *mêlée* which took place late in the fifteenth century, worked at Malines, is now at Valenciennes; and it is remarkable for its technical accuracy. The jousting is over; and a combat with sharp swords in progress. Broken lances, a helmet, a broken helm, fragments of crests, *grelots* and other debris shed in the contest lie on the ground among the horse's hoofs. The helmets are armets of the older form, of which there are existing examples spread over the collections of Europe. This type has hinged side-pieces and opens out from the middle for inserting and withdrawing the head of the wearer; and it is fastened together with a leathern strap. There is a small circular disk projecting from the back of the helmet, as well as a collar in front and over the neck behind, to which a necklet of chain-mail is fixed by a line of rivets. The comb of the helmet is holed for the attachment of a crest and the visor projects in a sort of beak. The disk is fixed to one side of the back of the head-piece by a thin iron connecting pin or bar. Its use or purpose is difficult to imagine and has given rise to much controversy, but none of the explanations advanced are at all convincing, for the bar or connecting pin is too slender to protect the neck from a sword stroke or even to shield from injury the strap at the back which holds the helmet together. This type fell into disuse at the commencement of the sixteenth century. The armour shown on the figures is fairly uniform. A long mail shirt with sleeves is worn, and it is much less covered with plate than might be expected at the end of the fifteenth century. The forms of the pauldrons, neck-guards, globose breast-plate, " bear-paw," or "cow-mouth" sollerets (as they were called), tuilles, tassets, and bases all mark the period, which other historic features on the tapestry confirm. Motons appear on only one of the figures, and they are pear-shaped; in the case of the other front figures there is no defence for the arm-pits beyond the chain-mail shirt. The lances are both grooved and plain, the vamplates, circular. An unusual feature is the presence of three long, narrow, label-shaped plates or bars, ridged down the middle, with small circular eyes at the tops, through which screws or rivets are passed, attaching them to the back rim of the armet. The back-plates are low, reaching but half-way up, and these three plates or bars form the only defence for the upper back ouside the mail shirts. They appear to be adjustable to a certain extent. The middle plate is the longest of the three, extending down the spine of the wearer to over the top of the low back-plate; while the side-bars, equal in length, reach well over the pauldron wings. The horses are all barded in leather, with chamfrons and crinets apparently of iron; and none of the animals are trapped. The bridles are of chain-mail, framed in iron. The tapestry measures 4·70 m. to 5·60 m. in size, and part of it is shown on Plate I (2).

In the year 1487 Johannes, Duke of Saxony, ran in *Gestech* with Cuntz Metzschen at Jena, and both riders kept their seats. They wore armour such as described in Plate IX (1): the motons were very ornate. On the duke's helm were two small black flags, on which the letter " M " was embroidered, in honour of his wife, Sophie of Mecklenburg. His trapper and shield were black, with violet, yellow, and white stripes.

A " Solemne Triumphe " was held at Richmond, which lasted a whole month, at which Sir James Parker was killed, in 1494.[1]

The two most important armouries are those at Vienna and Madrid; but for the study of the tourney that at Dresden is the best. Indeed, much of the armour there has remained, practically *in situ*, since it was in use, and many of the harnesses can be attributed with certainty, both as regards wearers and makers. In the *Tournierwaffensaal* several of the mounted models have sat their horses since the year 1591. At Dresden may be seen examples of the saddles, horse muzzles, weapons, bards and trappers; and even the textile costumes worn over and under the armour, as well as the small accessories and tools, may be studied. Besides these armouries, those at Paris, Berlin, Turin, Nuremberg, the Tower of London, and the Wallace Collection, are large and comprehensive.

The German *Turnierbücher* and jousting in Germany will be dealt with in the next chapter.

[1] *Archæological Journal*, LV, 299

CHAPTER VI

MUCH that is fanciful and unreal has been written about the tournament, and it is only in recent times that the knowledge of the subject has been placed on a more scientific basis, through the labours and researches of Querin von Leitner, Cornelius Curlitt, Boeheim, Dillon, Haenel and others, who have built on the valuable foundations laid by earlier writers on the subject. In France the subject has received but scant attention in recent times.

The contemporary literature in France and England concerning the tournament of the sixteenth century is much less voluminous than that written in the fifteenth, and the narrations of chroniclers greatly lack that technical knowledge which characterizes the work of their predecessors, who belonged to a higher class of society. The contrast, indeed, in their treatment of these meetings is very marked, in that comparatively little attention is devoted by the later writers to the martial sports themselves, while the pageantry and dresses closely connected with them absorb most of the matter of their narrations. This is perhaps an indication of a diminished public interest in the tournament in these countries; and but for the fuller and more circumstantial German records it would be difficult to present any comprehensive account of its ramifications during the sixteenth century and to the time when it fell into disuse. There are many records relating to the tournament in the College of Arms, London, and among the Ashmolean, Harleian and Cottonian MSS.[1]; whilst the *Chronicles* of Hall and Holinshed also afford much information. De Pluvinal, in *Maneige Royal*, published in 1625, gives some interesting particulars of jousting in its later stages, and Ménestrier, in *Traité des Tournois, Jousts, Carrousels, &c.*, when it had almost ceased being practised.

The institution had attained its highest development in most of the u ntries of chivalry in the first half of the fifteenth century, and the sixteenth saw its rapid decline. It had become more and more a mere sport and pastime, and had lost much of its former dignity in being so

---

[1] See Appendices A, B and C.

closely associated with mummeries and the pageant. All the safeguards instituted in the fifteenth century had become accentuated in the sixteenth to a degree making serious accidents very rare; and the introduction of barriers in combats on foot, and the employment of lances in these contests, apart from the preliminary casting, so often described in the narrations of such encounters of the fifteenth century, had greatly changed their character, and made them much less dangerous.

In admitting cavaliers to the tournament kings of arms were particular to exclude all who were not of noble birth, with the requisite number of descents. The bâton of illegitimacy, however, was no bar to the admission of the bastards of princely houses, who were generally accepted in society on an apparently equal footing with nobles of the highest rank.

The prizes awarded were often a wreath, a ring, a sword, helmet, jewel or a charger; at a joust held at Weimar in 1534 they consisted of a spur, a sword and a lady's slipper, all of gold.

Many new forms of jousting were introduced in Germany late in the fifteenth and during the sixteenth centuries, though most of them were derived from three main courses with but trivial differences from them. Some of the variants were conceived with a view to the introduction of some striking or humorous novelty; and, in fact, the passion for theatrical effect then prevailing in Germany, brought about some extraordinary mechanical absurdities as applied to jousting. The intricacies of the various courses would seem to have been somewhat perplexing even to the generations by whom they were practised, and they are, of course, much more difficult to disentangle now.

It was in Germany that the bulk of the jousting harnesses of the sixteenth century were made, and in that country the contemporary literature over the period in question concerning the tournament is most considerable.

The tournament records of the emperor Maximilian I and those of the ruling princes of the German Empire are of the first importance in the history of the tournament of the period, for it was at the courts of these sovereigns that such sports were most practised in their various phases, and when they reached their greatest development. The tournament, with its attendant pageants and mummeries, played a leading part in the weekly routine of the relaxation and amusements of these princes and their chivalry, a part perhaps second only to the chase; and these records bring the actual details of the various courses vividly before us in the many carefully executed drawings representing them which have been preserved. Most of them deal with the tournament of the sixteenth century, though some of the combats of the last quarter of the fifteenth are recorded and illustrated ; and while, perhaps, none of the drawings are strictly speaking contemporaneous with the events they depict many of them were copied from older pictures, so that taken as a whole the details given are more reliable than most of the other sources of information.

The most precious among these tourney-books is the *Freydal* of Maximilian I, a work of the year 1515, in which the emperor's combats in the lists, with the accompanying mummeries, are pictured.

The allegorical name " Freydal " is one of those assumed by the emperor in his knightly character. Maximilian was born in 1459, elected emperor in 1494, and died in 1520. He began his jousting career when quite a youth, and took a leading and personal part in the compilation of *Freydal*, dictating some of the text to his secretary Max Trytssaurwein in 1511 ; and, indeed, he corrected some of the proofs with his own hand. He selected for the book the examples of the various courses in which he was engaged, in almost all of which he appears as the victor. These instructions as to the choice of the subjects of the plates are of great value to the student, and are given in Appendix D. The personal character of the work adds much to its interest and importance in the history of the tournament.

The admirable reproduction of *Freydal* by Querin von Leitner, issued under the directions of Franz, Grafen Folliot De Grenneville,[1] leaves little to be desired. There are 255 plates arranged in series of *Rennen*, *Stechen*, foot combats and a *mêlée*, all depicting courses in which Maxmilian had " *gerennt, gestochen* und *gekämpft.*"[2] The work is valuable from many points of view, for it includes a register of the prominent personages of the time, and full particulars of the colours, trappers, arms and crests of the cavaliers taking part, together with the costumes of the mummers and others, besides some genealogical notes.

Freydal is one of a series of chronicles somewhat similar in character, comprising *Theuerdank*, *Weisskünig*, *Triumph of Maxmilian* and

---

[1] Vienna. 1880–1882.
[2] Courses run with pointed lances, those with coronals, combats on foot and a *mêlée*, as well as the mummeries in which he was engaged.

Ehrenpforte ; all were written with a view to the glorification of the emperor and his reign.   *Freydal* is the emperor's testament to posterity of his career in the tiltyard, and, with the accompanying mummeries he initiated, forms a knightly tribute to the memory of his much lamented consort Mary of Burgundy.   A poem in the work follows, which illustrates the spirit of vanity and the somewhat frivolous character of the monarch :—

RITTER FREYDALB [1]

Nun ver von kurtzweil lesen wil
Vnd lustbarlichen dingen,
der nem fur sich die ritterspil,
da ainr nach eer thut ringen,
als ritter Freydalb hat gethon
Aus ritterlichem gmute
Auf mengen adelichen plon.
Sein tugent vnd auch gute
ist allermenigclich offenbar,
wie er konndt tryumphiern
mit rennen, stechen kempfen zwar
Auch tantzen vnd thurniern
damit er in sein jungen tagen,
Als ir hie horen werden
grose freyd ynd ruem do hat erjagen,
(Seins gleich lebt nit auf erden).

Theuerdank is a narration of Maximilian's journey to Ghent to wed the heiress of Charles the Bold, with an account of his adventures by the way, and the story of his courtship.   It was written by the emperor for the instruction of Charles V when a youth.   There are 117 woodcuts by Hans Schaufflein

---

[1] In translation :—

THE KNIGHT FREYDAL

Now who would read of pastimes
And joyous deeds of pleasure?
Let him take up the tournament
In all its fullest measure.
This did the gallant Freydal
In knightly deeds of fame,
Thus rendering illustrious
The glories of his name.
His virtues and his goodness
Are manifest to all;
His many glorious triumphs
At tilt, at masks and ball.
Thus were his young days brightened
And the sunniest memories shed,
The cares of old age lightened
By brave records of the dead.

(His like will ne'er be seen again.)

Weisskünig is the story of his life and government.

The Triumph describes the progress and achievements of his reign, as typified by the picture of the triumphal car running through it. It was written in 1512, greatly at the emperor's own dictation; and the illustrations depict jousters fully equipped for some of the various courses of the tournament.

The Ehrenpforte is a monument to the glory of the Emperor's name and house.

In the tourney-book of Maximilian belonging to the Prince of Hohenzollern-Sigmaringen the spirited illustrations are by the hand of Hans Burgmaier, of Augsburg, an able coadjutor of the great armour-smith Koloman Colman of the same city, surnamed Helmschmidt.

Of great interest and importance are the three original tourney books of the Saxon Electors—Johanns *des Beständigen*, Johann Friedrichs *des Grozmüthigen*, and August, scoffingly called by Carlyle, if we remember rightly, the *physically* strong. They are in three volumes, which are preserved in the public library at the Japanese Palace, Dresden. The illustrations, which number over 300, are water-colour drawings on parchment, and they depict the courses of *Rennen, Stechen,*[1] and a *mêlée*, as run by those princes during their reigns; they afford characteristic records of these knightly sports from the year 1487 to 1566. The earlier jousts of the *Kurfürst* Johann begin towards the end of the fifteenth century, the others following in the sixteenth; while the third volume, executed in 1584, includes fifty-five drawings of the courses of *Scharfrennen* and *Gestech* run by the *Kurfürst* August, the last taking place in February, 1566, at Dresden. The drawings are by Heinrich Göding, of Brunswick, the court painter, and many of them would seem to have been copied from an earlier work.

There is also an old copy of one of the books in the royal library at Veste Coburg. Professor Haenel, the Curator of the Johanneum Collection of Arms and Armour at Dresden, has reproduced a selection of the plates in the three volumes of the joustings of the Saxon *Kurfürsts*, two of them coloured as in the originals, the others plain (published under the auspices of *Die Verein für historische Waffenkunde*, Dresden, 1910). The book supplies a long-felt want, for the original volumes are not easy of access.

[1] *Scharfrennen* and the *Gestech.*

In the *Gewehrgalerie* at the Johanneum, Dresden,[1] are twenty-nine paintings in oils by the same artist as those in the tourney-books, and they depict courses run in *Scharfrennen* by the *Kurfürsts*. These pictures are of even greater value than the drawings in the tourney-books in being painted on a larger scale, and giving more details both of the courses themselves and the general surroundings of the lists. One of them, like the last picture in the tournament-book, Vol. III, depicts the last joust of the *Kurfürst* August, run against his ennobled master-armourer Hans Dehn, in the year 1566; and it bears the title, "*Ein Rennen mit Hannss Dehnen gethan, der ist alleine gefallen. Ao 66 im Februar zu Dressten an der Festnacht.*" This oil-painting is hung in a bad light, and is darkened by age, but a close examination reveals the fact that the riders and horses are only models, stuffed with straw, their hoofs attached to low four-wheeled bogies. The figures are impelled to charge by a mechanical apparatus; ropes, running along the bogies and beyond, are visible, but the machinery itself for setting the models in motion is hidden from view. These models, as stated on the picture, formed part of a Carnival mummery, held at court. The painting exhibits the moment when Hans Dehn is in the act of being hurled from his horse by the *Kurfürst*, his lance falling to the ground; while the prince is holding up his left hand in the manner customary after impact. The *Kurfürst* wears a jousting-salade, with a crest of plumes; the usual shield; bases and jousting-cuisses. The legs and feet are unarmoured. The lance is stout, rounded, adorned with puffs, and headed with a small conically formed sharp tip; the vamplate is very large. The horse bears an enriched collar and a spiked chamfron, while plumes adorn the head and tail. The saddle is without cantle, the object of the course being unhorsing; the trapper, reaching down to the horse's houges, is painted with stars, foliations and the arms (viz. a lion *rampant*).

About the end of the seventeenth century the models of horses used for the display of armour in the Tower of London were mounted on casters, and guide books of the period and later state that they had been employed in practising tilting and running at the ring. This could hardly have been the case as regards these particular models, their purpose having been doubtless merely for convenience in moving and cleaning. These statements were, however, founded on the fact that there had been horses fitted with mechanical contrivances for impelling them

---

[1] The hall where the ancient firearms are on view.

PLATE III

MAXIMILIAN I ENGAGED IN *HOHENZEUGGESTECH*

forward towards one another for the purpose of practising the joust and its kindred military sports. In the years 1672 and 1673 patents were taken out in England for models of horses fitted with mechanical appliances for the purpose in question,[1] and the joust at Dresden on Twelfth-night, 1566, shows that they were not confined to this country.

The subjects of the paintings and embroideries on trappers in the sixteenth century were often humorous, religious, and sometimes even political in character. An example shows a barrel of gunpowder in the act of explosion and a pair of sweethearts standing before it kissing. Another exhibits a man standing in the street, clad only in his shirt, being well soused with water thrown from an open window. A religious example deals with the struggle in progress between the propaganda of reform as against the Church of Rome, wherein a monk and a Lutheran divine are seen fighting for the globe amid lightning and hail ; the waves of the sea, peopled by monsters of the deep, advancing menacingly towards them.

The mottoes are often curious and suggestive, for instance :—

" Was achte ich des Monden Schein,
wenn mir die Sonne gnedig sein."[2]

Another :—

" Niemand weisz mein Sinn
Ob ich ein Fuchs od Hase bin."[3]

The humorous devices painted were sometimes groups of owls, hares, mice or foxes. Trappers were usually armoried.

The contract price for a complete harness for the tilt-yard in the second half of the sixteenth century was usually from 100 to 200 *thalers* (£20 to £40), rather a wide margin ; though anything extra special in the way of enrichment would often cost much more. August *Kurfürst* of Saxony ordered from Peffenhaüser of Augsburg in 1582 a *" Stechkürass fur die Pallier*[4] *mit allen Doppelstücken, und alle Stücke zum Freirennen und Fussturnier 200 Thaler,"* i.e. a harness for jousting at the tilt with the reinforcing pieces thereto appertaining, together with the additional pieces for *Freirennen* and *Fussturnier*. A more ordinary suit *" ein anderer, schlichter, gemeiner Kürass"* is offered at 100 *thaler*. Four *thalers " Tringeld"* for each suit was usually added. A *Feldkürass*

---

[1] *The Armouries of the Tower of London*, I, 26.
[2] " What care I for the moon if the sun be gracious."
[3] " No one knows my heart, whether I am a fox or a hare."
[4] Joust at the tilt.

(a hoasting harness) was cheaper, say 60 to 80 *thalers* according to quality. Prices had advanced since the beginning of the century. In 1511, September 16, "Conrad Seusenhofer receives for two suits of armour for his Imperial Majesty and one for the English Embassy 211 *florins*."[1]

1512. Sept 13. "Payments made by Thomas Wuley on the King's behalf to a certain merchant of Florence for 2000 complete harnesses called Almayne rivets according to pattern in the hands of John Douncy, accounting alway a salet, a gorget, a breastplate, a backplate and a pair of splints for every complete harness at 16s a set."[2] Such last-named suits were for the soldiery and without armour for the arms and legs.

Hans Schwenkh's *Wappenmeisterbuch*, the tourney-book of Duke William IV of Bavaria, in the Royal Library at Munich, commences in 1510. It was compiled by Frederich von Schlichtegroll in 1807, it exhibits eight separate forms of the tourney, and covers the jousting of the duke in the first quarter of the sixteenth century together with later examples. The illustrations are faithfully reproduced on stone by the brothers Theobald and Clemens Senefeder, with an explanatory text by Schlichtegroll.

The tourney-book of Duke Henry of Braunschweig-Lüneburg is at Berlin; that of the Pole Zuganoviez Stanislaus of the year 1574 in the Dresden Historical Museum.

Several forms of jousting, combats on foot and the tourney prevailing in the fifteenth century have been lightly touched upon, and a more detailed statement of the leading courses now follows, together with an account of their more important variants.

The main courses of the jousts are :—

1. Courses run in the lists with lances rebated or tipped with coronals, without a tilt or barrier between the jousters ; the chief object in view being the splintering of lances and unhorsing.

2. Courses of courtesy run in the lists with sharp lances, also without a tilt ; the main desideratum being unhorsing.

3. Courses run with lances tipped with coronals, in which the jousters charged along a tilt which was between them. In this course the chief object in view was the splintering of lances.

There are many variants in the first two groups.

---

[1] *The Armouries of the Tower of London*, I, 37.   [2] Ibid., I, 49.

These three classes were practised more or less in all the countries of chivalry in the sixteenth century, though outside Germany it was the joust at the tilt which was commonly run. In the Fatherland and Austria these courses were known respectively as the *Gestech* or *Stechen*, *Scharfrennen* or *Rennen*, and the *Welsch Gestech* or Italian joust.

The type of joust run in the lists without a barrier or tilt, the lances tipped with coronals, is a very old one, though it had been subjected to a gradual modification and the application of safeguards as the centuries had advanced. The horses were blindfolded, so that they should not flinch or jib at the moment of impact, and so deflect the aim of the rider; and the animals were also sometimes rendered deaf by the stopping of their ears with wool, and they were often muzzled. Except in the case of one German variant of this class, the legs of the riders were without armour, these limbs being sufficiently protected by the saddle-steels. A chamfron, sometimes spiked, covered the face of the horse, and a crinet its neck. A cushion or mattress (*Stechkissen* or *Bourrelet*), filled with straw, hung from the saddle-bow, covering the chest of the animal, to act as a buffer when there were collisions, which frequently happened in the absence of a tilt; and, indeed, in such cases one or both chargers, with their riders, often fell. An illustration of this cushion is given in the *Tourney Book of René d'Anjou*, and another by Boeheim in his *Waffenkunde*, drawn after an actual example, which is believed to have belonged to Maximilian I, and now forms part of the superb collection of arms and armour at Vienna. The horse was usually barded in leather, which did not extend to the front, and a trapper, painted with various devices, covered its body. The saddle employed in Class 1, which weighs about 10·2 *kilos.*, has a high squared plate in front reaching to the jouster's breast, and there are short steels, though no cantle; so that unhorsing was of frequent occurrence. The head-piece of this class was the great jousting-helm. This course involved much more skill and initiative in the jouster and a more careful training of the horse than did the joust at the tilt. This class of joust was much practised in Germany under the general name "*Gestech*" or its abbreviation "*Stechen*," and was in three forms :

(a) *Das Gestech im hohen Zeug* or *Hohenzeuggestech*, known in France as *Joûte à la haute barde.*
(b) *Das gemeine deutsche Gestech. La Joûte Allemand.*
(c) *Das Gestech im Beinharnisch. Joûte au harnois de jambe.*

The joust in Germany was a ruder sport than that practised in other countries, and unhorsing very frequently took place.

Hohenzeuggestech is an older form of the group, its main object being the splintering of lances. In this course the jouster sat high up on his horse in a saddle formed like a well, and his body being well supported on all sides unhorsing was impossible as long as the animal kept its legs and the girths held. This form of saddle had been employed in the *Kolbenturnier* or baston course (i.e. a duel on horseback with heavy bastons or maces), which prevailed during the fifteenth century and which has been described. The protection on the saddle front in *Hohenzeuggestech* rises over the rider's breast, a broad band of iron encircles his body, and the steels are long and broad. The saddle weighs about 12 *kilos*. The horse ran blindfolded in a leather bard and trapper of cloth; the rider's legs and feet were encased in hose and well-padded shoes, no armour being necessary, as the saddle-steels afforded ample protection. The mobility of both man and horse must have been much restricted by the heavy armament and by the blind-folding and the thick cushion over the breast. The heavy Flemish horses " did not vanish from their posts like lightning and close in the centre of the lists like a thunderbolt," but charged at an amble.

Plate III pictures Maximilian armed for *Hohenzeuggestech*, as shown in *Freydal*, Plate 98.

Das gemeinedeutsche Gestech. In this course the object was unhorsing, or at least the splintering of a lance on an opponent's shield. In *Freydal* there are eighteen illustrations of this form of joust. The armour for the course underwent a complete change about the beginning of the fifteenth century, a special form of harness having been designed for it. The legs and feet were without armour.

Plate IV illustrates two harnesses for the German joust (*Gestech* or *Stechen*). Both date in the last quarter of the fifteenth century, that with tassets being the later of the two. They are now at Paris.

Plate IX (1) pictures a suit in the Wallace Collection, London,[1] for the *Gestech* (*Stechen*). It is very heavy, weighing about a hundredweight, leaving the wearer with little other mobility than was needed to couch and aim his lance; it had evidently seen some service, and bears the dents of many jousts. It is the only complete armour of this kind that we know of in this country. The great jousting-helm weighs about

---

[1] Catalogue No. 21.

PLATE IV

TWO HARNESSES FOR THE GERMAN JOUST OR *GESTECH*.   AT PARIS

PLATE V

HARNESS FOR *SCHARFRENNEN*. AT DRESDEN

twenty pounds: it is bucket-formed, and extends down in one piece over the top of the cuirass, to which it is fastened by three strong screws, two in front and one behind—the latter, placed vertically, is adjustable for getting the correct line of vision. The crown-piece curves gently over the wearer's head, and has a comb along the top pierced with twin holes for attaching the crest and torse or wreath which encircles its base. The eyelets for fastening the lining are bordered with laton, and the rivets are capped with the same metal, a golden-looking blend, something between bronze and brass. The *oculārium* affords but a very limited range of vision, and the front of the head-piece juts out in a sort of beak. The helm is very roomy, so that the wearer could move his head about freely under the cap of felt and leather lining, and small cushions stuffed with hair or feathers were over the temples. The breastplate is globose, and, as usual with armour for *Stechen* and also for *Rennen*, is flattened on the right side for better couching and aiming the lance. It is reinforced with a heavy plate over the abdomen, to which the taces, of five heavy lames, are riveted. The backplate is in three overlapping plates. A garde-rein (*Schwänzel*) of five lames protects the loins, and the tuilles, garnished with a figure like a horn, are tile-formed. The motons over the armpits, fastened in their places by straps of leather, are plain and very large—$9\frac{1}{2}$ inches across; that on the right side is pierced with a *bouche*, to leave space for the lance-shaft. On the right side is a lance-rest (*Rüsthaken*), and, as is usual in armour for both *Gestech* and *Scharfrennen*, there is a heavy queue, termed in German a *Rasthaken*, which acted as a counterpoise for holding the heavy lance used in the course in position, and for avoiding much strain on the lance-arm. The lance-shaft lies in the bed of the lance-rest, and is held under the queue behind it on the flattened part of the cuirass, the direction towards impact being guided by the hand. The cuirass is held together by hinged straps or strips of iron, which are pierced for fitting over staples and are secured by nuts. The pauldrons are each in five plates, with wings behind, and the coudes are pointed. On the top of each shoulder is a thin iron peg, which stands up diagonally, fixed to the armour by laton-headed rivets. These projections are roughly about two inches long, and are squared and topped like a nail. They were perhaps intended as winding pegs for the tassels or jagged ends of the mantling which usually streamed out from the jousting-helm. Such pegs are present on two similar harnesses at Paris. The right hand is without a gauntlet; the arm bears the poldermiton or *épaule de mouton*, stamped with the Augsburg guild badge; and on the bridle forearm and hand is the stiff and heavy mainfere, the jousting gauntlet. The jousting shield is of hard wood, covered with leather and gesso, about 15½ inches broad by 14 inches high : it is formed rectangularly at the top, somewhat rounded at the bottom, and is slightly concave and emblazoned. Pieces of horn are let into it to lend it elasticity and stability. It is fastened by cords to a pierced wooden block fixed on the breastplate and is held in position by a strap which buckles on to the helm. The harness itself bears the Augsburg guild stamp, a fir-cone and the letter "S" with an indistinct bar or bâton running through it. It is dated in the last quarter of the fifteenth century. No leg-armour was worn, so as to give the rider a better grip of his horse; hose covered the shanks, and well-wadded shoes, of cloth or leather, the feet.

There is almost an exact counterpart of this suit in a harness in the fine collection at Nuremberg, also forged at Augsburg, with the year of make, 1498, inscribed on the armour, the only difference between the two suits being that there are here tassets of laminated plates instead of the solid tuilles present on the Wallace suit, the tuilles being an indication of a somewhat earlier date. There are three similar harnesses at Vienna. The weight of the armour with shield is usually about 45·6 *kilos*. When arming, the different pieces are screwed on one after the other, the jousting-shield being adjusted last.

The lance is of fir or pine and is stouter than that used in *Rennen ;* its greatest diameter is 9 *centimetres*, length 373 *cm.*, and weight, with vamplate and coronal, about 14·3 *kilos*. An example may be seen in the writer's collection of arms and armour at Tynemouth.

Plate 9 in the tourney-book appertaining to the *Kurfürst* Johann (*des Beständigen*) pictures a *Gestech* at Leipsig in 1489, between Duke Hans of Saxony and Von Wunsdorf, in which the latter was unhorsed. The duke wears the jousting-helm, a spiked moton is over the armpit, and his lance is heavy and furnished with the circular form of vamplate, viz. that used in *Gestech*. The horse wears a collar of bells (*grelots* or *Schellenkette*), and a cushion over the breast; the body is covered with a trapper, painted with the royal arms. The equipment corresponds with the date of the armour shown on Plate IX (1).

The frontispiece of this work is taken from the tourney-book of the

Kurfürst Johann Friedrich (*des Groszüthigen*), Plate 81. It depicts the *Kurfürst* running in *Gestech* at the moment when his adversary is being hurled from his saddle. The victor's body-armour, vamplate, the chamfron of his horse and the coronal of his mighty lance are all painted the colour of steel. His crest, enriched by a crown at its base, is the Saxon emblem or badge (*Kleinod*), it is painted in a tawny colour with black stripes. The hose are striped in colours, green, pink, white and black ; the shoes are of black felt. The trapper, reaching down to the horse's houges, is banded in white, blue and two shades of red, and is sprinkled with the ciphers " XS " in gold and silver. It bears, twice repeated, the arms of Meiszen, Thuringen, Pfalz-Sachsen and Landsberg with the crested helm and shield of Saxony. The horses wear necklets of bells (*Shellenkette*). The trapper of the opposing champion is banded in shades of yellow and red sprinkled with foliations ; his crest a pair of silver horns with a coronet encircling the base and silver laterals of linden twigs and leaves. The details of the armour are very clear and the picture a good representative of its class.

Das Gestech im Beinharnisch is a course run with leg-armour, as its name implies. The object is unhorsing and the splintering of lances. The *Kuriss* saddle was employed. The presence of leg-armour rendered unhorsing much easier of accomplishment than without it, for the belly of the horse could not be so well gripped.

The joust of courtesy with pointed lances, as differentiated from Froissart's *justes mortelles*, was, as we have seen, much practised throughout the fifteenth century ; and it continued being run in Germany until soon after the middle of the sixteenth, when it became practically displaced by the joust at the tilt. This course was known in Germany as *Scharfrennen* or *Schweifrennen*, in France as *La Course à la queue ;* it is illustrated six times in *Freydal* and many times in the Saxon tourney-books.

The main desideratum of the course was unhorsing, and the form of the saddle had been designed with that object specially in view, though the splintering of lances also counted in the score, in fact, the jouster who sat his horse the longest against the greatest number of splintered lances, or without being unhelmed, was declared the victor. The objective of the lance in this course was either the beaver of an opponent or his jousting shield on the left side. The first-named mark was more difficult to hit than the other and the lance more liable to glance off, but when fairly struck it proved irresistible. As a rule the effect of impact was that the rider reeled in his saddle as he tried to maintain his seat, though usually one or other of the jousters was unhorsed, and, indeed, sometimes both fell, unless supported at the critical moment by the varlets. The lance was held with the point inclining slightly upwards, and, as in the other courses, the jouster promptly withdrew his hand and arm from the shaft immediately after impact, holding his arm upright, and the broken lance fell to the ground. It was the omission to do this which caused the accident resulting in the death of Henri II of France. The lance was a long, thin, rounded straight pole of soft wood, lighter than was used in *Stechen*, and was about 373 *centimetres* long with a largest diameter of about 7 *cm*., as against 9 *cm*. in the one for *Gestech*. The vamplate is in the form of a truncated cone. *Rennen* (*Scharfrennen*) was an even hardier course than *Stechen*, and demanded a still more careful training in man and horse and a surer seat.

The salient features of this form of joust are as follows :— The saddle employed in all its varieties was smaller and lighter than that used in the other courses, the weight being only a little over four *kilos.* ; it had a low pommel and no cantle, and was shaped, in fact, much like the British saddle of to-day. Jousting-cuisses (*Dülgen* or *Dilgen*, weighing 12 *kilos.*) hung from it and protected the lower limbs of the jouster, which were unarmoured. The armour was lighter than that used in *Stechen*, though somewhat similar in form, and the back plate was shorter. The helmet was a jousting-salade (*Rennhut*) forged in one piece, without any movable visor, but with a separate beaver reaching well over the top of the cuirass, to which it was screwed, back and front. It was well lined, and a cap of leather or silk was worn. The parts of the salade extending over the temples of the wearer were strengthend by extra plates (*Stirn-plätter*); and there was a thick reinforcing plate (*Magenblech*) over the abdomen, and to it the heavy taces and tassets were riveted. The horse was barded as in *Stechen*, a cushion or mattress protected the breast, and the animal was covered with the trapper. As in *Stechen* the cuirass was flattened on the right side, and to it the lance-rest (*Rüsthaken*) and queue (*Rasthaken*) were screwed. The queue was smaller than that on the harness for *Stechen*, the lance used in *Rennen* being lighter. There were no motons over the arm-pits, these weak places being well protected by the vamplate, which was larger and differently formed from that employed in *Stechen*. The shape was that of a truncated cone. The large concave shield of wood, covered with leather and plated with iron, was 6 to 8 *cm.* in breadth, it was screwed on to the beaver, and an armlet encircled the right lower arm.

Suits for both *Rennen* and *Stechen* were made so that they could be worn by a man of anything like a medium size; they were costly, and were frequently lent out by princes and the great nobles to their poorer brethren who lacked this equipment. A beautiful harness for *Scharfrennen,* made for the *Kurfürst* August of Saxony (1553-1586), by Sigmund Rockenburger, of Wittenberg, in 1554, is in the Dresden Museum. The form of the harness is graceful, and it is richly and tastefully etched with human figures, a double-headed eagle and foliations; in the centre of the breastplate is a spear-like projection—a fashion which did not last very long. The back-plate is unusually short and so is the garde-rein (*Schwänzel*). This harness is illustrated on Plate V. The weight is about forty *kilos.* The spurs have long shanks and are of both the rowel and prick kinds.

The store of armours for the tournament kept by the Saxon *Kur-fürsts* at Dresden greatly accounts for the number of historic suits preserved there.

In the *Turnierwaffensaal* at the Johanneum, Dresden, is a fine real-istic representation of a *Scharfrennen,* the jousters mounted and in com-plete armour down to the smallest detail. They are facing each other, with lances in rest. The armour is etched and gilt, and every detail is original except the under-garment, the hose and well-wadded shoes. The period is about the middle of the sixteenth century.

Plate VI illustrates Maximilian II, mounted and armed for *Scharf-rennen* in 1564. The armour is in the Collection at the Musée d'Artillerie, Paris.

Plate VIII (1) pictures a *Rennen,* held at Minden, between the *Kurfürst* August of Saxony and Johann von Ratzenberg. This particular joust was termed a " *Gedritts,*" signifying that the victor in the first encounter had still to dispose of a second antagonist in order to gain the prize; three were thus engaged, and hence the name. The *Kurfürst's* second adversary was Hans von Sehönfeld. The jousting-salade, large vamplate, jousting-cuisses and other details are clearly shown. Numerous illustra-tions of *Scharfrennen* are present in *Freydal* and in the Saxon tourney-books. There are many variants from the main course, the most impor-tant being *Geschiftrennen, la course à la targe futée.* It is of two kinds,

Geschifttartscherennen (*tartsche*, a shield) and *Geschiftscheibenrennen* (*scheibe*, a plate or disk) ; the wearing of a shield or a large plate or disk of iron over the breastplate being the main distinction between them. In both cases, when the centres of the shields were fairly struck by a lance a mechanism was set in motion by the freeing of a spring, which in *Geschifttartscherennen* dissolved the shield itself into fragments, the pieces flying over the jouster's head in wedged-formed particles. In *Geschiftscheibenrennen*, on the right impact having been attained the iron plate remained in its place and only the wedge in the centre flew out. The mechanism of the first-named was much more complicated than that of the latter.

Unhorsing was another of the objects in view in both cases. Both courses would seem to have had their origin in the game of Running at the Ring. There is an illustration of the mechanism at the back of the shield given in a picture-codex in the Armeria at Madrid, dating about 1544.[1] The general equipment in both cases was the same as in *Scharfrennen*.

Illustrations of *Geschifttartscherennen* are given in *Freydal*, both with leg-armour and without. In plates of that work, Nos. 29 and 45, the shields are seen flying in pieces in the air and both riders are unhorsed ; while in Plate 5, here reproduced in our Plate VII, both riders keep their seats, but the shields are seen dissolving into fragments over the heads of the jousters. There is but one illustration of *Geschiftscheibenrennen* in *Freydal*, viz. in Plate 41. There are also illustrations in the *Triumph of Maximilian*.

In *Bundrennen*, often called *Pundtrennen, Course appelée Bund*, the jouster here also endeavoured to strike the centre of his opponent's shield, but the main object was unhorsing. This was the most dangerous of all the courses, in the fact that a disrupting shield was employed, like that used in *Geschifttartscherennen*, but without any protecting beaver beneath it, so that the sharp lance was apt to glance off into the jouster's face or a fragment of the disrupted shield fly into it, sometimes injuring the nose or eyes. This course, says the *Weisskünig*, "was certainly amusing to look upon, though with often sorrowful results to one or other of the combatants."[2] In one of the plates of *Freydal* (No. 25), illustrating this course, the emperor and his opponent are both seen as

---

[1] *Waffenkunde*, p. 557.
[2] " *Er* [the Emperor] *hat auch under den pundten vilmal gerennt da im treffens baid shilt in de höch sprungen, das dann lustig ist zu sehen, aber sorgklich zu thun.*"

being unhorsed; while in other plates (Nos. 21, 62, 73, 93 and 204) the shields spring disrupted into the air, but the jousters retain their seats.

Anzogenrennen, Course au pavois,[1] is a kind in which a very long shield was employed, which was firmly fixed to the beaver by a large screw with a considerably projecting head. The immediate object was unhorsing, or at least the splintering of lances. A picture in the tourney-book of Duke William IV of Bavaria furnishes a good illustration of the course as run in the year 1512, and there are later examples in the tourney-books of the Saxon *Kurfürsts*. The arms and lower limbs are unarmoured, the harness the same as that employed in *Scharfrennen*. The shield is very long, extending from the slit for vision in the salade down to below the abdomen. The part over the breastplate conforms to the contour of that piece, while below it the shield becomes concave in form. There is usually a spike in the centre. There are twenty-five illustrations in *Freydal* (Plates Nos. 9, 17, 50, 58, 89, 97, 141, 180 and 240), all of which exhibit the opponents of Maximilian as being unhorsed; while in Plate 169 both riders retain their seats. In other plates both jousters are unseated.

Krönlrennen was a freak, probably of Maximilian's, first run in 1492. It is called "*Halbierung*" in the tourney-book of *Kurfürst* August of Saxony, and is a blending together of the courses *Scharfrennen* and *Gestech*, in that one jouster wore the armour usually employed in *Scharfrennen*, but used the lance headed with a coronal appertaining to the *Gestech*; the other, the harness for the *Gestech* with the sharp lance. The objects of the course were unhorsing and the splintering of lances. Plate 6 in *Freydal* illustrates *Krönlrennen*, and there is an excellent example given in the tourney-book of August of Saxony, Plate 1.

In *Pfannenrennen* the combatants ran without body-armour, except for a square metal shield on the breast, and the horses wore hoods.

Feldrennen closes the list under *Scharfrennen*. "Hoasting" armour was employed; the saddle was that used in jousting at the tilt. The horses were not always blindfolded, and the immediate object in view was the splintering of lances.

In the *tourney proper*, or *mêlée*, field-harness with *Kuriss* saddles were usually employed. Lances are splintered, and the combat continued with swords.

One of the fifteenth century forms was the *Feldturnier*, or field

---

[1] The word *Anzogenrennen* means merely jousting with the shield screwed on (*Angeschraubte Tartsche*).

course, a combat of groups on horseback. Ordinary field-harness, with or without reinforcing pieces, was usually worn. This form of contest is illustrated in the tourney-book of Duke William IV of Bavaria, showing that each cavalier was always provided with two swords. In what respects it differed from the ordinary *mêlée* is not apparent. Both swords and lances were employed.

The joust at the tilt has been already referred to more than once, and some account given of its leading features. There is reason to believe that it was practised as early as the first quarter of the fifteenth century, and we have mentioned cases of a *toile* having been employed at Arras in Burgundy in the year 1430, with some rather later instances. Viscount Dillon, in his paper "Tilting in Tudor Times," published in the *Archæological Journal* of the year 1898,[1] gives an extract from the *Chronicles of St. Remy* to the effect that the *toile* or tilt probably originated in Portugal. As already stated, the salient feature of this form is that it was run with a barrier between the jousters, along which they rode in opposite directions, their left sides towards it, until impact was effected. The first barrier was a *toile*, a rope hung with cloth extending along the length of the lists ; but as this did not prevent the horses from bumping against one another a tilt of planks, usually about six feet high, was devised, which effectually kept them apart, and collisions were avoided, thus rendering the sport much less dangerous. The use of the tilt made impact more uncertain than when running " at the large," and there was usually a considerable proportion of non-attaints. The main object of this course was the splintering of lances, though unhorsing was also in contemplation and not unfrequently took place. Unseating was, however, rendered difficult by the form of the saddle employed, the so-called *Kuriss* saddle, which had a cantle behind and a high pommel in front, thus making it much easier for a rider to keep his seat. The usual weight of this form of saddle was a little over 9 *kilos*. Jousting at the tilt soon greatly supplanted the earlier form in France, Italy and England ; but it took no root in Germany before the sixteenth century, at the commencement of which it is stated to have been introduced into that country and Austria from Italy. The name "*Welsch Gestech*" (Italian Joust), given it in the Fatherland, tends greatly to confirm this ; and, indeed, it was just at this time that Maximilian was introducing a new style of armour from Italy into his

[1] Vol. LV, page 297.

PLATE VI

MAXIMILIAN II ARMED FOR *SCHARFRENNEN*, AT PARIS

PLATE VII

GESCHIFTTARTSCHERENNEN

dominions. Though frequently practised in Germany during the first half of the sixteenth century, the joust at the tilt by no means displaced running "at the large" there. Several plates in *Freydal* furnish illustrations.

Plate VIII (2) depicts a joust at the tilt, run at Augsburg in 1510, between Duke William IV of Bavaria and the Pfalzgraf Friedrich of the Rhine. The illustration is reproduced from a picture in Hans Schwenkh's *Wappenmeisterbuch*, the tourney-book of the duke, who is seen jousting; it is a work which has already been referred to in these pages. The tilt itself, of three broad planks, is of massive construction. The harness worn in the earlier form was the *Stechzeug*, the kind that was used in the German *Gestech*, with no leg-armour, a style which has been already described and illustrated on Plate IX (1). The cuirass employed is flattened on the lance side, and there is a *Rasthaken* or queue as well as a lance-rest. Bases are worn by the riders, and a crest of plumes. The trapper of the duke's horse, dark in colour, is shot with painted rays over the body, and a picture of the Sun in Splendour encircles the horse's tail, which is further decorated with plumes. A collar of *grelots* is around the neck of the animal; the head is adorned with plumes, and the chamfron embellished with a picture of the sun. The lances with coronals are well shown; the former are long poles narrowing gently towards the heads, and the latter are in three short prongs.

Plate XI (1) pictures two fine suits at Paris for jousting at the tilt, one of them with the manifer or mainfere, the passe-guard and poldermiton in their places.

Plate X (1) illustrates a German harness, at Dresden, for this form of joust. It dates about 1580. There are three armours for jousting at the tilt in the Wallace Collection of Arms and Armour at London, Catalogue Numbers 484, 495 and 505. The first of these is a harness for *Realgestech*, as shown by the cross-ribbed shield, a device for affording a grip for the coronal of the lance on impact in order to prevent it from glancing off—another departure in the direction of greater safety for the jouster. This course was a late variety of the joust at the tilt.

No 505, illustrated on Plate IX (2) is perhaps somewhat earlier in date than the other two suits, for in the right side of the "volante-piece" is a little square door or window, for enabling the wearer to converse freely when open. This aperture is about three inches square in size and freely perforated so as to admit air to the wearer when closed. It is shut, of course, when the jouster is ready for his career. In other respects the three suits are very much alike ; and the " peaescod-bellied " breastplates of all of them tend to fix their date within narrow limits. The shields of Nos. 495 and 505 are practically the same in form and size. They fit round the front of the left side of the neck and cover the left shoulder and breast, running nearly straight down to the middle of the breastplate. The grand-guards are screwed to the upper parts of the breastplate and the shields are attached to them in like manner. The other reinforcing pieces are either present with the suits, or the armour is holed for them.

The sad accident which resulted in the death of Henri II, of France, at a *fête d'armes* held at Paris in 1559, was in a joust at the tilt with the Comte de Montgomeri. It was caused by the Comte failing to drop his splintered lance in good time.

The drawings of Hans Burgmaier in the *Triumph of Maximilian* afford illustrations of some of the varieties of the German jousting of the period.

Plate 45 illustrates the *Welsch Gestech* (Italian Joust) or Joust at the Tilt. The head-piece is the jousting-helm and the reinforcing pieces are in their places. The lance, tipped with a coronal, is lighter than that employed in the German *Gestech* and in *Scharfrennen* and the vamplate is circular in form. Feather plumes are worn.

Plate 46 pictures the *Gestech* or German joust (*Das gemeine deutsche Gestech*). The head-piece is the same as that on Plate 45. A cushion is worn over the horse's chest, and a *Rasthaken*, or queue, and a *Rüsthaken*, or lance-rest, are on the flattened right side of the cuirass. The lance is heavy and tipped with a coronal. The crests shown are very fanciful.

Plate 47 illustrates *Hohenzeuggestech*. The jousters are seated on the high saddles (*im hohen Zeug*) peculiar to the course. The jousting-helm is worn. Lances are tipped with coronals, as is the case with all varieties of the *Gestech*.

Plate 48. *Das Gestech im Beinharnisch*. This is a variety of *Gestech* in which leg-armour is worn, as the name implies.

Plates 50 and 55 picture *Bundrennen*, the peculiarity of the course being that no beaver is worn beneath the disrupting shield. This makes it the most dangerous of all the courses, and injuries to the face were frequent. The vamplate is large and formed like a truncated cone.

Plate 51 depicts *Geschifttartscherennen*, in which course the shield, when struck by the lance on a certain spot, dissolves in fragments over the jouster's head.

Plate 52. It pictures *Geschiftscheibenrennen*, a course similar in principle to the last-named, the difference being that the shield is a disk which, when properly struck, flies into the air, or the shield remains in its place but the plug in the centre flies out.

Plate 53. The cavaliers are here accoutred for the pan joust (*Pfannenrennen*). There are one or two other varieties of the joust depicted.

Several combats on foot of the fifteenth century, perhaps the most dangerous items of the articles of a *pas d'armes* of that period, have been fully described in Chapters III, IV and V, in the narrations by contemporary chroniclers of actual encounters. The character of these contests underwent a great change in the sixteenth century, through the introduction of barriers over which the combatants fought. These bars or barriers reached up to the breasts of the fighters, and prevented their grappling with each other or getting out of bounds. They made their appearance probably in the last decade of the fifteenth century. As the tilt had been conceived with a view towards mitigating the danger of the joust, so barriers were adopted towards minimizing the risk of serious injuries in fighting on foot, and, indeed, the new style was hardly more dangerous than the game of football as played to-day. This latest phase is well described by Viscount Dillon in " Barriers and Foot Combats," a paper published in the *Archæological Journal* of 1904.[1] The special features of the armour for combats of this kind are its massive character, the presence of an apron (*Kampfschurtz*, a sort of continuation of the taces), and the large, thick, globose bascinet. A fine armour for foot fighting in the lists may be seen in the Tower of London. It is a grand piece of work, weighing about 93 lbs., sent by Maximilian of Austria to our Henry VIII. The Vienna Collection possesses seven complete armours for fighting on foot, which vary considerably, both in form and weight. The weapons employed in these contests in Germany and Austria, as given in *Freydal*, are the sword in different forms, including the " bastard " (a hand and a half-sword) the dussack, the *Kurisschwert* or armying-sword, and even the two-handed sword (*Zweihänder* or *Schlachtschwert*), the dagger, battle-axe (including the *bec de faucon*), mace, halbard, *ranseur*, guisarme,

---

[1] LVI, page 276.

Aalspiess (a short-shafted spear with rondel-guard), *Langspiess* (a short lance), *Würfspiess* (a javelin), *Stange* (a quarter-staff), and *Drischel* (the military flail).

The *Fussturnier*, which originated in the sixteenth century, was a fighting in groups on foot over a barrier, and in it and some other courses the challengers were termed "Maintenators" and their opponents "Aventuriers." Each combatant had to deliver three thrusts with the lance and four strokes with the sword. Dr. Cornelius Curlitt gives the following extract from *Acten des Dresdener Oberhofmarshallamtes* of the year 1614:—"The one who shivers the greatest number of lances in the most adroit manner shall have the lance prize; and he who in five strokes strikes the bravest and strongest with the sword shall have the second prize." The locking gauntlet was forbidden, and the lower limbs were without armour. A harness for this kind of fighting, by Anton Peffenhaüser, worn by the *Kurfürst* Johan George of Saxony in 1613, is now in the Dresden Museum. The head-piece is a burgonet.

An important later form of joust is the *Freiturnier*, or Free Course, which grew out of the old German *Gestech*, and, like it, was run "at the large," that is without a tilt. There is a harness for this course at Dresden, reproduced on Plate X (2). The passguard is much larger than that worn in jousting at the tilt, reaching nearly to the left shoulder. Leg-armour was worn. The harness illustrated in Boeheim's *Waffen-kunde* (Fig. 655) as being for the *Welsch Gestech*, or joust at the tilt, is really for *Freiturnier*, a form of joust which does not appear before the second half of the sixteenth century.

As already stated, the suit in the Wallace Collection, numbered 484 in the catalogue of that institution, is for *Realgestech* or *Plankengestech*, a variety of joust at the tilt. It first appeared about 1540, and did not differ materially from the main course; nor did the armour employed differ except for the cross-ribbing on the shield. This course, like the others, fell into disuse in the seventeenth century, though it was the last to survive except the one called *Scharmützel*, often a sort of general siege or skirmish, with a view to practice for actual warfare. A *Scharmützel* was held at Dresden in 1553, when four bands of horsemen attacked a mock fortress, defended by a garrison armed with *Aalspiesse* and military forks, and supplied with four hundred earthenware pots for missiles, to be thrown empty. Cannon were employed on both sides, presumably fired in blank, though this is not stated.

The foregoing comprise the most distinctive forms of the tourney.

There were permanent lists in Germany, as also at Calais; and in England, at Westminster, Hampton Court, and Greenwich.

The quintain and running at the ring have been described in Chapter I, and there only remains the *Karoussel*, or *Carrousel*, to be mentioned. The name is derived from *carosello*, a ball of clay, which was hollow. The game was a favourite one at the court of Louis XIV, where it gave rise to handsome dresses and costly display. The players, arranged in opposing bands or sides, were mounted and threw these missiles at one another, catching them on their shields. There were several varieties of the game.

Harness for the tilt-yard was usually made thicker than that for field purposes and was thus somewhat heavier. Much taste and labour were expended on its ornamentation.

Though the best armour was imported from Italy and Germany, a large proportion of that in use in England was made at home, and, indeed, there is plenty of evidence that this is so. Henry VIII, like Maximilian, took a strong personal interest in all that related to arms and armour, and was very desirous that the form and quality of harness made in England should be improved. With this object in view, he arranged with the emperor for German smiths to be sent to Greenwich, and some really fine armours were made there during his reign and later, many of which have been preserved, though the iron billets used in forging them were imported from Innsbruck, English iron not having been found to be of a sufficient tensile strength for the best purposes. Whether this inferiority lay in the process of puddling the iron or to the presence of any considerable proportion of deleterious elements, such as sulphur and phosphorous, is another matter. Henry VIII established his "Almain Armouries" at Greenwich about the year 1514.[1]

The form of " Hoasting " armour underwent several important changes during the course of the sixteenth century and to the time when body-armour fell into general disuse. The changes had their origin, mainly, in new departures in the fashion of the civil dress; indeed, the shape of the doublet of each period is faithfully reflected in that of the cuirass of steel. This following of the modes of the day by the smith sometimes resulted in the production of harness which, however effective from a spectacular point of view, proved most unsuitable for service in the field.

[1] *The Armouries at the Tower of London*, I, 18.

This was greatly owing to the abandonment of the principle of a glancing surface on the armour, thus tending to effect lodgment for strokes from weapons of attack, instead of deflecting them.

The elegant form of " Gothic" armour of the connoisseur had been modelled, as we have seen, after the shapely Florentine dress of the fifteenth century : but a radical and far-reaching change took place at the commencement of the sixteenth, following on a new departure in civil costume. This style, *armatura spigolata*, is usually known as " Maximilian," named after the emperor, and would seem to have been introduced by him in his extensive dominions from Italy, after his Italian campaign in 1496. That " Maximilian" armour was of Italian origin is clear by the very name it bore in Germany at the time, viz. " *Mailander Harnisch*." The leading features of this type are :— the globose form of the breast-plate ; the abnormally wide-toed solerets, following the new fashion in shoes, " bear-paw " or " cow-mouthed " as they were commonly called ; the heightening of the shoulder or neck guards (pieces often, though erroneously, termed pass-guards, a mistake pointed out by Viscount Dillon in one of his valuable and suggestive papers on armour) ; and the substitution of laminated tassets in place of the solid, tile-formed tuilles. The head-piece is the armet, the most perfect as well as the most familiar form of helmet—of which, however, there are several varieties. This armour was usually made fluted, though sometimes plain. When fluted, the whole surface down to the jambs, which are always smooth, is covered with narrow, regular radiating flutings, differing in that respect from " Gothic" armour, with its broad, sweeping flutings and ridgings.

Tonlet armour (*à tonne*) has a deep skirt of hoops called " jambers," standing out all round like a more modern crinoline, and moving up and down like the laths of a Venetian blind. It also had its origin in Italy, and was copied from the civil skirts of the doubtlet of the period, called " bases " ; which when reproduced in steel were clumsy and unwieldy. We have here an apt illustration of the lengths people will sometimes go in slavishly following a particular fashion, however clumsy or unsuitable it might be. This style of armour was greatly employed in fighting on foot, though a variety was adapted for use on horseback. A fine and historic armour for fighting on foot, made by Conrad Seusenhofer of Innsbruck, may be seen in the Tower of London.

Bards probably had their origin in the twelfth century, though there is little mention of them in English records before the close of the thirteenth, but in the fourteenth they would appear to have become fairly common. The chamfron, crinet and peytral are observable in engravings of the fourteenth century, when they were probably of *cuir-bouille*. In the *Histoire de Charles VII* it is stated that a combat, *à outrance*, took place in the year 1446, between the Seigneurs de Ternant and Galiot de Balthasin,[1] in which the latter was mounted " *sur un puissant cheval, liquil selon la costume de Lombardie estoit tout couvert de fer.*" A complete equipment of steel plate for the horse was attained in the second half of the fifteenth century, when, according to a picture in the arsenal at Vienna, painted in 1480, " *Der Ritter sitz auf seinem bis auf die Hufe verdecten Hengst.*" A fine bard which had belonged to Henry VIII, weighing 92½ lbs., may be seen in the Tower of London. Bards for the tourney were usually of leather.

The expression " trapped and barded," so frequently met with in records, is often misunderstood. The bard is a defence for the horse, while the trapper is its outside textile covering.

The importance of lightly-armed troops in warfare became steadily greater, and even as early as the beginning of the sixteenth century a large proportion of the armour for the field was made lighter, and demi-harnesses were employed for light cavalry.

The imitation in steel of the civil costume was carried to absurd lengths, as is glaringly shown in the so-called " *Pfeifenharnis* " (pipe-harness), forged after the picturesque dress of the period, with its pipings, puffs or rolls, points and slashes. Illustrations of it may be seen in the *Triumph of Maximilian.* In a suit in the Wallace Collection (catalogue No. 555) the details of the dress have been faithfully and minutely reproduced in metal. The very fabric of the civil costume has been imitated and the slashes are gilded. Harness was freely and delicately etched, engraved, damascened, and decorated with repoussé work; and some of the ornamentation did away altogether with the glancing surface of the armour, thus greatly militating against its efficiency for military purposes.

A fine armour in the Zeughaus, at Berlin, affords an excellent example of the best work of about the middle of the sixteenth century. It is by Peter von Speyer, of Annaberg, made for the *Kurfürst* Joachim II, of Brandenburg, whose arms decorate the breastplate. The helm is

---

[1] This duel is described in Chapter V.

of the type of armet without collar.   The peak in the cuirass tends to be placed lower down as the century advances, until at length the " peascod " form is reached, as shown on Plate IX (2).   Here the breastplate is of the true Elizabethan " peascod " form, converging to a retreating point at the bottom.   You have this shape exactly in portraits of the Earl of Leicester, and, indeed, of the queen herself.   The tassets swell out over the hips, another feature observable in the portraits.   This form continued, with some modifications, up to nearly the end of the century.

PLATE VIII

A *SCHARFRENNEN* AT MINDEN IN 1545

A JOUST AT THE TILT AT AUGSBERG IN 1510

CHAPTER VII

L'HISTOIRE *Du Bon Chevalier, Sans Paour et Sans Reproche, Gentil Seigneur De Bayart,* gives some account of Bayard's combats in the lists. The Chevalier was born in 1476 and died in 1524, and his first fights on foot and on horseback took place when he was a raw, growing stripling of eighteen. This was on the occasion when the Burgundian Chevalier, Claude de Vauldray, came to Lyons in 1494 to accomplish a deed of arms—"*à course de lance et coups de hache*"; and the young Bayard, though without possessing an equipment for the joust or means of procuring one, conceived the idea of engaging this redoubted champion in combat. The difficulty as to horse and armour was solved by the coming forward of a kinsman, L'Abbe d'Esnay, with the necessary cash. After several chevaliers of the French court had encountered De Vauldray, Bayard entered the lists to do battle. No particulars of the combat itself are given by the chronicler, but the account states that the youngster bore himself right gallantly; and the verdict of the ladies on the stand erected for their accommodation, expressed in the Lyonese dialect, "*Vey-vo cestou maloûtru, il a mieulx fay que tous los autres.*"

Soon the young Bayard, advancing towards fame and fortune, caused a proclamation to be made for a *pas d'armes* to be held at the town of Ayre, in Picardy, on the 20th July, 1494, *Pour l'amour des dames.* The articles of combat provided that "hoasting" armour be worn, and on the first day three courses be run with rebated lances and afterwards twelve strokes exchanged with the sword, all on horseback; on the morrow the combats to be on foot at barriers, high as the *nombril,* with lances and later with axes. Prizes were offered to the successful competitors as follows:—For the first day a bracelet of gold, enamelled with Bayard's device, of the value of thirty *ecus;* and for the second day a diamond worth forty *ecus.* The proclamation runs:—

"*Pierre de Bayart, jeune gentil-homme et apprentif des armes, natif de Daulphiné, des ordonnances du roy de France, soubz la charge et conduicte de hault et puissant Seigneur monseigneur de Ligny, faisoit crier et publier ung tourney au dehors de la ville d'Ayre, et joignant les murailles à tous venans, au vingtiesme jour de juillet, de trois coups de lance sans lice, à fer esmolu, et en harnoys de guerre ; et douze coups d'espée, le tout à cheval. Et au mieulx faisant donnoit ung brasselet d'or esmaillé de sa livrée, et du prix de trente escuz. Le lendemain seriot combatu à pied, a poux de lance, à une barrière de la halteur du nombril ; et après la lance rompue à coups de hache, jusques à la discrétion des juges et de ceulx qui garderoient le camp. Et au mieulx faisoit donnoit ung dyamant du pris de quarante escus."*

On the first day, on the trumpet sounding, *le bon Chevalier* presented himself for the first course, his adversary being a neighbour from Dauphiny named Tartarin, in which the latter broke his lance within six inches of the head, thus forfeiting a point ; and jousting between other cavaliers lasted until evening. On the second day Bayard fought at barriers against a Messire Honotin de Sucre, first with lances and afterwards with axes. Bayard struck his adversary two heavy blows over the region of the ear, the second of which bore him to the ground. Other foot encounters followed, after which the prizes for the two days were awarded by the judges to *le bon Chevalier*, as having done the best on both days, but he refused to accept them, and they were adjudged to other champions who came next in order of merit.[1] The Chevalier's next tourney was at Carignan, in Italy, at which he gained the prize.[2]

Chapter XXII tells how *le bon Chevalier* fought at barriers at Andre with Don Alonce de Soto-Majori. Bayard had wished the combat to be on horseback, owing to some trouble in his legs which hindered locomotion ; but the Spaniard insisted all the more on fighting on foot, and this was finally arranged to take place. The weapons selected were estocs and daggers, and the fight commenced with an exchange of thrusts with the former, in which Soto-Majori was slightly wounded in the face ; then Bayard, making a feint, thrust his sword right through the neck of his adversary, inflicting a fatal wound. The Spaniard, in his death agony, clutched the body of the Frenchman with his arms and both combatants fell to the ground. Bayard then drew his dagger, crying, "*Rendez vous, Seigneur Alonce, ou vous estes mort*" ; but he had

[1] Chapter X, 1.   [2] Chapter XIII.

hardly uttered the words when the Spaniard expired. The Chevalier then knelt down and thanked God for his victory.

The Chevalier's next combat was at Monervyne, in the Kingdom of Naples, thirteen Spaniards against the same number of Frenchmen, which took place during a truce between the two armies, the leaders of this encounter being the Seigneur d'Oroze and *le bon Chevalier* respectively. A condition of the articles of combat was that any cavalier on being unhorsed should render himself a prisoner to the side opposing him. The fight began, and the Spaniards unchivalrously aimed their lances at the horses of their adversaries instead of at their riders; but, in spite of this dishonourable ruse, the honours of the battle are stated to have lain with the Frenchmen.

Other examples of Bayard's prowess and chivalry in the tournament are given in the chronicle. The dates given by chroniclers of jousts and *pas d'armes* are apt to vary somewhat, partly owing to the different methods of computing the regnant years of a king.

A manuscript in the College of Arms, London, gives an account of the *pas d'armes* held at Westminster in honour of the marriage of Katharine of Arragon with Prince Arthur, the heir to the throne, in the seventeenth year of King Henry VII (1501). This narration is apparently the work of an official present at the meeting, and an abridged account of it follows here. Besides jousts and *mêlées*, there were fights at barriers, pageants, and mummeries most splendid, costly, fanciful and elaborate. A tilt was erected in the open space before Westminster Hall, and adjoining the lists were gaily decorated stands and galleries for the king, court and other spectators. For the knights, nobles and esquires taking part there were within the lists pavilions, which were removed before the jousting began. The first jousting is thus described :—

"And at furst curse ran the Duke of Bokyngham and the Lord Marquyes ; and the duke brake his staff right well, and wt great sleight and stringht, upon the Lord Marquyes ; and at the secunde curse the Lord Marquyes brake his staff oppon the Duke in like wise ; and then the residue of the Lords and Knights ranne orderly togiders, and, for the most parte at every curse, other the on staf, other the other, or moost comonly bothe, were goodly and wt great art and strength, brokyn of meny pecys ; that such a feld, and justs ryall, so noble and valiantly doon, have not been sene ne hard ; the which goodly feats, and those of the descripcion apperyth weil pleynn, and more opyn, in the bokys of the Harolds of Armys."

There is nothing said of the lances employed in the first day's jousting, as to whether they were rebated or not, but the courses which follow on the succeeding days are expressly stated to have been run with pointed lances "at the large."[1] We may thus assume that the running of the first day was at the tilt (else why its erection at all ?), and that lances with coronals were employed. Afterwards there was a *mêlée*, the weapons being "armyng swords" (i.e. *estocs*). On the fourth day jousting was again followed by a tourney (*mêlée*).[2] The lances were tipped with coronals, and the weapons in the tourney were estocs, as before. Many of the cavaliers were unhorsed in the jousting and in the *mêlée* : "Sume of their swords were brokyn in two peces, and sume other their harneis was heuen off from their body, and felle into the feld." Then the prizes, consisting of diamonds, rubies and rings of gold, were awarded.

In 1502 a "Solemne Triumphe" was held in the Tower of London.

Plate 118 in *Das Turnierbuch Johan des Beständigen*, *Kurfürst* of Saxony, depicts a course with sharp lances, run at Naumburg in 1505, between Duke Hans of Saxony and Georg von Brandestein. The duke keeps his seat, but his opponent is unhorsed. The armour is of the kind usually employed in this course (*Scharfrennen*).

In the *Turnierbuch* of Duke William of Bavaria is a picture of an *Anzogenrennen*, held in the year 1512. The body armour employed is that used in all the varieties of *Rennen*, though the shield in this course is much larger than in the others, extending up to the *ocularium* of the jousting-salade, thus covering the face. This shield has been described under the heading *Anzogenrennen*. The armour with the shield is illustrated by Boeheim.[3]

There was jousting at Paris in 1513, at which the Duc de Valois was the chief tenant, and many courses were run.[4]

Jousts were held at Lille, in the same year, in a large hall paved with black marble, and the horses were shod with felt to prevent their slipping.[5]

In 1515, in honour of the marriage of the king, jousts took place at Paris, which had been proclaimed by the Dauphin, as follows :—

"Nemelie, that he with nine aides should answer all commers, being gentlemen of name and armes. First, to run fiue courses at the tilt with péeces of advantage[6] ; after fiue courses at random[7] with sharpe speares, and twelue strokes with sharpe swords ; and that doone, he

---

[1] Without a tilt.

[2] The term "tourney" is very frequently employed by chroniclers to express the mêlée, though also often applied in a general sense.　　[3] *Waffenkunde*, Fig. 631.　　[4] Monstrelet, *Continuation*, Chap. CCXXXIX.

[5] *Arch. Journ.*, LV, 306.　　[6] Reinforcing pieces.　　[7] Without a tilt.

and his aids to fight at the barriers with all gentlemen of name and armes. First, six foins with hand speares, and after that eight strokes to the most aduantage if the speares so long held, and after that twelue strokes with the sword; and if any man be vnhorsed or felled with fighting on foot, then his horse and armour to be rendered to the officer of armes; and eueri man of this challenge must set vp his armes and name vpon an arch triumphant, which shalbe made at the place where the iusts shalbe, and further shall write to what point he will answer, to one or all."

When this *fête d'armes* was proclaimed in England, "the duke of Suffolke, the marquis of Dorset and his four brethrern, the lord Clinton, sir Edward Neuille, sir Giles Capéll, Thomas Cheneie and others sued the king to be at the chalenge, which request he gratiouslie granted." "The Dolphin desired the duke of Suffolke and the marquess Dorset to be two of his immediate aids, which they thereto assented." Four shields were set up—viz. silver, gold, black and tawny—under which the venans were to write their names, electing, in their order, whether to run at the tilt, in the open with sharp lances, to fight on foot with one-handed swords, or lastly, with two-handers. This *pas d'armes* continued over three days, during which 305 cavaliers each ran five courses, some with sharp lances, and several were killed. In the joust in the open the Duke of Suffolk wounded an antagonist almost to the death. The Dauphin was wounded in the hand, so that he was unable to take further part. Many other particulars and details of this passage of arms are given by Holinshed.[1]

Among the Ashmolean MSS. is one relating to the proclamation of jousts to be held at a later date and to letters-of-safeguard issued to intending venans. The document is of the year 1520, and runs as follows:—

"The lettres of savegarde given by the said King of England [Henry VIII] unto Thomas Walle al's Norrey King of Armes, for the proclamacōn of the same Ioustes in the parties of Almayn and the contrye of Germania, wch Norrey proclaimed thē welle in French for the lowe contreys, as in High Dutch as hereafter followeth &c."[2]

In foot contests there was a rule that no one who had seen a challenger fight on foot on any previous occasion was allowed to engage him. It is difficult to understand the reason for this condition, and it was often waived on permission being given by an intended opponent.

Charles V, in January, 1518, two years before he became emperor, took part in a tournament at which twelve horses were killed; and in another in the March following, when seven cavaliers lost their lives.[3]

Henry VIII, like his friend Maximilian of Austria, took great delight

---

[1] *Chronicles*, III, 605.   [2] See Appendix A.   [3] *Archæological Journal*, LV, 302.

in the tourney and in the pageantry so frequently combined with it, and much money and labour was expended in staging the many functions of the kind held during his reign. Henry greatly encouraged these martial games and frequently took part in them; indeed, Hall remarks "that the king was not minded to see young gentlemen inexpert in martial feats." This chronicler positively revels in picturing these brilliant scenes, devoting himself more especially to their spectacular aspect, and giving full details of the dresses and equipment of those taking part, together with particulars of the general surroundings, though little is said of the martial games themselves. The pageantry and mummeries associated with the tournament were often of almost incredible puerility, and they detracted greatly from the dignity of these warlike sports. There were many childish conceits at these gatherings, all showing that the tourney had reached an advanced stage of its decline. Such costly shows went greatly out of fashion after the death of Henry VIII.

Jousts, combined with pageants, were held in honour of the coronation of the king, and Holinshed thus describes them:—" For the more honour and innobling of the triumphant coronation, there were prepared both iusts and turneis to be doone in the palace of Westminster, where, for the king's grace and the queen's, was framed a faire house, couered with tapestrie, and hanged with rich clothe of Arras, and in the said palace was made a curious founteine and ouer it a castell, on the top thereof a great crowne imperiall, all the imbatelling with roses and pomgranats gilded," and many other conceits.

The tenans in the jousting on this occasion were Thomas, Lord Howard; his brother, Sir Edward Howard; Lord Richard, the Admiral; Lord Richard, brother to the Marquis of Dorset; Sir Edmund Howard; Sir Thomas Knevit and Charles Brandon, Esquire. Their bases and trappers were of green velvet, charged with roses and pomegranates of gold fringed with damask gilded.

The venans were Sir John Pechie, Sir Edward Neville, Sir Edward Guildford, Sir John Carr, Sir William Parr, Sir Giles Capell, Sir Griffith Dun and Sir Roulande. Their bases and trappers were of tissue, cloth of gold, silver and velvet.

The second day was devoted to the *mêlée*. No details of the jousting itself or of the tourney are given. Both Hall and Holinshed describe this meeting.

PLATE IX

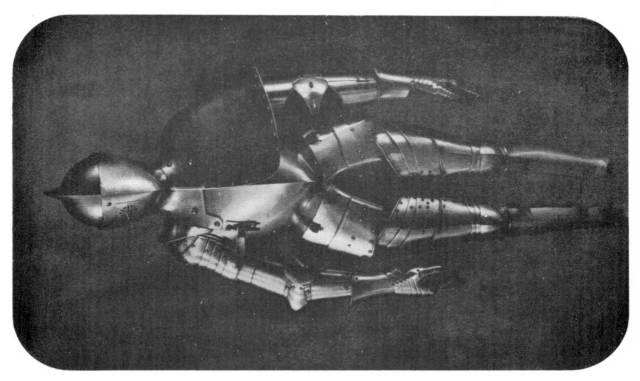

SUIT IN THE WALLACE COLLECTION FOR JOUSTING AT THE TILT

A HARNESS FOR THE GERMAN JOUST. WALLACE COLLECTION

On the twelfth of January following jousts were held in the park at Richmond "vnknown to the kynges grace, whereof, he beyng secretly informed, caused hymself and one of his priue chambre, called Willyā Compton to be secretly armed, and so came into the Iustes vnknowen to all persones and vnloked for. The kyng ranne neuer openly before, and there were broken many staues, and greate praise geuen to the two straungers, but specially to one, whiche was the kyng." "Master Compton was sore hurte and likely to dye."[1]

Holinshed tells us that in May, 1510, the king with his aides challenged all comers to fight at barriers at Greenwich, viz. casting the spear and twelve strokes with two-handed swords. Henry much distinguished himself by his great strength and judgment.

On the 13th November in the same year Henry, with Charles Brandon and "Mayster" Compton, answered all comers for two days, the first at the tilt, the second at the tourney. "At these iusts the king brake more staues than any other, and therefore had the pryse : at the Turney in likewyse the honor was his."[2]

The original Roll of the "Iusts" held at Westminster on the 13th February, 1511, in honour of Queen "Katherin" on the birth of Prince Henry, is now in the College of Arms, London. It is of parchment, $14\frac{1}{2}$ inches broad, the figures of the combatants and others being from seven to eight inches in height; and the whole is in an excellent state of preservation. The roll is headed with the words "Viue le noble Roy H. VIII," followed by a large device of a rose and pomegranates surmounted by a crown, impaled with the letters H and K. Some of the figures are armed at all points, while others are in civil dress, thus constituting an invaluable record of the costumes of the day.

The picture of the procession to the lists is headed by " Le Maistre de Armurerye du Roy," in civil dress, with his guard, and immediately after him follow the sergeant-at-arms, holding his crowned bâton of office; then five trumpeters, one of them a negro. In their order march after them a band of courtiers, and "Les Officiers d'Armes," being heralds and pursuivants, in tabard-shaped surcoats. Then come the four tenans, each riding under a " Pauilion," with their varlets. Two led horses immediately follow the king, and they afford a good opportunity for observing the saddles employed in jousting at the tilt. After them ride " Les pages du Roy," the marshal of the lists, " Le

---

[1] Hall's *Chronicle*, p. 513.   [2] Hall, 516.

grant Escuyer," and "Le maistre des Pages." The tenans are seen approaching the gaily-decorated stand, in which the queen and her court are seated, and the venans are reaching it on the other side. The picture closes with the king on horseback in civil dress—"Le Roy desarmey"—holding a broken lance in his hand. He is preceded by his helm-bearer, on horseback, carrying the head-piece of his majesty on a truncheon. The helm is surmounted by a royal crown, enriched with gold, pearls, diamonds and rubies.

The roll concludes with a poem, in which the name of the king figures among a band of heroes, the others being Hector, Cæsar, Judas Maccabæus, Joshua, Charlemagne, King Arthur, Alexander, David and Codefroi de Bouillon.

The " tenantz " were—

His Grace the King   (Cœur Loyal),
Lord William of Devon (Bon Vouloir),
Sir Thomas Knevit   (Valliant Desyr),
Sir Edward Nevyle   (Joyeulx Penser).

They all subscribed to the articles of combat, which follow here—

" And for as moche as after the order & Honnor of Arms hyt is not lefull for any man to enterpryse Arms in so high a presens without hys Stocke and name be of Nobles dyscended. In consyderation theis four Knights be of so fer & straunge partes. they shall present themselff wt their names and Arms portend [pictured] in their shylde.

Item these four Knights shall present themselves in the feyld at the paleys of Rychmond or elles where hyt shall please the Kynges Grace. at the tyme of Candelmas next or nigh theirupon in harneys for the tylt wt out tache or breket, *wolant pece on the hedde*[1] Rondell on the garde rest. aduntag (sic). fraude. deceyt or any malengyne.

Item to every comer shall be Runne six courses pvyed [provided] allway yf the comers be of sush greate number that they cannot reasonably be for on [one] day Hyt shallbe lefull for the four challengers to enter the felde the Second day and so to answere all the comers to the full nomber be served of soche as be noble of name or of Armes and wt out report.

Item all speres to be garnished and brought to the ffeyld at the pvision and chardge of the Chalengers, of the wch speres the answerers to have the Choice.

Item yf yt happe any Man as God defend to kyll his fellows Horse by way of fowle Runnyng. He shallbe bound yf so doth to give the horse yt he rydeth on to his felow or the pryse of the Horse so kyld at the dyscresion of the Iudges.

Item who stryketh his felow beneth the wast or in the sadell with full course be [by] way of fowle Runnynge he shallbe dysalowed for two speres before broken.

Item who stryketh his felow uncharged & disgarnyshed of his speare he shallbe disalowed at the descression of the Iudges.

Item who breaketh his spere above the Charnell [coronal] to be allowed[2] two speres well broken after the old custom of Arms.

Item who breaketh his spere morme to morme [coronal to coronal] to be allow'd three Speres after the Custome of Arms.

[1] The italics are ours.   [2] Disallowed ?

Item who breaketh most speres ys [is] bette worthey the pryse.

Item who stryketh Down Horse and Man is better worthe the pryse.

Item who stryketh his felow clene out of the Sadell is best worthe the pryse. Item if any Gentleman chalenger or defender breake a staff on the Tylt to be disalowed a staff.

Item yf yt is the pleasurs of the Kynge our most Dred Souaigne Lorde, the Queens Grace and the Ladies with the advice of the Noble and dyscret Iuges to give pryses after their deservings unto both the Parties.

Item that every Gentleman answerer do Subscrybe his name to the Artycalles."

Hall's florid account of this meeting, in a much abridged form, is as follows :—The jousting was combined with a pageant picturing a forest in which stood a castle of gold, and before it sat a gentleman weaving a garland of roses for the prize. Jousting began on the twelfth, and on the morrow there was a grand procession to the lists. The king was on horseback, armed at all points, riding under a " Pauilion " of cloth of gold and purple velvet, embroidered and powdered over with the letters " H " and " K " of fine gold, surmounted by an imperial golden crown and valanced with hanging wire of the same precious metal. The king's bases and the trapper of his charger were of cloth of gold, fretted with damask gold ; his crinet and chamfron were of steel, and on the latter was a plume garnished with golden spangles. Then followed his three aides, each riding under a " Pauilion " of crimson damask and purple, powdered over with the letters " H " and " K " in fine gold, valanced and fringed with damask gold, and on the top of each canopy a great " K " of goldsmith's work. After them marched a number of gentlemen and yeomen on foot, clad in russet and yellow cloth; then twelve children of honour, mounted on great coursers richly caparisoned. Then in the counterpart rode the " venantz," headed by Sir Charles Brandon,[1] who appears first on horseback in a long robe of russet satin, like a recluse, and he petitions the queen for permission to joust in her presence. His request having been granted, he doffed his cloak and appeared in full armour, with rich bases, and his horse nobly trapped for running at the tilt. In attendance on him were divers men clad in russet satin. Next came young Henry Guilford, Esquire, himself and horse in russet cloth of gold and cloth of silver, embroidered with a device like a castle or turret, and all his men in russet satin and white, with hose of the same and bonnets of a like colour; and he also petitioned the queen for permission to run. After him rode the Marquis of Dorset and Sir Thomas Bulleyn,[2] dressed

---

[1] Created Duke of Suffolk in 1514.   [2] Father of Anne,

as pilgrims in tabards of black velvet, with palmer's hats over their helmets and long Jacob's staffs in their hands. Their horses were trapped in black velvet, which, like their hats and tabards, was garnished with scallop shells of fine gold; their servants were in black satin, with the same kind of shells pinned to their breasts. Then came Lord Henry of Buckingham, Earl of Wiltshire, himself and his horse draped in cloth of silver, embroidered with a "posye" of golden arrows and roses, and above the flowers the figure of a greyhound in silver holding a tree of pomegranates in gold. Then entered Sir Giles Capell, Sir Roulande and many other knights, richly armed and apparelled.

The jousting began and was gallantly achieved, the prize being awarded to the king. The proceedings were followed by music and the dance, closing with a pageant.[1] What a contrast between this passage of arms and the tournament held in 1278, *temp*. Edward I, as described in Chapter II.

Ashmole, No. 1116, fol. 109-10b, runs as follows :—" Iustes holden at Westminster the XIIth daie of February by the Kinges grace called Cueur Loyal, the Lord William of Devon Bon Voloir, Sir Thomas Knevit Valiant Desire, and Edward Nevell Joyous Penser, with the articles and courses of the said Iustes," etc. The articles begin thus— "The noble lady Renowne considering the good and gracious fortune. . . ." The "courses" (checques) were tilting tablets for recording the scores for two days (Wednesday and Thursday, February 12th, 13th, 1511), marked with strokes, and accounts of the "best Ioustres."

In the tournament illustrated on the Herald's College Roll it is stated that 264 courses were run at the tilt and but 129 attaints made. The tenans scored seventy-seven of these, the king himself making thirty-eight hits out of fifty-two courses. Of the venans, one made no hits at all and six only struck once in six courses.[2]

Another meeting took place on the 1st May following, at which the tenans were the king, Sir Edward Howard, Charles Brandon and Sir Edward Nevil; the venans being the Earl of Essex, the Earl of Devon, the Marquis of Dorset and Lord Howard.[3]

In the fourth year of King Henry's reign—

"the King had a solempne iust at Grenewiche in Iune: first came in ladies all in White and Red silke, set vpon Coursers trapped in the same suite, freated ouer with gold, after which folowed a Fountain curiously made of Russet sattin, with eight Gargilles spoutyng water,

---

[1] Hall's *Chronicle*, p. 516.   [2] *Arch. Journ.*, LV, 338.   [3] Hall's *Chronicle*, 520.

PLATE X

GERMAN ARMOUR FOR JOUSTING AT THE TILT. AT DRESDEN

AN ARMOUR FOR *FREITURNIER*. AT DRESDEN

within the fountain sat a knight armed at all peces. After the Fountain folowed a lady all in black silke dropped with fine siluer, on a courser trapped in the same. After folowed a knight in a horse litter, the Coursers and litter apparareled in blacke velvet with siluer droppes. When the Fountain came to the tilt, the Ladies rode rounde aboute, and so did the Fountain and the knight within the litter. And after them wer brought twoo goodly Coursers appareled for the iusts: and when they came to the tiltes ende, the twoo knightes mounted on the two Coursers, abidyng all commers. The king was in the fountain and Sir Charles Brandon was in the litter. Then suddenly with great noyse of the Trompets, entered Sir Thomas Kneuit in a castle of cole blacke, and ouer the castell was written, 'The dolorous Castle,' and so he and the erle of Essex, the lorde Haward and other ran their courses, with the King and Sir Charles Brandon and euer the king brake moste speres."[1]

There were royal jousts held in October, 1513, the king and Lord Lisle answering all comers. His Majesty was attended by twenty-four knights clad in robes of purple velvet and cloth of gold, and many lances were broken.[2]

In 1515 Henry, with the Marquis of Dorset, challenged all comers to a joust, and the king "brake three and twentie speres beside attaints and bare downe to ground a man of armes and his horse."[3]

In the same year on twelfth-night the king held a *Scharmützel*, being the attack and defence of a mock fortress, at Eltham.[4]

Royal jousts were held again in June, 1519, at which 506 lances were splintered.[5]

Royal jousts in March, 1520.[6]

In the eighth year of his reign the king proclaimed solemn jousts in honour of his sister, the Queen of Scotland,[7] to extend over two days. The tenans on the first day were the king himself, the Duke of Suffolk, the Earl of Essex and Nicholas Carew, Esquire. The venans numbered twelve. On the second day the king ran against Sir William Kingston, a tall and strong knight, and unhorsed him. The apparel of the tenans and their horses "was blacke velvet, covered all over with braunches of honey suckels of fine flat gold of damaske, of lose worke, every lefe of the braunch moving, the embroudery was very conning and sumptuous."[8][10]

There was another passage of arms in the year following, at which 506 lances were splintered.[9]

The following documents occur among the Harleian MSS.:—"Justs at Greenwich, the 20th daie of Maye, the 8th yeare of the Raigne of our Soveraigne Ld. K. Henry VIII." The score of each jouster is given.

[1] Hall's *Chronicle*, 533.   [2] *Ibid.* 564.   [3] Holinshed, III, 609.   [4] *Ibid.* III, 613.   [5] *Ibid.* III, 625.
[6] *Ibid.* III, 636.   [7] Margaret Tudor, afterwards married to the sixth Earl of Douglas.
[8] Hall, 584.   [9] *Ibid.* 591.   [10] Probably the same meeting mentioned by Holinshed under 1519.

"*Coppye de Chapitres (ou Articles) des certaine Faits d'Armes, tant a Pied, comme a Cheval, qui par deux Gentilmomes d'Almaigne touchant une certaine Emprise.*"[1]

The jousts and tourneys of the Field of the Cloth of Gold were held on a truly magnificent scale, and, indeed, everything was done to make them a triumphant spectacular success. The cavaliers of the two nations, like the ladies present, vied with each other in the richness of their dresses and appointments, and the two monarchs greatly distinguished themselves in the tilt-yard. The lists themselves are stated to have been 150 paces long, and were placed in a plain surrounded by a ditch. Stands were erected for the officials and spectators, and pavilions were pitched for the use of the cavaliers taking part. The jousting was with blunted lances, each challenger to run eight courses. The two kings entered the enclosure on June 11th, 1520, armed at all points, at the time appointed. The horse of his Majesty of France was trapped with purple satin broached with gold and embroidered with raven's plumes hatched with gold, and on his helm he wore a lady's sleeve. The trapper of the King of England was of cloth of gold tissue, fringed with damask and knitted together with golden points. In attendance on King Henry were Sir Henry Guilford, Master of the Horse; Sir John Pechie, Governor of Calais; Sir Edmund Guilford, General of the Forces; and Monsieur Morel, attached to his suite by King Francis. They all wore the royal livery.

The jousting began, the onset was sounded, and King Henry ran against Monsieur Grandevile, and the helm of the Frenchman was fractured. The Duc de Vendôme ran five courses against the Duke of Suffolk, each breaking his lance on the other's body. After many more jousts had been accomplished the signal to cease for the day was given, the heralds crying "*Desarmée*" and the trumpets sounded *à l'hostel* (to lodgings).

On Tuesday, the 12th, ten gentlemen of the French king's Swiss Guard tilted against eleven of the band of Monsieur de Tremouille.

On Wednesday, the 13th, the King of France, with his aides, and King Henry, with his following, rode at the tilt, after which there was much jousting between the knights of France and England; and towards evening King Francis left for Ard and the English monarch departed for his castle of Guisnes.

---

[1] See Appendix B.

On the Thursday the French king tilted with the Earl of Devonshire and others, and King Henry ran against Monsieur Montmorencie and Rafe Brooke. On the Friday there was fighting at barriers, and on the Saturday a banquet was given by the French king and his suite at the Castle of Guisnes. A Frenchman was killed when fighting on foot.

On the Monday the fêtes were in abeyance, owing to a great storm, but on the Tuesday the two kings came to the lists, armed at all points, and jousting was resumed. Wednesday and Thursday were devoted to the *mêlée*, and on Friday, June 22nd, "the two kings with their retinues did battle on foot at barriers.[1] The French cavaliers wore doublets of cloth of silver and purple velvet, while those of the English were of cloth of gold and russet velvet. The weapons were spears and swords.

On Saturday, after a banquet, there was again fighting at barriers, first with spears and afterwards with two-handed swords.

The *pas d'armes* was followed by masks, more banqueting and the dance. Both Hall and Holinshed describe this historic meeting.

Among the Ashmolean MSS. are the following concerning the Field of the Cloth of Gold :—" *Ce sont les noms des princes, prellatz, et grans seigneurs de France, qui estoient en la compaignie de Roy de France quant le Roy [Henry VIII] Dengleterre et led' sr le Roy [François] sentrevyrent et ordonnerent les Iousts et Tournoys qui sensuyvent.*" Prefixed to the title is a stanza of five lines inviting to the jousts.

" The proclamacõn in Frenche of the Articles of the Iustes and other feates of armes at the meeting of the aforesaid Kinges [Henry and François] at Guisnes, proclaimed throughout the realme of France by Thomas Benolt al's Clarencieux King of Armes. *Comme ainsi soit louange.*"[2]

Imperial royal jousts were run in the month of March of the thirteenth year of the reign, of which Hall gives an account ; and there were others in the year following.

On March 10th, 1524, King Henry ran a great risk of losing his life in the tilt-yard, for when jousting with Brandon, Duke of Suffolk, he forgot to shut and clasp down the visor of his helmet. Brandon, who was short-sighted, did not perceive this, and in his career aimed his lance at that part of the king's head-piece, striking it at the side of the face, unhelming his Majesty, though without causing him any

---

[1] Another account says that on that day the two kings preferred to look on.   [2] See Appendix A.

injury. As already mentioned, in a joust held on Shrove Tuesday in the year 1525 Sir Charles Bryan nearly lost an eye from a somewhat similar cause.

King Henry, like his friend Maximilian of Austria, is always represented as the successful jouster, and, although his strength, skill and good fortune are generally admitted, some explanation is required to account for his invariable success. It has been suggested that it may have been due in some measure to the prerogative of the queen, by which a joust could be stopped if there should be any probability of the king's defeat.[1]

"On May-day *anno* 1536 was a great jousting held at Greenwich, at which the chief challenger was the Lord Rochford, the queen's brother; and the defendant was one Henry Norris, of the king's bedchamber, with others. They managed their arms with great dexterity, and every course which they ran came off with the loud applause of the people."[2]

"Another solemne Challenge was proclaimed and perfourmed by certaine English Knights, viz. Sir John Dudley,[3] Sir Thomas Seimer, Sir Francis Poynings, Sir George Carew, Anthony Kingston and Richard Cromwel. *Anno* 1540."

Royal jousts were run on the thirty-first year of the reign, in celebration of the king's marriage with Anne of Cleves.

Lacroix, in *Military and Religious Life in the Middle Ages*, pictures the degradation of a knight convicted of dishonourable conduct, copied from a wood-cut bearing the initials " J. A." (Jost Amman). The culprit is exposed on a scaffold, clad only in his shirt, his armour is broken in pieces before him and thrown at his feet, and his spurs are cast upon a dunghill. His shield is dragged by a cart-horse through the mire, and the tail of his *destrier* cut off. A herald-at-arms cries three times, "Who is there?" and each time the name of the knight is given. The herald then cries, "No, it is not so; I see no knight, but only a false coward." The culprit is borne on a litter into a church, where the burial service is read over him, and the world of chivalry knows him no more.

There is no record of any royal jousts on the accession of Edward VI to the throne, and such pastimes would seem to have been greatly in abeyance during that short reign.

The same would seem to have been the case during the reign of Queen Mary; but there were fights at barriers in 1554, when Philip II arrived in England. The challengers, against all comers, were Don

---

[1] *Archæologia*, LXIII, 32.   [2] *Harleian Miscellany*, X, 306.   [3] Afterwards Duke of Northumberland.

Fredericke de Toledo, the Lord Strange, Don Ferdinando de Toledo, Don Francisco de Mendoça, and Garsulace de la Vega.

The prizes were as follows, viz. :—

" 1. He who cometh forth most gallantly, though without superfluities, shall have a rich brooch.
2. The best stroke with the pike shall have a ring with a ruby.
3. The best stroke with the sword shall have a ring with a diamond.
4. He that fighteth most valiantly shall have a ring with a diamond.
5. The prize of all together in rank at the foyle was a ring of gold with a rich diamond.

He that giveth a stroke with a pike from the girdle downwards shall win no prize.
He that shall have a close gauntlet or anything to fasten his sword to his hand shall win no prize.
He whose sword falls out of his hand shall win no prize.
He that striketh his hand in fight on the barriers shall win no prize.
Whosoever shall fight and not show his sword to the judges shall win no prize."

The prizes were thus awarded by the judges, in the above order, to :—
Don Fredericke de Toledo.
Don Diego Ortado di Mendoça.
Sir John Parrat.
Ruygomez.[1]   And
King Philip, in highest honour."[2]

During the reign of Queen Elizabeth vigorous efforts were made to revive the ancient glories of the tournament, which were for a time not without a certain measure of success, under the auspices of the maiden queen. Sir Henry Lee rode as the queen's champion until advancing years caused him to relinquish the self-imposed office in favour of the Earl of Cumberland, who wore a glove of her Majesty's on his helmet.

A drawing, from a MS., of tilting, tourney and barriers is reproduced in Lord Dillon's paper in the *Archæological Journal*, Vol. LV, which affords a good deal of information regarding the detail of such combats during the reign.

There were jousts and barriers on the accession of Queen Elizabeth to the throne in 1558, in which the Duke of Norfolk and the earls of Surrey, Warwick and Leicester took part.[3]

The *fête d'armes* at which Henri II of France was fatally injured was held at Paris in 1559. The tenans on the occasion were the king, the Prince of Ferrera, the Duke of Guise and others. The course in which the accident befel was an extra one, run in the face of remon-

---

[1] The famous minister of Philip II.
[2] See Ashmolean, MS. 845, 171a; and Harl. MS., Codex 69, Art. 20.
[3] *Archæological Journal*, LXI, 304.

strances on the part of the other challengers. The cause of the injury would seem to have been that the Comte de Montgomeri, Captain of the Scottish Guard, failed to drop his shivered lance immediately after impact, as he ought to have done, and the jagged end striking the king's visor, a splinter passed through the slit for vision and pierced his brain. The king's case was hopeless from the first, though he lingered in agony for nearly a week. The king's accidental death was not avenged on Montgomeri at the time, but Catherine de Medici had him executed fifteen years later. Lacroix, in *Military and Religious Life in the Middle Ages*, gives a picture of this fatal encounter, copied from an engraving of the sixteenth century.

Viscount Dillon, in his paper "Barriers and Foot Combats," reproduces a picture of Spanish officers "At Barriers" in Brussels, 1569 (after Hogenberg). The details are interesting as showing the manner of fighting on foot at the time.

As stated in the Ashmolean MS., No. 837, fol. 245, a tournament was proclaimed at Hampton Court by Clarencieulx, King of Arms, on Twelfth-night, *anno* 1570, to take place in the month of May following. The MS. begins with a preamble, being a general exhortation to revive the tournament, which "had of late fallen a sleepe." Next come the *chapitres d'armes* (the articles) for the tilt, tourney and barriers. A copy of the document follows here :—

"For as much most noble Queene, as ther ar within this yor ma^{ties} Courte a greate nombre of noble menne and gentlemenne excellent men of Armes, and yet (as it wer) of late fallen a sleepe from eny kinde of such exercyse : Therfore by your ma^{ties} lycense, to revyve theim withall, ther ar fower Knightes Errant which haue thought goode to challenge all commers at Shrovetyde next as followeth. Videlicet.

Tilt

Vpon Shrouesonday at the Tylt, six courses a pece. And who so doth best of the Defendanntes in those six courses, shall have for his prize a cheyne of gold.

Tourney

Vpon Shrovemonday at the Tourney, two blowes at the passage, and tenne at the ioyninge. All grypes, shockes, and fowle playes forbidden. And who so doth best of the Defendantes at that feate, shall haue a Diamonde.

Barriours

Vpon Shrouetuesday at the Barriours, three pusshes with the short pyke, and tenne blowes with the sworde with open gauntlet : no Barriours to be layde hande vpon, nor eny weopen to be taken holde of. And he of the Defendantes that doth best ther at, shall haue a Rubie.

[The entire page is scored out. On the back of the page, which is written by Glover, a second hand has written, the other way up :—]

The proclemacion that was procleamed at hampton court by Clarencieulx Kyng of armes on twelffe daye at nyght in A°/1570/ the chalengers names was the erle of Oxfford Charles howard S^r henry Lee and christoffer hatton a pencioner.

Theys excercyses was not Fulffylled tyle maye deye next after on which daye was the tylte at westmynster and the second daye of maye the torney and on Sonday byeing the vj of maye the barrioures."

Another MS. in the same collection (No. 845, fol. 164) gives a list of the participants, with their "checques" (which are tablets for recording the scores made). Examples of these registers are given here, under the heading of the document in question :—

[Endorsed :—Tournay.

Two blowes at the passage : and tenne at the ioyninge : All gryppes shockes and foule playe forbidden.]

[A list of names is also on folio 164 b.]

[fol. 164.]

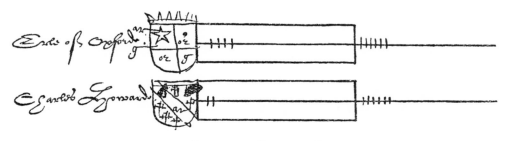

SCORING "CHECQUES."

[54 more, as above, 25 without arms.]

The tenans on the occasion were the Earl of Oxford, Lord Charles Howard, Sir Henry Lee, and Christopher Hatton, a "pencioner," and a list of their opponents, with their "Checques," is given in the Ashmolean MS. No. 845, fol. 167. (See page 128.)

The prize for the best lance among the tilters was "a cheyne of gold," which fell to the Earl of Oxford, who ran forty-two courses and splintered thirty-two lances, a very good performance. The prize for the tourney was a "Diamonde"; that for "barriours" a "Rubie," which was won by Thomas Cecil, one of the venans.

In 1590, after the seige of Paris had been raised, King Henri IV

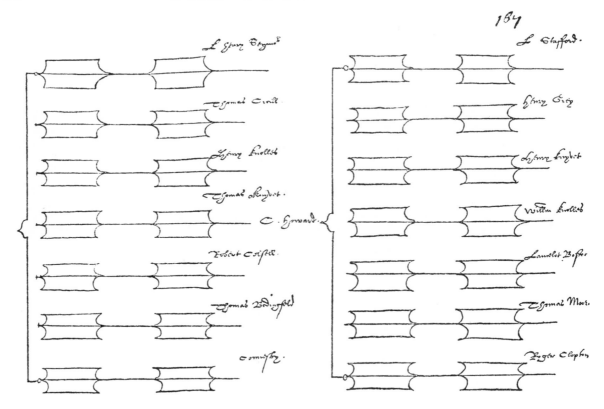

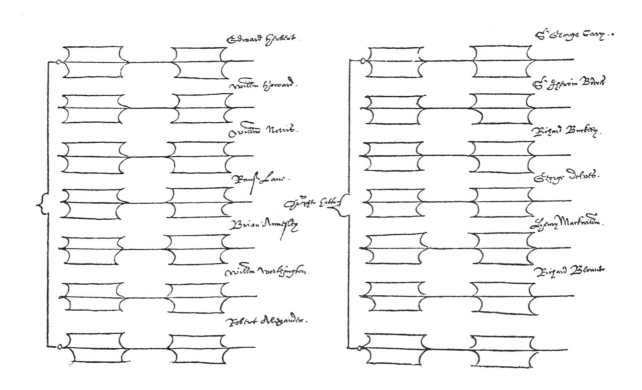

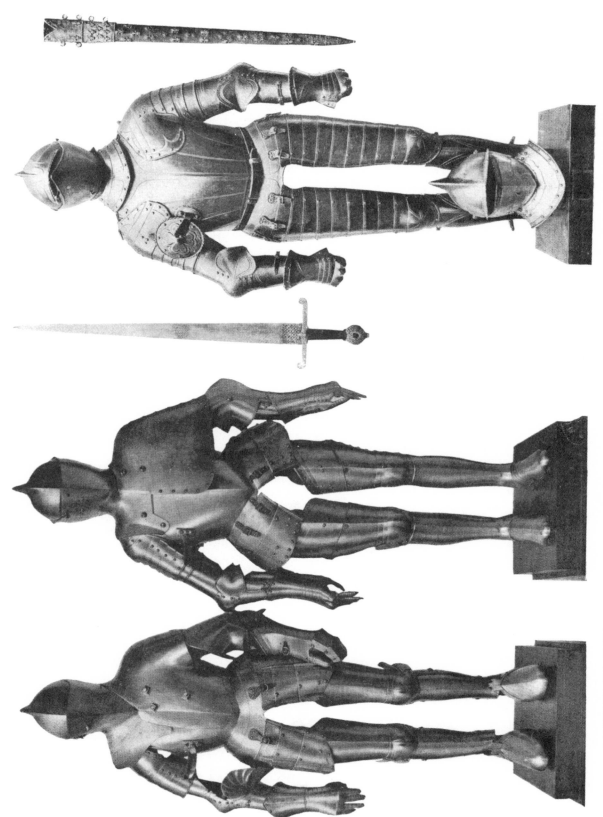

PLATE XI

FIELD HARNESS OF ANNE DE MONTMORENCY

HARNESSES FOR JOUSTING AT THE TILT.   AT PARIS

challenged the Duc de Mayenne to single combat, in order that by a decisive result the calamities of France might be stayed, but nothing came of it.

A tournament was held at Westminster under the leadership of Walter, Earl of Essex, which is chiefly remarkable from the fact of its having taken place during the night. It was on the occasion when Anne de Montmorency, Constable of France, came to London to receive the Order of the Garter, in June, 1572. Queen Elizabeth gave a supper in celebration of the event, at which she presided, and in due time she retired to her apartments. The weather being warm, however, it pleased her Majesty to walk from her chamber on to the open terrace of the palace, where the French duke and his suite were assembled, with many of the English courtiers. The Earl of Essex entered the terrace quite suddenly, accompanied by twelve gentlemen armed at all points and well mounted.

"The Earl and his horse were furnished with white cloth of siluer, and the rest in white sattin, who after reuerence done to her Maiesty, marched to the east side of the Court, and there in troope, stood firme. Forthwith entered Edward Earle of Rutland, with a like number, in like sort armed and apparelled all in blew; and hauing presented his reuerence, stayed on the west end. Before either of these bands, one Chariot was drawen, and therein a faire Damsell, conducted by an armed Knight, who pronounced certain speeches in the French tongue, vnto her Maiestie. These Ceremonies passed, the Queene commanded the armed men to fall vnto fight, which they performed with great courage, and commendation, chiefly in the Earl of Essex, a noble personage, valorous in armes, and all other wayes of great vertue.

Of the Actors names in this Triumph (it seemeth) no note is kept: yet are many of them still liuing."

The ordinances and regulations which controlled the routine of a tournament, some of them compiled for general use and others framed for particular contests, have been repeatedly referred to in these pages; but the method of the keeping of scores is nowhere clearly indicated, and, indeed, is but rarely mentioned. The score was marked in strokes by a king of arms, sometimes by a pursuivant,[1] on a scoring tablet, termed a "checque," which was tricked with a shield of the arms of the owner, as shown on page 127. The scoring-board itself was in the form of a parallelogram, with three horizontal lines, the middle line projecting some distance beyond the others, and on the projection of this middle line the number of courses run (usually from two to eight)

[1] The duties of "pursuivants d'armes" are given by Sainte-Palaye in his *Mémoires sur L'Ancienne Chevalerie* (I, 32), and among them is that of registering the scores, "*& afin de n'en point perdre la mémoire, on y portoit des tablettes pour enregistrer les faits & les circonstances les plus remarquables.*"

were registered. The attaints were noted on the top line; and they were often differentiated as hits on the body or head, which had a different value in the tale.[1] The middle line inside the parallelogram was for the staves well broken, and the bottom line for those "ill-broken—that is, broken within a foot of the head of the lance or on the tilt, on the adversary's saddle, etc.—these being deducted from the score or disallowed. The proportion in the number of attaints varied greatly, though on the average it would appear that the misses made in jousting at the tilt (i.e. when the jousters failed to touch each other in their careers) were greater in number than the hits made; while in jousting "at the wide" the proportion of attaints was much greater. The registration was done by vertical strokes on the horizontal lines.

As many as ten jousting cheques have been found, which help to a knowledge as to how the scoring was managed, though more light is needed on the subject.

The rules and regulations concerning the conducting of tournaments in Tudor times were based on those framed in 1466 by John Tiptoft, Earl of Worcester, Constable of England, which are given in our Chapter IV; but there is no rule among them directly mentioned concerning the method of scoring the points. There are, however, pictures of the scoring cheques, reproduced by Mr. ffoulkes in his paper in *Archæologia*, Vol. LXIII, Plate IV, Nos. 2, 3, which appear at the ends of two of the versions of the Tiptoft rules; viz. those in Harl. MS. 2413, fol. 16, and Ashmole MS. 763, fol. 149. Two cheques out of the fifty-six in Ashmole MS. 845, fol. 164, are reproduced on our Fig. 1. They are those of the Earl of Oxford and Charles Howard, being registers of their scores at the passage of arms which was proclaimed by Clarencieulx in 1570.

This somewhat intricate subject can only be lightly touched upon in these pages; but we may refer any of our readers who may wish to pursue the subject further to Lord Dillon's paper, "Tilting in Tudor Times," published in the *Archæological Journal*, Vol. LV, and to that written by Mr. Charles ffoulkes in *Archæologia*, LXIII, entitled "Jousting Cheques of the Sixteenth Century."

Three writers on certain features in the routine of a tournament are mentioned in the last-named monograph, *The Romance of Three*

---

[1] "He that on horsebacke directeth his Launce at the head, is more to be praised, than he that toucheth lower. For the higher the Launce hitteth, the greater is the Runners commendation."

King's Sons, written about the end of the fifteenth century,[1] from which the following extract is given :—

"All these thinges donne thei were embatailed eche ageynste the othir and the corde drawen ageynste eche partie, and whan the tyme was, the cordes were cutte and the Trumpettis blew up for euery man to do his deuoir. And for to assertayne you more of the Tournay there was on eche side a stake, and at eache stake two Kynges of Armes, with penne, and Inke, and paper, to write the names of all of them that were yolden, for they shold no more Tournay."

This refers to the *mêlée*, not the joust.

King René d'Anjou, in *Traicte de la forme et Devis d'ung Tournoi*, gives an illustration of a *mêlée* in which the attendants are seen cutting the cords with axes, but there are no kings of arms present noting the score.

Another reference occurs in the account given in the Landsdowne MS. 285 of the combat between the Bastard of Burgundy and Lord Scales in 1466, a contest which has been already described on these pages. It is entitled *The Ordenaunce of kepyng of the Feelde*, and runs—

". . . . At ev'y corner a Kyng of Armes crownyd and an Harauld or Pursevaunte within the seide feelde, for reporte makyng of actes doon within the same : Garter and othir Kynges of Armes and Hauraldes to be sett in the scaffolde before the Kyng on the right hande of the staire of the Kynges place judiciall' to make report generall' and to marke all that should be doon in the seide feelde."

And we may infer that a score of the points, for and against, was kept on the occasion.[2] Hall, in his narrative of the Field of the Cloth of Gold, states definitely that the scores of the combatants were marked down by the proper officials, English and French.

The Duc d'Alençon and three French gentlemen, with the earls of Sussex and Leicester, challenged all comers, in 1551, to fight at barriers, and they had forty-five opponents.[3]

Jousts were run at Westminster, in conjunction with a great pageant, on January 22nd, 1581, in the presence of Queen Elizabeth. The fêtes extended over several days, and many lances were broken at the tilting. The crowd was so great at the pageant that many citizens were maimed and some killed. Those taking part in the tilting were Henry Gray, Sir Thomas Perot, Anthony Cooke, Thomas Radcliffe, Robert and Francis Knolles, Rafe Bowes, Thomas Kelwaie, George Goring, William Tresham, Robert Alexander, Edward Dennie, Hercules Meantus, Edward Moore, Richard Skipwith, Richard Ward, Edward Digbie, Henry Nowell and Henry Brunkerd. During the running

---

[1] Harl. MS. 326, fol. 113 v°.   [2] *Archæologia*, Vol. LXIII.   [3] *Archæological Journal*, LXI, 305.

Sir Henry Lee entered the tilt-yard as The Unknown and, after breaking six lances, retired again. The challengers each ran six courses against all comers. A *Scharmützel*, being the attack and defence of a mock fortress on which cannon were mounted, took place later, and this was followed by the tourney and barriers. Taking part in these were the Earl of Arundel, Lord Windsor, Sir Philip Sidney and Fulke Greville, Esquire.[1]

A tournament was held on the 15th May following, as mentioned in Ashmole MS. No. 845, fol. 166, a copy of which follows :—

"The Tournay holden at Westminster on monday the 15. of May. 1581. when as the prince dolphine of Auuergne and other the frenche commissioners were here.

This mark at the end signifyeth that that party hath perfourmed his blowes at the passage and at the joyninge."

[46 more figures like this, with a line at the right end. They are arranged in two columns.]

The challengers were Monsieur the brother of the French King, the Prince Delphine,[2] the earls of Sussex and Leicester, the Count S. Aignon, Messires Chamuallan and Bacqueuile. The venans were led by Lord Thomas Howard.

Another tournament took place at Westminster on November 17th in the same year, and a list of names of those taking part is given in Ashmole MS. No. 845, fol. 165 :—

"1581. 24. R.R. Elizabeth

Therle of Arundell	)	The Lord Windesore
Henry Greye	)	Henry Windesore
Sr Henry Lee	)	Phellip Sidney
Sr Thomas Perot	)	Thomas Ratclyff
Foulke Grevill	)	Rawffe Bowes
Edward Norrys	)	Thomas Knevet
Anthony Cooke	)	John Pagingeton
George Gyfford	)	Thomas Kailloway
Robart Alexander	)	George Goringe
Edward More	)	Henry Bronkard
William Tresham	)	Rychard Warde
Everard Digby	)	Tyrrell
Storry	)	
William Knolles	)	Robart Knolles.

[1] The Continuation of the *Chronicles of England*, by John Stow and others.
[2] The Prince Dauphin, not the Dauphin of France.

These be the names of the noblemen and gentlemen, that for the honour of the Queenes Majestie did their endevour at the Tylt at Westminster on the xvijth day of Nouember, beinge the first day of the xxiiijth yere of the reigne of queene Elizabeth, whome God of his greate mercy longe contynue to reigne over this sinnefull realme of England. Amen."

In 1585 there is what is described as "the last joust on the Thames," but which was really a form of water quintain :—

"From ech end of the riuer came a bote running with six ores, in the stern of which on the top stood a man armed in a red wastcote, with a staffe in his reste, hauing a but end of corke ; now ech meeting other with their staues, both fell into the water, where spare botes were redi to succour them, for ouer went their horsses." [1]

Ashmole MS. No. 1109, fol. 154 b, gives a list of names of persons taking part in a tournament held at Windsor on November 17th, 1593.

"[In Officio Armorum Lib.] M. 4 : Justes. fo : 42

Course at Feild at Windsor the 17th of Nov: 1593. A° regni Reginæ 36.

The Earle of Cumberland	The Earle of Southampton.
The Earle of Essex	Robert Knowles.
The Lord Fitzwalter	Cary Reynoldes.
The Lord Compton	Henry Nowell.
Sr Charles Blount	Sr Tho: Gerrard.
Sr Vnknowen	Robert Dudley.
The E. of Essex [sic]	Sr William Knowles.

Judges { The Earle of Worcester
The Lord Sandes
The Lord North
The Lord Norrys "

In 1606, in the reign of James I, there was a fight at barriers in celebration of the ill-fated marriage of the Earl of Essex. Sixteen combatants fought on each side, first singly and then in threes. One party was led by the Duke of Lennox, the other by the Earl of Sussex.[2]

Another fight at barriers took place on Twelfth-night, 1610, when Henry Prince of Wales, with six aides, met sixty-five defendants at Whitehall. The weapons were pikes and single swords, and the prince, then in his sixteenth year, is stated to have greatly distinguished himself.[3]

Harleian MS., 111, 215, 4888, 20, is a general challenge at tilt, tourney, and barriers, "signed Lenox, Southampton, Pembroke, Montgumbray," dated 1612. It was in defence of these propositions—
"1. That in Service of Ladyes, Knights have no free-will. 2. That it is Beautie maintains the World in valour. 3. That noe fare Ladie was ever false. 4. That none can be perfectlye wife but Lover." The

---

[1] Continuation Holinshed, IV, 645.   [2] *Archæological Journal*, LXI, 305.   [3] *Ibid.*

challenge was addressed, " To all honourable men, Men at Armes, and Knight Adventurers of hereditarie note, & examplarie noblesse, that for most memorable actions doe wield either Sword or Launce in quest of glorie."

Ashmole MS. No. 837, fol. 129-32, gives a long account of " The manner of first cominge into the Tiltyard " of Charles Prince of Wales in the year 1619. It is interesting from many points of view, and we reproduce it here nearly *in extenso*. Like all accounts of the tournament of the period but little information is given of the martial sports themselves, though a great deal is written concerning the dresses, etc. This MS. affords abundant evidence that the last stage of the tournament had been reached.

" The manner of the first cominge into the Tiltyard of the Most high and mighty Prince Charles Prince of Wales sonne and heir apparent of our Souereign Lo: Kinge James on Friday the xxiiijth of March 1619 wch was in the most princely and Royall manner that had been sene many yeares before.

The day and tyme drawing neare the Tiltyard at whitehall was prepared wth many scaffoldes on both sides & the vpper end where stood his Majestie himself wth many other great estates and on the one side sate in a place prepared of purpose at the vpper end the Embassadors on the other side next to St James parke gate was erected a most rich & stately Pauillion of green yellow & white damaske laid on wth broad lace of siluer & gold wth a very deep valence of cloth of silver frendged about wth a deep freng of gold & siluer garnished about wth The princes Armes & badges. on the top of it was set an Eglet in her nest loking vp at the sonne wth this motto at it Nec Degener heres. All wch being ready & exceedingly well cleared & ordered by Sr Edw: Zouch K^t Marshall. The E: of Arrundell being appointed to be Erle Marshall of England for that day about 12 of the clok came into the Tiltyard on horseback attended by diuers of his owne gent on foot wth truncheons in their handes on whome likewise attended the Kt Marshall & all the officers of Armes in their Coates of Armes on horseback vntill his Majestie was ready to come thither. All things beinge / in a readines

[fol. 129 b] & the tiltyard in a very good order his Lordship attended wth the Kt Marshall Clarenceux & Norry & all the heralds & pursuiantes of armes rode to Denmarke house to fetch the Prince his highnes and let him vnderstand that his Majestie were [sic] redy & expected his coming wherevpon he proceeded in manner followinge.

First marched on foote all the Princes band of his Artillery yard led by their captaine, Mr Conisby. next to them went many of the Kt Marshalls men well suited wth truncheons in their handes before their Master who for the most part coasted vp & downe to keep the street & passage clene from people. /

Then six of the Kings Trumpetters sounding the serg^t Trumpeter wth his mace before them riding

The reason why the Princes trumpets did intercede betw: the officers of Armes and the Prince and had place of them & the Kinges trompetts was because they were part of the Princes Show, and therefore not thought fitt to be diuided.

Next to them the pursuiantes & heraldes of Armes wth the two provinciall kings of Armes Clarenceux & Norry vnto all whome the Prince his highnes had very bountefully distributed to euery of them 9 yardes of rich taffata of his coullors vist 3 yardes of white 3 yardes of yellow & three yardes of green all fringed very richly wth a deep frenge of silver & gold spangled and likewise to each of them a white Bever hatt wth a fair gold & siluer band and larg plumes of his coullors /

Then followed 6 of the Princes Trumpettes very richly clad in grene veluet coats laid wth gold & silure lace & white Beruers & fethers

Next them rode his 3 pages one after another brauely mounted very richly clad aleso in grene sattin suits laid exceding thich [sic] wth gold & siluer lace white beuers & plumes,

[fol. 130 a] & their horses in rich caparasans of greene velvet embrodered wth gold & silver each of them / of [sic] attended by querries in rich suites of the Princes coullors on foot.

Next rode the Erle Marshall wth his marshalls rod

Then the Prince his highnes alone all armed in white armour & bravely mounted on horseback wth wonderfull rich caparisans & plumes attended by diuers of his cheife gent on foot most richly araied in greine suites of sattin laid very thick wth siluer & gold lace white bevers & fethers each of them carying in their handes one of the Princes staues After the Prince rode Sr Tho: Howard Master of the Princes horse.

And after him followed 3 spare horses wth plumes & rich embrodered caparisans of his coullors : / led by Querryes or officers of the stable. / :

In this manner they proceeded from Denmark howse to the Tiltyard gate where the artillery men first made a stand & deui[d]ed themselues in a lane for the Prince to passe When his highnes came at the vpper end of the tiltyard he alighted & went into his pavillion to sitt & repose himself whilst the other Tilters were brought in who tarried at the mewes vntil the Kt Marshall & the officers of Armes came for them who proceded in manner following every one in his rank the officers of Armes going before the new runners.

[fol. 130 b] euery one in his rank

Thus appointed to Runn.

new	The Prince	& The E: of Dorset
new	Marquess Bucks	& Sr Sigismond Alexander
new	Marquess Hamilton	& E: of Warwick
new	E: of Oxford	& The lo: walden
	E of Rutland	& E of Salsbury new /
	E of Montgomery	& Sr Thomas Somerset
	E of Desmond	& Sr Hen Riche
	The lo: Gerard	& Mr Hen: Alexander

it is to be noted that because the : E of Montgomery was hurt in the arme in practisinge about 3 dayes before Mr Cary 2 sonn to Sr Robt Cary the Princes chamberlein was appointed to Runn for him at wch tyme it was concluded that hereafter if at any tyme any man shold be hurt that he could not run himself but that he appointed another to run for him (if he were inferior to him hurt and desyred to run in his place) he should come into the tilt wth his beuer close or if he would haue his beuer open he should then come in the due of his place. /

Iudges. /.

[fol. 131 a] The Prince brake _____ staues
The E: of Dorset _____
The Marques of Buck _____
The marquess Hamilton _____

After all was done the the [sic] Prince and all the Tilters once passing round the tilt passt round on alonge before the Prince and so attended him to Somerset howse again.

Fees giuen to the officers of Armes

Of the Prince in scarfes of his coullors each scarfe coat 9 yards of rich taffata fringed wth deep frenge of gold & siluer, and 12 white beuer hats wth gold & siluer bandes and faire fethers of his coullors yellow white & grene.   And 20^{li} in money for his fee

of the marquess Buck —— 13^{li} 6^s 8 for his fee
of the E: o[f] Oxford —— 10^{li} for his fee
of the E: of Salsbury   10 for his fee & scarfes of his coullors

xxiiij⁹ Martij A° dni 1620./
                    A° Regni Regis Jacobi 19

	The Prince	The E: of Dorsett
	Marquess of Buckingham	The marpuess Hamilton
new	The E: of Lincolne	Sʳ Sigismond Alexander
	The E of Desmond	Lo: Walden
new	The lo: Compton	Lo: Gerard
new	The lo: Scroope	Sʳ Tho: Somerset
	Sʳ Hen: Riche ———————	Mʳ Hen: Alexander
	Sʳ Hen. Mildmay ———————	Sʳ Sigismond Alexander

Judges:
The E: of Bridgwater
The viscount Doncaster
The viscount Falkland
Sʳ Fulk Greville
T: Arrundell

At this tyme the Prince his highnes came from Denmark howse to the Tiltyard through the Strand as followeth /

First went the band of Artillerymen marching along vntill they came to the gate of the Tiltyard and there made a stand & deuided themselves in a lane for the Princes highnes to pass through

The seriant Trompetour and the K. Trompettes.

Next followed on horsback the officers of Armes in their coates.

Then the Princes Trumpetes richly clad in coates of grene velvet laid wᵗʰ gold lace /

Then the Princes 3 pages one after another bravely mounted & most richly clothed. /

[* Blank] Then the Prince his highnes alone armed wᵗʰ * of his gent on foot carrying his staves most richely arayed going on both sides./

Then followed Sʳ Tho: Howard master of the Princes horse on horsback

After whom followed seuerall spare horses led by the Querryes or officers of the stable and in this manner they preceeded into the Tiltyard and at the vpper end of the tiltyard by the parke gate was set vp a pauillion of yellow & grene damask laced wᵗʰ gold & siluer lace where the Prince reposed himself vntill the rest of the runners were brought in who stand at the mewes in a redines vntill they were sent for by the Kt marshall & the officers of Armes. and then they cam in according to their degrees two & two together before the E: of Lincolne being a new runner went 4 officers of Armes & 4 before the lo: Compton & two before Sʳ Henry Mildmay being allso new runners.

The E: of Lincolne gaue to the officers of Armes 10ˡ and fouer scarfes of his coullors of 3ˡ prise & fethers each of them

The lo: Compton gaue them 6 13ˢ 9ᵈ & 4 scarfes of like valew & fethers

['This is an original paper, with notes and corrections by one of the Heralds. This art. is recorded in the Heralds' MS. M. 3, f. 1–3ᵇ.' Ashm. Catal.]"

One more illustration of a tournament of the seventeenth century is afforded by Ashmole MS. No. 1127, fol. 196–99 b; and it aptly illustrates the advanced stage of degeneration now reached by these once brilliant and chivalrous martial games:—

"Extracted out of P. Boitells Generall history of all that hapned most remarkeable as well in France as in other forrain Country's in the yeares 1618. 1619: 1620 Printed at Paris in the year. 1620.

p. 87, 88   The Colours of the Madame are Blew Incarnate, White & Amaranthus, the Blew represents heavenly & exalted thoughts, the Incarnate chast and honest Inclinations, the White purity & sincerity of faith, the Amaranthus Constancy.

p. 90   The Knight of the Royall Amaranthus sends his Challenge abroad for the Celebrating of a solemn Turneament, the Princesses & Lady's of the court had scaffolds erected for them, & for judges of the Combatt were chosen the Count Guy St George, the Count de la Bassie, & the Count de la Valdisere.

The trompetts beginning to sound from the new palace, there appeared presently after 12. trompeters clad in Blew, Incarnate White & Amaranthus representing yᵉ winds after whom a Camell was led by fowr African Moores, habited in the same livery & bearing lances cover'd with blew damask, twelv Lackey's follow'd clad after the same manner & after them 12 Pages upon spanish Genetts richly harness't & representing the

p. 92   12 houres of the day, their cloakes were of the same colours, their heads cover'd with perrukes compos'd of golden threads with crowns composed of flowrs de Lyses /

[fol. 198b] roses, heyacynthusses & Amaranthusses beneath each of which there seem'd to shine a Great Sun made of plates of Gold & at their shovlders they had two wings of

p. 92   silver   In their left hands they carry'd sheilds which had devises painted on them, & the name of yᵉ Knight written, & in their hands silver lances with bannerolls of the same colour.

After which came six winged coursers drawing slowly a tryumphall Charriott wᶜʰ signify'd the Charriott of the morning, it was of a great heigth & vast biggness adorn'd all about with paintings, & built with rare workmanship, On the top of this Charriott was plac't

p. 93   Aurora or the Morning quaintly attir'd & accompany'd with joy & Laughter who playing upon the Lute & the Theorbo, after they had taken a round about the place, address'd themselves at length to the Infanta's, & both of them together joining in Consort with Aurora sung certain Italian verses.

After the tryumphall Charriott follow'd six peers magnificently attir'd, with a great

p. 94   number of Heron's plumes & Jewells about their hose, & scarfs of the same colour, & these were the Marquese of Lullin, the Marquese of Vogueres, the Baron of St George, the Marques of Caraglio, the Marquese of Pallavicini, & Mounsieur de Lodes.

[fol. 199] At Length the Prince enter'd the lists as Challenger as being of the most active address & most skillfull of his weapon of all the rest, & the Combatants were these following knights.

Mounsieur de St Reran, under the name of Almidour the Constant, the Count de

p. 95   Montué, Sirnamed Fulginart without fear, Mounsieur de Cavorrett stlled the Fierce Dragon, Mounsieur de Maserez call'd Palmiades the faithfull, Mounsieur de Roussillon tearmed Learques the Couragious, Don Astanio Bobba named Primislas the Strong, Mounsieur de Druent entitled Cloridant the brave, Fulvio Delle Lanze, stiled Altomar the bloody, the Knight d'Aglie with the title of Prodicles the warriour, the Count de Ferrusasque titled Termodont the angry, the Marquese Formo call'd Erolind the Cruell, this noble troop made their Entry three & three in a rank, their livery consisting of all yᵉ fowr colours, but the Prince made choice cheifly of the Amaranthus, & therefore his plume of that colour shew'd it self eminently above the rest, his mantle was of cloth of silver, & under it he had a rich suit of armour made after the manner of the ancients with breeches of silk made after yᵉ same fashion, sprinkled all about with pearles & Jewells, he was mounted upon a stout prancing

[fol. 199b] horse, cover'd with stately capparisons of the same livrie, with / the laces fringes & tassells of silver, & all inrich't with floures & roses of the same mettall he enter'd in between two knights whereof the one was clad in blew, the other in Incarnate.

After the severall Combats were ended the prise was adjudg'd to the Knight of the royall Amaranthus, which donne the trompettes sounded a retreat, & then the Knights each of them retir'd in their Order to the new palace.

p. 85   This Ceremony was celebrated by the Prince of Savoy, upon occasion of the marriage between him & Christina the sister of Lewis the just King of France at his return to Turin from Rivolles where Inviting the Lady's to a Ball he Instituted a Turneament under the title of the Knight of the Royall Amaranthus fighting under the Colours of Madame, the Princess."

The tournament lingered long in Germany.

The decline of armour had become acute by the close of the sixteenth century, and to this there were many contributory causes. Far too much stress has been laid on the extended use of firearms as being the main reason for this, though the ever-increasing penetrative force of the musket-ball had tended greatly to diminish the value of steel harness as a sure means of defence. As a matter of fact, full armour could not be constantly worn during a long campaign without injury to health, besides being a great clog to mobility on the march and in the field. Another potent factor towards the disuse of armour lay in the fact that harness for the soldiery was made in certain standard or arbitrary sizes, each piece being numbered, so that the suits rarely fitted individual cases. They were thus apt to chafe the bodies of the wearers and to cause sores beyond endurance, so that pieces of armour were frequently cast away on the march, all penalties notwithstanding. The man-at-arms of an earlier age became the pistolier, *Landsknecht* and cuirassier of later times.

Early in the seventeenth century another decided change took place in the form of the breastplate, which followed the cut of the doublet of civil life, in the gradual shortening of the waist, and body-armour became stumpy and inelegant.

The latest phase of cap-à-pie armour is well illustrated by a harness in the Musée d'Artillerie, Paris, which was presented by the Republic of Venice to Louis XIV, in 1688. It is very uncouth in form. During the last half of the century plate armour gradually disappears, the pikemen being the last infantry arm to employ it. A " pair of plates " were the last pieces worn, and, except in the case of the cuirassiers, they also were abandoned in favour of the buff coat pure and simple.

After a career of six centuries, the tourney had practically run its course, and had now become almost a thing of the past. Its influence on the ages had been in the main for good, in restraining the licence of troublous times and in inculcating a respect for women. It had fostered a spirit of courtesy, honour and chivalry, sentiments which extended themselves far beyond its borders. Sainte-Palaye remarks, " *Chevalerie est la fontaine de courtoisie, ce qui arrose le reste du monde"*; but as the means for luxury increased, and as time rolled on, the old simplicity fell away and corruption set in, and though the forms remained the spirit had fled. All *raisons d'être* for the tourney beyond those of exercise and pastime had long since passed away, through the continuous decline in the importance of the man-at-arms in warfare, the ever-increasing efficiency of firearms, and the necessity for greater mobility of armies in the field.

The history of the tournament would not be complete without some account of the revivals attempted in the nineteenth and twentieth centuries. They lack, however, a sense of reality, being, in fact, merely more or less well-staged plays.

The Eglington Tournament, held in Ayrshire in 1839, though a good deal based on Sir Walter Scott's legend, the "Gentle and Joyous Passage of Arms of Ashby de la Zouche,"[1] was, in many respects, also a revival of a *pas d'armes* of Tudor times. It was carried through in the face of some ridicule, much discouragement and many difficulties; but all obstacles were gallantly surmounted by the enthusiasm, tenacity and liberality of the Earl of Eglingtoun and his coadjutors. The very elements were against it, for torrents of rain fell frequently during its course, converting the lists into a pond, spoiling the decorations of the stands, and wrecking the temporary banqueting-hall erected at the castle. The training of the horses in so short a time presented the greatest practical difficulty, for here the promoters were at a great disadvantage as against the early and persistent drilling of the chargers for employment in the *fêtes d'armes* of the olden times. The lists at Eglington Park measured 600 yards by 250, the tilt or barrier being 300 yards long, running down the centre. A handsome pavilion was pitched for the use and comfort of the Queen of Beauty (Lady Seymour) and her train of ladies. There were other tents for the accommodation of the knights taking part, and a grand stand was erected for the presiding queen, her maidens, and the guests of the promoters. Seats were placed at the eastern end of the arena for about two thousand spectators. Thirty-five knights took part in this passage of arms, and among them were Prince Louis Napoleon, the Marquis of Waterford, Earls Eglingtoun, Craven and Cassilis, Lords Alford, Glenyon, Cranstoun,

---

1 *Ivanhoe* was published in 1820.

A. Seymour, W. Beresford, Drumlanrig and Maidstone. Lord Gage and Sir Charles Lamb acted as Marshals of the List, the rôle of King of Arms being sustained by the Marquis of Londonderry. There were several rehearsals, the last of which took place on July 13th. The first to joust at the tilt on that occasion were the Earl of Eglingtoun and the Lord Cranstoun. Several courses were run by these champions and two lances were broken. Other encounters followed with varying fortune. The " Lord of the Tournament " was the Earl of Eglingtoun ; the Judge of the Lists, Lord Saltoun ; and the inevitable Jester, a Mr. M'Ian from London.

The procession was arranged by Sir Charles Lamb and Lord Saltoun. The tournament began on August 28th, 1839. The morning was fine, and by one o'clock some ten thousand persons had assembled, and crowds continued to arrive. A pitiless rain much delayed the starting of the procession from the castle, and it was sadly shorn of its fair proportions; for the Queen of Beauty and her maidens had to betake themselves to carriages instead of riding on horseback as intended. The procession reached the lists in the afternoon, about three, in a much bedraggled condition, and the presiding queen, her attendants and the castle house-party, took their seats on the grand stand prepared for them. After flourishes of trumpets, the rules, regulations and limitations for the guidance of the proceedings were proclaimed by a herald. The number of courses to be run by each pair of jousters was settled at three, or at most four. The harnesses employed, some of them collected in England, the rest abroad, varied greatly in regard to period: the armour of the Earl of Craven is amusingly stated to have been worn by an ancestor of the Earl's (Baron Hilton) at the field of Cressy. Reinforcing pieces were employed.

On the weather clearing a little, the scene presented was a brilliant one. There were the knights armed at all points, and their horses gaily trapped in cloth painted in rich colours with their arms and devices. Merging with the rich dresses of the ladies, they offered a fine and moving spectacle. The *pas d'armes* commenced with the quintain, after which jousting at the tilt began. The tilting was far from satisfactory, for the attaints achieved were very few in number. This was owing to the lack of skill on the part of the riders, the insufficient training of the horses, and the mistaken notion that the careers were to be run at the gallop instead of at an amble. The first joust was run between the "Knight of the Swan" (the Hon. Mr. Jerningham) and the "Knight of the Golden Lion" (Captain J. O. Fairlie). They took up positions for their careers, and the trumpets sounded the onset. There were no attaints in the first three courses, but in the fourth the Knight of the Golden Lion broke his lance on the shield of his adversary. The second challenge was by the Earl of Eglingtoun to the Marquis of Waterford, and in the first course both lances were splintered. There was no attaint in the second, but in the third the Earl again splintered his lance. The third joust was between Sir Francis Hopkins and R. J. Lechmere, Esq. In the first encounter Sir Francis shivered his lance, and in the second both lances were broken, but that of Sir Francis was disallowed as being " ill-broken." In the fourth career Sir Francis again shivered his lance. The fourth tilt was between the Lords Glenlyon and Alford. There were no attaints in the first two courses, but in the third Lord Alford broke his spear. Next came combats on foot at barriers with two-handed swords, after which jousting was resumed. The last joust of the day was between the Marquis of Waterford and Lord Alford. The first course was without attaint, and in the second a hit was disallowed, the lance breaking just above the head; but in the third the Marquis shivered his lance " as it ought to be broken." During all this the rain fell at intervals and with increasing violence, which sadly marred the brilliancy of the scene, and the banquet had to be abandoned owing to the wrecking of the temporary banqueting-hall by the storm. In the evening there were combats with broadswords in the drawing-room of the castle, and a duel between Prince Louis Napoleon and Mr. Lamb is stated to have afforded some excellent sword-play. The tournament was to have been continued on the following Thursday, but the weather was so boisterous that the completion of the *pas d'armes* was postponed to Friday, August 30th. The weather was fine and sunny, and the procession to the lists was this time complete in all its parts, the queen and her ladies being on horseback. The first tilt of the day was between the Lords Glenlyon and Alford, and there was but one attaint in the three courses. The Earl of Craven and Captain Fairlie then took up positions for their careers. Both lances were shivered in the first course, in the second there was no attaint, but in the third the Earl again shivered his lance. This was the best joust of the tournament. To be brief, there were six more jousts, making altogether nineteen courses, and but two attaints. Running at the Ring followed, and a *mêlée* brought the tournament to a close. The combatants in the latter were—The Lord of the Tournament (Earl of Eglingtoun), the Knight of the Dragon (Marquis of Waterford), the Black Knight (W. L. Gilmour, Esq.), and the Knight of the Gael (Lord Glenlyon): *against* the Knight of the Black Lion (Viscount Alford), the Knight of the Red Rose (R. J. Lechmere, Esq.), the Knight of the White Rose (Charles Lamb, Esq.), and the Knight of the Swan (Hon. H. Jerningham). Mr. Jerningham was hurt in the wrist by a sword-stroke in the *mêlée*, but this was the only casualty worth recording during the tournament. Several of the knights were unseated, and in one case both horse and rider fell, a few bruises resulting. The prize was awarded to the Earl of Eglingtoun. It was a coronet, with which the Queen of Beauty gracefully crowned him, in the manner of the Lady Rowena in the lists at Ashby de la Zouche. There was a banquet in the evening, at which Lord Eglingtoun expressed the hope that this attempt at a revival of the tournament might result in its being continued among the nobility and gentry of these islands. This pious wish, however, failed to be realised, the very ethics of the institution being so totally at variance with the sentiment prevailing in modern times. The banquet was followed by a dance.

THE TOURNAMENT AT BRUSSELS IN 1905

In marked contrast to the Eglingtoun Tournament, in the way of accuracy of detail and historic truth, was the *pas d'armes* in the Rathausplatz, at Brussels, in 1905, held nearly three-quarters of a century later. This revival in what was once Burgundian territory was most appropriate, the more so as it took place in Brussels itself. It was in the Rathausplatz there, one of the most striking sites in Europe, that the Comte de Charolais, afterwards Charles the Bold, ran in his first tournament in 1452. The Comte was then but eighteen years of age, and tilted in as many courses on that occasion, breaking sixteen lances " as they ought to be broken "—a very good performance, viz. sixteen attaints out of eighteen runs. It was this tournament, held in the city of Brussels some four and a half centuries before, in the reign of Philippe le Bon, that was selected for reconstruction in the months of

July and August, 1905.[1]   Charles was born in November, 1433, and the tournament in question was held in commemoration of the anniversary of his birthday.   He was killed in battle on the fatal field of Nancy in 1477.   In the month of August of the same year his daughter and heiress, the Princess Maria, was wedded to Maximilian of Austria, and the brilliant traditions of the tournament passed over to his court.

The collection of illuminated MSS. in the Burgundian Library, now transferred to the National Library at Brussels, with the *Armorial de la Toison d'Or* and other Burgundian records, now in the National Library at Paris,[2] furnish reliable and inexhaustible material for the correct staging of a modern revival of a tournament on the lines of one of the fifteenth century.   It is thus no wonder that the reconstruction, in the summer of 1905, of the *pas d'armes* of 1452 was attended by such success as to prove of great educational value.   The middle of the fifteenth century was, perhaps, the most picturesque period of the tourney : its rich weapons and armour, the caparisons of the horses, the arms of the champions and others, the lists, the music, and even the very musical instruments of the period, together with the sumptuous accessories of the brilliant Burgundian Court, were reproduced in 1905 to a marvel.

The reconstruction, as presented at Brussels, began with the entry of Duke Philip of Burgundy into the lists in the Rathausplatz, with a splendid train of the ladies of his court, the Marshal of the Lists, the King of Arms (Jean Lefébre de Saint-Remy, the reputed writer of the *Armorial de la Toison d'Or*), the Comte de Charolais, with his five jousting associates and many historic figures of the camp and tourney throughout Christendom, the four judges of the tournament, heralds, pursuivants, etc.   The Duke having taken his seat as supreme umpire on the gaily decked tribune prepared for him, the trumpets sounded and the jousting began.   Many courses were run in character.   This was followed by the quintain, and afterwards by combats on foot and a *mêlée*; then the prizes were presented.   Figures of the knights of 1452, such as those of the Comte de Charolais, Jacques de Lalain and Fredrich de Renesse, were faithfully reproduced in all their details. Some excellent post-cards were published in Belgium, picturing some

[1] A short account of the *pas d'armes* of 1452 is given in our Chapter V.
[2] The *Armorial* was written a little before 1467, and, through the Princess Maria, the Order of the Golden Fleece was transferred to the Courts of Austria and Spain.

of the principal scenes of the tournament. Plate XII (1) depicts the Comte de Charolais armed at all points for the *mêlée*, and Plate XII (2) Jean de Clèves. The *fêtes d'armes* and its rehearsals extended over several weeks.

"TRIUMPH" HELD AT EARL'S COURT, LONDON, ON JULY 11TH, 1912

The object of the promoters of this revival was to reproduce an Elizabethan tournament of about the year 1580, such an one as is described in this chapter. This idea was very creditably carried out, though falling short of the Brussels reproduction of 1905 in the matters of technique and minuteness and correctness of detail. It must be remembered, however, that in 1580 the tournament, then itself a revival in England, had reached an advanced stage of decadence, and that the materials available for reconstruction are scanty and uncertain, as contrasted with the ample records of the century preceding. The Earl's Court reproduction is stated to have been devised by Mrs. George Cornwallis-West and Mr. Seymour Lucas, R.A., with the technical assistance of Mr. (now Sir) Guy Laking. The stage management of the play was in the competent hands of Mr. (now Sir) Frank R. Benson. It is interesting to see so many historic names and titles, corresponding with those of Tudor times, borne by the jousters at Earl's Court. The rôle of Marshal of the Lists was sustained by Lord Lonsdale, and the judges were Lords Shrewsbury and Talbot, Essex, and Dudley, with Major-General Brocklehurst. The Queen of Beauty was the Viscountess Curzon.

The procession to the arena was headed by trumpeters and four pursuivants, marching on foot; then rode the marshal, armed at all points, with the herald (Sir F. R. Benson). The four judges, clad in black robes, followed, their esquire (Sir Guy Laking) bearing the umpire's bâton. After their entry into the lists the trumpets again sounded and the Queen of Beauty, with her train of maidens, all mounted on palfreys, gaily decorated with roses, each led by a henchman, rode into the arena. The Queen was attended by an esquire, and her palfrey was caparisoned in silk. She was clad in a ruff, a robe sparkling with diamonds, and a long mantle.

The knights were arranged in trios, each cavalier preceded by an

PLATE XII

THE COMTE DE CHAROLOIS, AS REPRESENTED AT BRUSSELS
IN 1905

JEAN DE CLEVES, AS REPRESENTED AT BRUSSELS IN 1905

esquire, bearing his lance, and followed by other esquires. The first champion was the Duke of Marlborough; his motto was *Fiel pero desdichado*, his colours a dark blue, and his proof armour was etched with gold. The second was Lord Craven; his motto was *Virtus in actione consistet*, his colours green, and he wore the famous armour made for Philip II of Spain. Lord Compton completed the first trio, and his motto was *Je ne cherche qu'un*. The second trio followed, and all did homage to the Queen of Beauty, now seated on her throne. The herald then proclaimed that the six knights would joust at the tilt, for a rich and noble prize. The Lord Chrichton and the Duke of Marlborough were the first to joust, and five courses were run by each pair. On completion the verdict of the Queen of Beauty was that the Duke had well jousted, but that Lord Ashby St. Ledgers, whose motto was *Ferro non gladio*, had jousted best, and he received the prize, viz. a gold cup of the value of £600, from her hands. The tilt was then removed and a *mêlée* followed, in which twelve knights were engaged. There was, of course, a banquet in the evening followed by a dance.

There was also a revival at Rome.

There now only remains the judicial duel to be described, an institution which had much affinity with the tournament, and which, indeed, formed an integral part of it, both in sentiment and fact. This important branch of the subject is dealt with at some length in the next chapter.

CHAPTER VIII

TRIAL BY COMBAT, ITS SCOPE AND HISTORY

CURIOUSLY interlinked with the procedure of the law courts, forming, indeed, an integral part of the law of the land, was the judicial duel; an institution applying to both civil and criminal jurisdiction.

It was allowed in certain cases, such as on a civil writ of right for the recovery of land, and in criminal charges of treason or felony on an appellant making a sworn declaration before a judge. This law, though falling greatly into disuse after the reign of Queen Elizabeth, remained on the statute book until early in the nineteenth century.

Among the Asmolean, Harleian and Cottonian MSS. are many tracts, treatises and other documents relating to the laws and manner of conducting judicial duels, with other matter concerning these combats; and abstracts from the MSS. are given in Appendices E, F, and G, respectively.

The custom of trial by combat or legal duel, the ordeal of battle, was introduced into England by the Normans.[1] As far as can be ascertained it was unknown to the Anglo-Saxons, though the ordeal of hot water appears in one of Ine's laws;[2] and, indeed, trial by ordeal appears repeatedly among the laws of the Anglo-Saxon kings. The principle involved was the same in both cases, viz. that the Almighty would not remain indifferent when solemnly invoked, but would intervene miraculously so that the ends of justice might be furthered. The simple faith of the times would act as a deterrent to appeals to the judgment of God and would thus tend to limit the number of cases. The consciousness of innocence or guilt would also contribute towards the vindication of the cause of justice in actual combat.

The proofs by fire and water (*vulgaris purgatio*), holding, carrying or walking over hot iron or heated plough-shares (*ferri candentis*

---

[1] *Origines Juridiciales*, p. 65.   [2] Pollock and Maitland, *History of English Law*, I, 39.

judicium), being thrown into deep water, bound hand and foot, may be said roughly to have preceded that by judicial combat; but they form quite another and earlier branch of the subject. The number of cases given in history of these earlier forms of ordeal which defendants are stated to have passed through triumphantly is considerable, but most of them must surely be either apocryphal, or the intensity of the ordeals themselves was much exaggerated.

Ordeal by combat is found among the laws of nearly all the German tribes; and it flourished greatly in France until cases of more than suspected miscarriage of justice brought it into disrepute. An edict passed at Lyons in the year 501 established the institution as a regular form of trial. It appears among the ancient laws of the Swedes and Lombards.

In civil cases a claimant would declare that some ancestor of his had been in seisin of certain property but had been unlawfully deprived of it by another, and he would offer battle to the "tenant," as the owner was then called, for its restitution, by the body of a champion. The tenant, or defendant, could then choose between an appeal to the Grand Assize, an inquest where the question of right is determined by the verdict of neighbours,[1] in which institution may be traced the germ of the more modern jury; or to the ordeal of battle, in his own body or by champion. No one was compelled to defend his seisin of a free tenement by battle, though a claimant could offer combat in the lists, which, however, might be refused by a defendant. When a civil court ordered a combat it was fought on foot in a small circular or oblong enclosure, similar to that used in the foot fighting, with shields and staves (bastons) at a *pas d'armes* of the fifteenth century. The course of procedure in criminal cases for the most part differed widely from that followed in civil cases and was under quite another jurisdiction; and it largely consisted of accusations made against the honour of certain persons, or of alleged treason. It was customary for an accuser to justify his charge by an offer of single combat in the lists, "God showing the right"; and such a mode of settlement was greatly in unison with the chivalric spirit of the age. To bring such a matter to an issue an accuser offered battle by throwing down his glove, which when lifted by a defendant signified that the challenge was accepted. The king was appealed to, and, in the event of the case being remitted to the ordeal of battle, he assigned the place and day for the combat. He further, in consultation with the constable and marshal,

---

[1] Pollock and Maitland, *History of English Law*, I, 147.

decided on the preliminaries, the conditions of battle to be observed being regulated in accordance with fixed ordinances, which in England were drawn up by the constable for the time being. The combat would be on horseback, fighting *à outrance*, with lance and sword, in lists similar to those erected for the tourney. Charges of homicide or murder might in this country be remitted to the ordeal of battle, with shields and bastons and in civil garments. Should an accused or claimant fail to appear in the lists on the day appointed he could be outlawed.

The judicial duel may be regarded as the prototype or parent of the chivalrous duel on foot at a *pas d'armes*.

The custom never took deep root in England, though during the reign of King Henry II, when the monarchy had become more settled, and in the times of his immediate successors Richard and John, disputes relating to the possession of land were very rife, greatly owing to the fact that so many manors and smaller holdings had been forcibly and illegally riven from their rightful owners in the preceding reigns since the Conquest, by the barons and their adherents. The ordinary law courts experienced great difficulty in dealing with them on the principles set forth in the written statutes, which then as always inclined to favour the man in possession; and the rough and ready settlement by combat was ordered, more especially in cases where there was a hopeless conflict of testimony between litigants and no means of getting at the truth by the evidence of any living witnesses.

The actual number of judicial duels would seem to have been small in England, for in the great majority of cases before the courts the judges managed to declare that there should be no combat.

Certain persons were excused from battle. They comprised the citizens of London, who were exempted by charter; the clergy; "*sexagenarii*"; and "those blind by accident after issue joined.[1] Women were not exempted by law and, indeed, sometimes fought.

The early ordinances, forms and manner of carrying out this singular institution in practice in England are given in *Origines Juridiciales*.[2]

A short and imperfect summary follows on these pages:

[1] *Origines Juridiciales*, p. 79.
[2] Published in 1671, by William Dugdale Esquire, Norroy King of Arms, later Sir William and Garter King of Arms; the ordinances, etc., being those in operation in the reign of Henry II, set forth by Ranulph de Glanville, Justice of England, page 65.

TRIAL BY COMBAT IN CIVIL CASES

In cases where this mode of trial for the possession of certain lands or other property was allowed by the court, and a combat followed, the further tenure of a holding in question would depend solely on the principle of battle, without any later appeal to the Grand Assize being permissible.

Before a trial by combat could be sanctioned the claimant in the suit was summoned before the court with his champion, who, once fixed upon, could not be changed, unless in the case of his "natural death" taking place in the interval before battle; but should he die "by his own fault, the lord shall lose his Sute."

The defendant might either defend his cause in person or fight by deputy; but should he elect to be represented by champion and the one chosen should die in the interim it would become a question to be argued before the court as to whether or not the defendant should be allowed to appoint another in his place. The challenger or demandant was not allowed to fight in person.

Should the defendant, the "tenant," be vanquished in the fight, then "the lord shall lose the land and the claimant shall have it"; but it often happened that a champion had been hired for some fee or reward, and if this should be proved the principal would lose his suit. Some particulars are given of a case of this kind[1] "betwixt Thomas fitz Hugh de Staunton and the prior of Lenton for the advousen of the church of Harlaston, in Northamptonshire." Both parties to the suit were represented by champion, the appellant being a churchman, and they fought on foot in the lists, armed with bastons (i.e. polygonally-shaped maces or cudgels of heavy wood, tipped with horn: "basculi cornuti, bastons cornuz").[2]

TRIAL BY COMBAT IN CASES CRIMINAL

This was conducted much on the lines of knightly usage in combats on horseback *à outrance*, except, as already stated, in charges of homicide or murder.

---

[1] *Origines*, p. 68.
[2] Bastons were sometimes headed with a double beak, like a pick. Their usual length was three feet, though shorter ones could be used in the event of combatants mutually wishing it.

The cartel setting forth the charge, subscribed to on oath, was laid before the judges of chivalry by the appellant, the accuser, stating that "he was ready to maintain the same with his body." This document was then considered by the judges, and should combat be allowed it was served on the accused, the defendant; and if within an interval of six weeks he had not responded, judgment was registered against him by default, his coat-armour being reversed or ignominiously fastened under his horse's tail, in disgrace.

Should the accused stand on his defence both parties were cited to appear in the field outside the lists, which were quadrangular in form with a gate at each end. Judgment seats were provided for the constable and marshal, and at their feet were stationed a competent number of experienced knights and "a doctor or two of civil laws," all for the advice and assistance of the court.

The appellant first came to the gate at the right end of the lists, clad in complete armour, attended by his esquires, and the constable and marshal demanded of him through their herald his name and purpose. On his answering, he was conducted into the lists by a knight and herald and placed before the judgment seat on the right hand. A similar course of procedure was adopted towards the defendant, who was placed facing the accuser on the left hand.

The choice of the weapons stipulated in the cartel lay with the defendant, and the advisory knights inspected and measured them for both sides, so that there might be no inequality in that respect between the parties; and the knights must answer for it that there be no enchantment or magic practised on either side.

It was then demanded of the principals if their purpose held, and they affirmed the same, laying their hands on the Evangelists. The appellant then briefly rehearsed the terms of the cartel of defiance, making oath as to its truth, after which the defendant affirmed also on oath his denial of the charge.

These preliminaries over the parties prepared for battle, which was to continue from sunrise to sunset; the herald crys, "Let them goe together," and the onset is sounded by trumpet call.

Should the appellant not overcome the defendant during the day the latter was deemed guiltless, and the procurator of the constable and marshal publicly proclaimed the fact: but to secure what was termed "a perfect victory," a confession of guilt by one of the parties was necessary.

The cartel was then sealed with the common seal in testimony that the combat had duly taken place, and all the legal formalities been observed.

A picture of a legal duel on a murder charge, of the reign of Henry III, has been preserved, and the names of the combatants are written upon it. It has been reproduced by Hewitt in *Ancient Armour and Weapons of War*,[1] and the parties are represented fighting. A gallows is depicted in the group with the vanquished combatant hanging from it. This was no knightly battle—the champions fought on foot in their civil dresses of leather or cloth, bare-headed, with quadrangular bowed shields, and bastons garnished at their heads with spurs, like those of a pick.

Rules and ordinances for the regulation of judicial combats in France were promulgated by Phillip IV, surnamed le Bel. An abridged account of them follows:—[2]

Four things to be established before the Gage of Battle may be adjudged.

1. The institution applies to grave suspicion in cases of murder, manslaughter, treason or the like offences.

2. Every true man if he knows himself to be accused to present himself before the court without waiting to be cited or summoned.

3. That no gage be granted for accusations of theft or robbery.

4. On a gage of battle being granted the appellant to furnish particulars as to where the alleged wicked deed was done, the name of the party dead; or full details of the treason alleged to have been committed.

Should the judge allow the combat the advocate of the appellant is to lay the case before the court in sober terms; but should the defendant deny the charge the appellant must say that, although he cannot prove it by witnesses or other evidence, yet he can avouch it in his own body or by another for him, in an enclosed field in presence of the king.

The appellant is to throw down his glove and retain counsel for arms, horse, etc., necessary for the gage of battle. The defendant may reply to the accusation that the appellant has falsely and maliciously lied; and that in his defence, by the help of God and our Lady, he will avouch his innocence with his body or by some other for him; and that he will be ready on the day and at the place fixed upon for the combat. Then he is to take up the gage thrown down by the appellant, and a decision will be given by the count as to whether trial by battle will be allowed or not.

---

[1] Vol. I, p. 375.   [2] *Theatre of Honour and Knighthood*, Chap. II, p. 423, written at Paris *anno* 1619.

If recourse to a duel be permitted the parties will swear to be on the ground on the day appointed; the combat to be overlooked by wise and honest men, clerks, knights, and esquires, without favour to either party; but should either appellant or defendant fail to keep his tryst he shall be proclaimed recreant, and afterwards arrested.

Regulations as to the procedure for the combat follows:—the parties to bring sustenance for themselves and their horses for the day; the lists to be 40 paces in width by 80 in length, and within them two pavilions are to be pitched for the use and comfort of the combatants. The herald is to come on horseback to the gate and to cry three times: firstly, before the arrival of the appellant; secondly, when the combatants have entered the lists; and thirdly, when they have taken their oaths. The appellant should be first in the field on the day of battle, before the hour of noon; the defendant not later than four in the afternoon. The parties make their affirmations and the sign of the cross, and appear before the stand on which the judge is seated, and he commands them to raise the visors of their helmets, after which they return to their pavilions. The herald, after having called them for the third time, motions them to kneel before a table on which a crucifix and missal are placed, when a priest admonishes them; and the marshal takes off their right-hand gauntlets and hangs them on the arms of the cross. The combatants then mount their horses, the pavilions are removed from the lists, and the marshal cries, "Gentlemen doe your Deuiore," throwing down his glove, and the combat begins.

The body of the vanquished, dead or alive, shall be delivered by the judge to the marshal, his points cut and armour cast piecemeal in the lists, and his horse and armour shall appertain to the constable and marshal of the field. The victor shall depart honourably from the lists, on horseback.

Ashmole MS., No. 764, p. 7, furnishes the following:—"*De la droite ordonnance du Gaige de Bataille par tout le royaume de France Philipe par la grace de Dieu Roy de France a touz ceulx qui ces presentes lettres verront salut.*" This letter of King Philip IV, written in 1306, limits the practice of wager of battle, and is prefixed to regulations for the whole course of the combat (44-54 b).

In Favine's *Theatre of Honour and Knighthood*,[1] rendered into English in 1622, judicial duels are thus defined:—"It was the custome of our auncient French to vndertake the hazard of armes and combat, to justifie

[1] Chap. 2, p. 423.

themselues in an Accusation, fordged against their honour and good fame; and to sustaine the truth of some iust cause, whereof the proofes were doubtfull, yea, wholly hid and concealed." In France the oaths were administered over the bones and relics of saints and martyrs.

In *La Vie de Bertrand Du Guesclin*[1] is an account of a singular legal duel between Jews, named Daniot and Turquant, which took place in Spain; and the narration aptly illustrates the superstitious character of the times and country. These Jews were accused of assasinating Blanche de Bourbon at night in her bed; and on being charged with the crime Daniot averred that he had not entered the bed-chamber of the princess at all, and had done his best to prevent Turquant from committing the murder. This Turquant denied on oath, stating that his accomplice had taken an equal part with himself in causing the death of the princess. On hearing of this direct conflict of testimony Bertrand Du Guesclin is stated to have suggested a judicial duel in the lists (*champ-clos*) between the parties, and this having been assented to the fight duly took place. The combatants, who were well mounted and in complete armour, fought with swords, and after some severe passages Turquant wounded Daniot in the arm so severely that he was incapacitated from further combat, owing mainly to the loss of so much blood. The *coup de mort* was about to be given to the vanquished champion and a confession of his guilt demanded when just at that moment a thick cloud appeared above the heads of the combatants, and issuing from it a flash of lightning struck them both dead.

Among the Monstrelet illustrations is a picture of a highly improbable judicial duel between a man and a dog, the man being accused of murdering the dog's master. The picture was copied from an ancient painting which hung in the great hall of the Castle of Montargis, and is supposed to picture an event recorded by Colombière in *Theatre d'Honneur et de Chevalerie*. The fight is stated to have taken place in the reign of Charles V of France (1364-1380).[2] The scene represents the duel in progress within a large circular enclosure or lists, around which are galleries and promenades like a theatre, the numerous spectators being richly dressed nobles and ladies. Companies of soldiers are on guard and there is a large band of trumpeters. The defendant is clad in a leather jerkin, torn in places, and slashed drawers; he is armed with a baston or club and a large circular shield. The dog, a large stag-

---

[1] *Anciens Mémoires Du XIV Siècle*, I, 505.　　　　[2] See Montfaucon, Tom III, Pl. 18.

hound, is seen gripping the murderer by the throat, and justice is vindicated.

"On the seuenth of June 1380 a combat was fought afore the kings palace at Westminster, on the pauement there, betwixt one sir John Anneslie knight, and one Thomas Katrington esquire; the occasion of which strange and notable triall rose hereof. The knight accused the esquire of treason, for that which the fortresse of saint Sauior within the Ile of Constantine in Normandie, belonging sometime to sir John Chandois, had béene committed to the said Katrington, as capteine thereof, to keepe it against the enemies, he had for monie sold and deliuered it ouer to the Frenchmen, when he was suffientlie prouided with men, munition and vittels, to have defended it against them: and sith the inheritance of that fortresse and landes belonging thereto, had apperteined to the said Annerslie in right of his wife, as néerest cousine by affiniti vnto sir John Chandois, if by the false conueiance of the said Katrington, it had not beene made awaie, and alienated into the enemies hands: he offered therefore to trie the quarrell by combat, against the said Katrington, wherevpon was the same Katrington apprehended, and put in prison, but shortlie after set at libertie againe." It was decided to try the case by combat, and the constable and marshal were duly notified. Lists were erected and crowds assembled on the day appointed to witness the fight. On being called three times by the herald-at-arms the parties entered the lists for fighting, and the articles of combat were publicly read, and after each had been duly sworn the fight commenced "first with speares, after with swords, and lastlie with daggers. They fought long till finallie the knight had bereft the esquire of all his weapons, and at length the esquire was manfull overthrowned by the knight," who was declared the conqueror. The esquire died soon after from his hurts. The king was present at the fight.[1]

Mr. Hewitt[2] describes a legal duel of the reign of King Richard II, between a chevalier of Navarre and an English esquire, which is figured in Cotton MS., Nero, D VI. The engraving has been reproduced in Strutt's *Regal Antiquities*.[3] Holinshed gives an account of the duel, as taking place in 1384, between John Walsh or Wallis and an esquire of Navarre named Martilet; the charge being that the former had forced the wife of the latter. Martilet was slain, his body drawn, hanged and beheaded.

---

[1] Holinshed's *Chronicles*, II, 727.   [2] *Ancient Armour and Weapons of War*, II, 342.   [3] Plate 58

Froissart describes a judicial duel which took place at Paris in the year 1386, in the reign of Charles VI of France, between the Chevaliers Jean de Carouge and Jacques le Gris, both knights of the household of the Comte d'Alençon. Owing to the singular nature of the charge the event caused a great stir at the time and drew a multitude of spectators from far and near. De Carouge leaving France to take part in the crusade in Palestine, his young and handsome wife, a modest and virtuous dame, awaited his return in their strong castle of Argenteil. Jacques le Gris having conceived an unlawful passion for the lady determined to gratify it during the absence of her lord. He paid a visit to the castle one morning and was received by the lady with all honour as being a companion at arms of her husband; and was being shown over it when he asked to see the dungeon. She suspecting no evil, took him down to it alone, when he suddenly locked the door, took advantage of her and forced her. On the return of de Carouge from the Holy Land his wife complained to him of the outrage, which was solemnly denied by the defendant; and the husband called together his friends and kindred to advise with them as to his proper course of action. Parliament was applied to, and a combat to the death between the parties was arranged to take place, de Carouge to act as champion for his wife, le Gris to defend his honour in his own person. Lists were erected at Paris behind the Temple, together with accommodation for the vast number of spectators expected to be present. King Charles was at Sluys at the time superintending the arrangements for a contemplated invasion of England, but he hurried back to Paris to sit as umpire on the occasion. On the day of battle the two knights entered the lists, with their sponsors, armed at all points; and the onset was sounded for a joust *à outrance*, which was run without hurt to either party. They then dismounted and attacked each other with swords. De Carouge was first wounded in the thigh, but continued fighting and at length passed his sword through the body of his adversary, killing him instantly. The body of le Gris was delivered over to the common hangman by the marshal and dragged to Montfauçon, where it was gibbeted.

Juvenal des Ursins, in *Histoire de Charles VI*,[1] also gives an account of this duel, which differs materially from that of Froissart, and is more likely to be correct. It states that when the vanquished knight lay wounded on the ground and when de Carouge was about to administer

[1] Page 371.

the *coup de grâce* he demanded a confession of guilt, but le Gris with his last breath solemnly asseverated his denial of the crime; and innocent he was later proved to be, for some time afterwards another person on his death-bed confessed to having committed the outrage. The motive of the lady in charging the wrong person is not apparent. The duel is also described in *Les Annales de France*.

In 1398 the Dukes of Hereford and Norfolk accused each other of treason, and a duel took place between them, though King Richard had in vain tried to reconcile them. Holinshed gives the following account of this combat:—"The duke of Aumarle was that daie high constable and the duke of Surrie marshal, and they entered vnto the lists with a great companie of men apparelled in silke sendall, imbrodered with siluer both richlie and curouslie, euerie man hauing a tipped staffe to keepe the feeld in order. About the houre of prime came to the barriers of the lists, the duke of Hereford, mounted on a white courser, barded with gréene and blew veluet imbrodered sumptuouslie with swans and antelops of goldsmiths worke, armed at all points. The constable and marshall came to the barrier, demanding of him what he was, he answered 'I am Henrie of Lancaster, duke of Hereford which am come hither to doo endeuer against Thomas Mowbraie duke of Norfolke, as a traitor vnto God, the king, his realme, and me.' Then he entered the listes, and descended from his horse, and set him down in a chaire of greene veluet, at the one end of the lists, and there reposed himself, abiding the comming of his aduesarie." King Richard then entered the lists with great pomp "accompanied with all the péeres of the realm," and took his seat upon the tribune. "After him entered the Duke of Norfolk, his horse barded in crimcon velvet, embroidered with lions in silver and mulberry trees," and he took his seat in a chair, "which was of crimosen veluet, courtined about with white and red damaske." The herald then gave the signal for the combat to begin, but the course proved abortive, and the king cast his bâton, the heralds crying " Ho, Ho." A council was then held by the king resulting in both dukes being banished the realm.[1]

---

[1] Holinshed, II, 844. Harleian MS., III, 6079, Art. 36, gives an account of this duel.

TRIAL BY COMBAT IN GERMANY[1]

Application had to be made by an appellant to the civic authority of a town before a judicial duel could take place, and this having been done the following answer would be given:—

"We have received your letter and are very sorry to see that your hearts are so moved with rancour and hatred as you seem to bear to one another. In which regard we pray you that you would desist from combat if it may be; and that you would end your quarrels by the way of mildness and gentleness without the adventuring of handy strokes and without shedding human blood. Consent to our request, and so much the rather because we entreat you most instantly."

Should the demand for a trial by combat be still persisted in the following answer was returned:—

"Seeing that you still persist in your hatred and challenge, and that the way of gentleness can take no course of kindness between you, we do order and appoint that you shall appear on such a day before us to hear the ground and subject of your quarrel, wherein we mean to do you justice."

A day may then be assigned for the combat if it be allowed.

The preliminaries and regulations are similar to those which prevailed in France and England, with, however, the difference that in each of the pavilions pitched in the lists for the accommodation of the combatants, a bier, a coffin, four candles and a shroud for the dead were placed; and both the appellant and defendant were confessed by a priest. If not slain the party vanquished remained infamous for the rest of his life; he was never allowed participation in aught knightly, and his beard was to be kept close-shaven.[1]

Trials by combat in Germany were more complex and far-reaching than was the case in France and England, and the weapons employed in conducting them more varied and specialized in character.

A paper was read on February 20th, 1840, before the Society of Antiquaries, London, by Mr. R. L. Pearsall,[2] entitled, "Some Observations on Judicial Duels, as practised in Germany"; a short résumé of which follows here. The paper is largely based upon a curious manu-

---

[1] *Theatre of Honour, etc.,* p. 459.　　　　[2] *Archæologia,* XXIX, 348.

script of the year 1400, in the Royal Library at Munich, containing some text and a number of wood-cuts on vellum, representing various forms of duel in Germany. The work is by Paulus Kall "Master of Defence"[1] to the then Duke of Bavaria; and the illustrations refer to judicial and perhaps other duels as practised in the Fatherland about the end of the fourteenth century, as well as to some others of a still earlier period. This MS., together with others at Munich and Gotha, references to which Mr. Pearsall has omitted to give, form the ground-work of his paper.

Strange though it may seem, the legal duel was resorted to as a court of appeal in extreme cases of quarrels and accusations between man and wife; and Fig. 2 in Paulus Kall's book affords an illustration of the manner in which such combats were conducted. It depicts a man, bareheaded, buried in a pit up to his loins, holding a short staff in his right hand, the left arm bound to his side. The woman is clad in her chemise only, which is bound together below the middle by a lace passing between the legs; the right sleeve of the garment extends beyond the hand "*ein dünne Elle*" in a bag which contains a stone, and this constitutes her weapon of attack. At first sight the combat would appear to be an unequal one. It might be thought for a moment that the wood-cut had been conceived in a humorous sense, but there is no doubt whatever that such duels did really take place in Germany, though cases of the kind were probably comparatively rare after the twelfth century; and, indeed, Mr. Pearsall had not been able to find any record of an actual combat of the kind later than the year 1200, when a man and his wife are stated to have fought under the sanction of the civic authorities at Bâle. We may take it, however, from other evidence that the practice continued up to the close of the fourteenth century and perhaps even later. Reference is made in the paper to a book of drawings, also at Munich, executed as late as the end of the fifteenth century, among which is a representation of such a duel, though possibly traditional in character. The man here is depicted as buried up to the waist in a tub; he wears a skull-cap, and is armed in the same manner as shown in the other drawing, with a short staff, the left arm tied to his side. The woman is fully dressed and in the act of swinging a weapon which looks like a sling, in which is a stone. Mr. Pearsall further refers to "an ancient codex of defence" in the library at Gotha, one of the drawings depicting a duel between a man and his wife, the former fighting from a tub; and the man is shown

---

[1] Probably a fencing master.

to have vanquished the woman and drawn her into the tub headforemost, in which she appears with her legs kicking in the air. This incident explains why the chemise, as shown on Fig. 2 of Kall's work, was tied with a lace between the legs; and that wood-cut also illustrates the mode of action on the part of the duelists in attack and defence. The woman's weapon is thus seen not to be a sling at all, but one similar in principle to the extended sleeve with a bag at the end in which is a stone; the object being to inflict a swinging blow on her opponent, who parries with his staff. Another cut, the source of which Mr. Pearsall does not mention, represents a more deadly form of duel between a man and a woman, who fight bareheaded and naked to the girdle, with small falchions, like knives; and wounds are shown on both their persons.

A singular form of duel, pictured in Paulus Kall's book, is that with "*shilts*," used as weapons both of attack and defence, sometimes alone, and at others in conjunction with daggers held in the disengaged hand. To judge from the wood-cuts this great oblong shield is about $4\frac{1}{2}$ feet long by about 18 inches broad; and though the examples depicted differ somewhat, they are all garnished at the head, foot, and sides with a greater or less number of projecting spears or spurs, for the purposes of attack. The combatants are wearing greyish-brown tight-fitting dresses and hoods; the faces, hands and legs are left bare. The preliminaries completed, the duelists are conducted into the lists by an official; each combatant brings a bier and is accompanied by his relations and a confessor. The principals are then sworn, their weapons handed to them, and the onset sounded. It would appear from the surrounding details and the character of the officials concerned, that this form of duel appertained to members of the privileged class.

A fourth kind of duel was fought with spiked clubs (or more usually with swords) and "*der Hutt*," a shield formed like a hat; and Kall's woodcut pictures the duelists as being clad in garments of cloth. The shields vary in size from very small to very large, the latter kind being employed in conjunction with spiked clubs, the former with swords. Another form of duel is with the "*streit-axt*" (*bec de faucon*), the variety of battle-axe with a hammer on one side of the head and a spike, like that of a pick, on the other. Here the champions fight in complete armour; and besides axes they carry swords and daggers. In the Gotha codex is a drawing entitled, "*Dass ist wie sich ainer versorgen sol der zu gewapenter Hand fechten sol*," meaning that this is the equipment for a duel with gauntlets. The duelist is shown as being anointed with oil by his armourer preparatory to combat; and the items of his body armour stand ready to be put on in their turn. Some of the woodcuts in Paulus Kall's work afford representations of such duels; and the text furnishes directions as to how they were to be conducted. It was from this kind of legal duel, more especially, that combats on foot in the lists at a *pas d'armes* had their origin.

The last form of duel referred to in Mr. Pearsall's paper is one with two-handed swords; and a woodcut of Paulus Kall's illustrates a combat of the kind, in which the duelists are clad in jerkins and long hose. The swords appear to measure about five feet in length. These clumsy and unwieldy weapons were for striking and parrying, but could not be employed effectively at close quarters.

An original manuscript in the possession of Mr. Richard Bull, F.S.A., at the commencement of the nineteenth century, contains the orders, rules and regulations issued by Thomas Duke of Gloucester, the Constable of England, in the reign of King Richard II, 1377–99, for observance in cases of trial by combat.[1] They differ little from those of an earlier period, but the particulars given of the lists may be noted with advantage. They run :—

" The Kinge shall finde the feeld to fight in and the listes shalbe made and deuised by the Constable and it is to be considered that the listes must be 60 pace longe and equally made without great stones the grounde flat and 40 paces brode in good order and that the grounde be harde stable and firme and that the lists be strongly barred abowt with one dore in the este an other in the weste with good and stronge barres seven foote highe or more than a horse can leape over them."

The weapons were to be " glayues,"[2] long sword, short sword and dagger.

There are other copies of these rules extant besides the one given in the *Antiquarian Repertory*, viz., Ashmole MS. 856, 83–89, and that among a MS. Collection of Ordinances of Chivalry of the fifteenth century, belonging to Lord Hastings. The last-named document is copied in Lord Dillon's paper on these Hastings MS.,[3] published in *Archæologia*,

---

[1] *Antiquarian Repertory*, II, 210.
[2] The glaive here mentioned is not the weapon usually known by that name, but the lance : for it will be observed in some later rules given on these pages that " spears of equal length " were to be issued to the combatants. Lances were often termed glaives at this period, and in such combats were shortened to five feet.   [3] Appendix B.

Vol. LVII, and is reproduced in our Appendix H, but with the long pre-amble left out. These three copies of the rules for conducting judicial duels in the reign of Richard II vary somewhat; for instance, glaives[1] are mentioned in the two first copies as being among the weapons employed in these combats, but not in the last.

RULES FOR JUDICIAL COMBATS IN THE REIGN OF RICHARD III [2]

A case lodged by an appellant should be pleaded in the court before the constable and marshal, and if the accusation cannot be substantiated by witnesses, a recourse to trial by combat may be granted by the Crown. Should a judicial duel be decided on, the time and place of combat are fixed by the constable; the weapons to be "glayves," long-swords, short swords and daggers. Sureties to be found by both parties to keep their day, and no attempt shall be made to injure the plaintiff or defendant before the day of battle.

The general rules and arrangements do not differ materially from those of earlier reigns, though here it is mentioned that spears of equal length were issued to the combatants, thus explaining the term "glayves."

If the charge be one of treason the vanquished shall be stripped of his armour, and a piece of the railings of the lists broken down, and he shall be drawn through the lists by horses to the place of execution.

A judicial combat took place at Quesnoy in 1405, Duke William, Count of Hainult, sitting as judge. The parties were two gentlemen, Bournecte the appellant and Bounaige the defendant. The accusation was that of murder. Lists were erected at the expense of the Duke, and the fight commenced by each combatant hurling his lance at the other, but without effect; they then drew their swords, and Bournecte soon overcame his adversary, who confessed his crime, and was ordered by the judge to be beheaded. This was a duel between members of the privi-leged class.

A challenge for a duel between Henry Inglose, Esq., and Sir John Tiptoft, Knt., to be fought before the Duke of Bedford, high constable, in 1415. (Cotton MS. Titus. C. 28.)

A trial by combat took place at Arras in the year 1431, the Duke of Burgundy sitting as judge. The charge was one of treason, and about

---

[1] Clayues.   [2] *Antiquarian Repertory*, I, 152.

the time of the duel many allegiances were being transferred from Burgundy to France. The appellant, Maillotin de Bours, had charged the defendant, Hector de Flavy, with having expressed the intention of deserting the Burgundian interest in favour of that of France and with other contemplated acts of treason. On this information the Duke had de Flavy arrested and lodged in prison. The defendant, however, had many influential friends at Court, and through their good offices and representations he was at length received in audience by his sovereign, when he solemnly denied the charge, alleging that it was de Bours himself who had suggested the treason. The Duke then sent for the appellant, and the discussion between the parties waxed very violent until at length de Bours flung down his glove and demanded a trial by combat, God showing the right. The defendant, with the Duke's permission, took up the glove and a day was fixed for the combat to take place, both parties giving security to keep their tryst. Lists were prepared and erected. Within them was the model of a sepulchre, for de Flavy had been dubbed a knight before the Holy Sepulchre at Jerusalem. On the day of combat the Duke took his seat on the tribune prepared for him. De Maillotin first entered the lists armed at all points, attended by the Seigneur de Charny and other sponsors. He held a lance in one hand and one of his two swords in the other, and after making his obeisance to the Duke he retired to his pavilion. Sir Hector de Flavy entered the lists in like manner; he was influentially attended, and his charger was led in by the two sons of the Comte de St. Pol. After saluting the Duke he also retired to his pavilion. Both knights on re-entering the lists were led before the judge and swore on the Evangelists that their cause was just and true. They then took up their positions for combat and the onset was sounded, the fight beginning by each hurling his lance at the other, but without hurt to either. They then attacked with swords, each champion displaying the utmost courage and dexterity. The Duke at this juncture quite unexpectedly cast his bâton, thus putting an end to the fight. He commanded the attendance of the combatants to dine at his table on the morrow, when he reconciled them to each other.[1]

"In the foure and twentith yeare" of the reign of King Henry VI (1446) "the prior of Kilmaine appeached the earle of Ormond of treason. For triall whereof the place of combat was assigned in Smithfelde, and the barriers for the same there readie pitcht. Howbeit,

---

[1] *Chronique de Monstrelet*, Liv. II, Chap. CII.

in the meane time a doctor of diuinitie, named maister Gilbert Worthington, parson of saint Andrews in Holborne, and other honest men, made such sute with diligent labor and paines taking to the kings councell, that when the daie of combat approched, the quarell was taken into the kings hands and there ended "[1]

" In the same year also, a certeine armourer was appeeched of treason by a seruant of his owne. For proofe whereof a day was giun them to fight in Smithfield, insomuch that in conflict the said armourer was ouercome and slaine; but yet by misgouerning of himselfe. For in the morning, when he should come to the field fresh and fasting, his neighbours came to him, and gaue him wine and strong drinke in such excessiue sort, that he was therewith distempered, and reeled as he went, and so was slaine without guilt. As for the false seruant, he liued not long vnpunished; for being conuict of felonie in court of assise, he was judged to be hanged, and so he was, at Tilburne."[2]

A good example of a judicial duel, fought in the year 1455, is given in *Histoire des Ducs De Bourgogne*.[3] It took place at Valenciennes, a town then belonging to the county of Hainault, which, with so many other rich manufacturing territories had fallen under the dominion of the dukes of Burgundy, by marriage or conquest. The privilege of sanctuary had been conferred on the town by its ancient counts, and the old rights and charters had been confirmed by the dukes their successors. A person named Mahiot Coquel, a tailor of Tournay, had murdered a man in that town, and he took refuge from justice in Valenciennes, claiming the right of sanctuary. Soon after his arrival a near relative of the murdered man named Jacotin Plouvier, met him in a street of the town and threatened vengeance against him for the murder of his kinsman; upon which Coquel applied to the magistracy, demanding their aid and counsel. The syndic then sent for Plouvier and reproached him with having the intention of violating the franchise of his town; but he denied this and claimed the right of lawful combat as against Coquel, at the same time throwing down a gage of battle. This, after some hesitation, Coquel lifted up; and a combat was allowed as being the law of the land, without being any infringement of the principle of sanctuary, which only applied to protection from the officers of justice. The parties were lodged in prison in separate cells, and seconds were appointed to arrange the preliminaries for the fight; when the Comte

---

[1] Holinshed, III, 210. [2] *Ibid.* [3] II, 182.

de Charolais, afterwards Charles the Bold, on being informed of the case, acting in the capacity of lieutenant-general for his father Duke Philippe le Bon, of Burgundy, ordered the matter to be referred to his council for judgment.   The town authorities then applied to the Duke their sovereign lord for the maintenance of their ancient rights, when all opposition to the combat was withdrawn ; the Duke announcing his intention of being present, with his son the Comte de Charolais, to view the fight.   Lists were erected, not in the form usual for the tourney, but round and with only a single entrance.   The judges of the fight were the provosts of the town of Valenciennes and of the county of Hainault, the Duke and his son being merely spectators.   Two seats draped with black cloth were placed facing each other in the middle of the lists, and the combatants were conducted to them and sworn on the Evangelists.   The two champions were clad in leathern garments, close-fitting and laced down the middles, the arms and legs bare.   These corselets were well greased so that neither of the parties could easily grip the other.   Their hands were rubbed with ashes for the better grasping of their weapons, and each held a piece of sugar in his mouth as a preventive against their throats becoming parched with the heat. Their weapons were knotted clubs, equal in weight and length and obtusely pointed at the narrower ends, and triangular shields, painted red.   When the signal for combat had been given Mahiot Coquel, who was the shorter and weaker man of the two, grasped a handful of sand with which the lists were strewn, and threw it into the eyes of his opponent.   This nearly blinded Jacotin for the moment, and he received a heavy blow in the face from the club of his adversary, but on recovering somewhat he set upon Mahiot and seizing him by the arm threw him violently to the ground, then placing his knees on his stomach, to the horror of the spectators, he kept steadily prodding Mahiot between the eyes with the pointed end of his club until he was dead.   The body was then dragged by the hangman from the lists to the gallows.

Lacroix in *Military an Religious Life in the Middle Ages, &c.*, gives a picture of a judicial duel of the knightly kind, fought on foot. It is copied from a miniature in the *Conquêtes de Charlemagne*, a MS., in the National Library at Paris.   The combatants are armed at all points ; their weapons are swords ; and the lists, of open railings, are octagonal in form.

The general course of procedure in these matters continued much the same up to and including the reign of Henry VIII. A manuscript of that reign, sometime belonging to Sir Edward Wyndham, Kt., Marshal to the Camp, gives particulars.[1] The form and size of the lists and counter-lists are as before ; also the kind of weapons to be employed. The defendant, if he appear not, is called by proclamation, made by the marshal of the king of " Heraults of that province wherein the Battail is to be deraigned." The bill of challenge of the appellant and the answer of the defendant is read to them and they take their oaths :—

1. That their appeal and defence is true.
2. That neither hath advantage of the other in weapons.
3. That each will do his best to vanquish his enemy.

The combatants being ready, the constable and marshal, sitting at the king's feet, order the onset to be sounded, pronouncing the words in high voice, "Lesses les aller et fair leur devoir."

"In the fight if either of the parties do give sign of yielding or if the king, being present, do cry 'Hoe,' the constable and marshall do part them and observe precisely who hathe advantage or disadvantage either of the other at that instant, for if they should be awarded to fight again, they are to be put in the same position as they were before."

"If the king take up the matter they are brought honourably out of the lists, neither having precedency over the other."

If the "Battail" be performed and one party be vanquished then "in case of Treason the rayles of the lists are broken down, and the party vanquished is drawn at a Horse-tayl and carried presently to execution."

The last instance of a duly authorised legal duel in France was that between François de Vivonne de la Chataignerie and Guy Chabot de Jarnac, which took place at St. Germain-en-Laye in 1547, in the presence of the king (Henry II.) It is doubly remarkable in that it contributed a new and subtil stroke of the sword, the "coup de Jarnac," and that it led to an edict being issued against duelling. This ordeal by combat resulted in the death of de la Chataignerie.

Judicial Duel in 1548, 2nd Edward VI, between one Newton, a Scot, and a gentleman named Hamilton ; the former being charged with uttering opprobrious epithets against His Majesty of England. Lists were erected in the market-place of Haddington, and at the time appointed the parties entered them for combat, clad in their doublets and hose, and

[1] *Origines Juridiciales*, p. 78.

armed with sword, buckler and dagger. The fight began with great spirit, Hamilton following his adversary up to the very railing of the lists, whereupon Newton struck him on the leg with his sword inflicting a great gash, upon which he fell to the ground and was slain. This ending of the fight was looked upon as a miscarriage of justice.[1]

The Abbé de Brantôme reports a trial by combat which took place about the middle of the sixteenth century, without the sanction of either king or parliament. The appellant was a Seigneur de Fandilles who charged the defendant, the Baron de Guerres of Lorraine, with an odious crime; and it was mutually agreed that the matter be referred to the judgment of God, in battle in the lists. The fight took place on foot with "bastardes" (hand and a half swords) in the lists at Sedan, a M. de Bouillon acting as judge. De Fandilles severely wounded his adversary in the thigh with a stroke of his powerful weapon, and the loss of blood was so great that the defendant could hardly keep his feet, at length falling to the ground. The lists were as usual freely strewn with sand, and the baron clutched handfuls of it which he threw into the eyes of his opponent, who was blinded for the time being and incapacitated from continuing the combat. This ending of the duel by means of an action strictly forbidden by the laws of the duello caused great disputes between the seconds and friends of both parties; and the matter was further complicated by a fall of the stand which afforded accommodation to the judge and spectators. This was certainly an irregular judicial duel, without any sanction at law, though the legal forms were observed.

Brantôme narrates several other duels.

In Harleian M.S., Vol. III, 505, 7021–22, is a catalogue of judicial combats anciently granted by the kings of England.

In the reign of Queen Elizabeth judicial duels had become rare, and the crown employed all its influence in their restraint. Fierce polemics had arisen in regard to the lawfulness or otherwise of the practice, and the conscience of the nation had been thoroughly aroused against them by reason of cases of more than suspected miscarriage of justice coming to light. Strong influence was brought to bear on the law courts to place all possible obstacles in the way of granting licences for such combats, and judges, at that time more especially, usually managed that disputes concerning the possession of land should be settled in the law courts without any resort to the ordeal of battle. Many treatises were

---

[1] Holinshed III, 890.

written against the practice, examples of which follow : Ashmole MSS., No. 856, p. 10. "Duello foild. The whole proceedings in the orderly dissolveing of a designe for single fight betweene two valient gentlemen ; by occasion whereof the unlawfulnesse of a duello is preparatorily disputed, according to the rules of honour and right reason ; written by the Lord Henry Howard Earle of Northampton." 126–145, p. 11. "A Discourse touching the unlawfulnesse of private combates, written by Sir Edward Cooke Lord Chiefe Justice of England, at the request of the Lord Henry Howard Earle of Northampton." (3 Oct., 1609.) 146–148. "Ex MS. in Bibl' Hatton."

Cotton MS. Titus. Fol. 33. A treatise on duels, in two books. (239.) Fol. 38. Two papers on measures taken against duels. (402.) Fol. 44. A paper concerning laws against duels. (416.)

On the 18th June, 1571, a judicial duel was ordered to take place, the principals being Simon Low and John Kime, who were to fight by proxy in the persons of George Thome and Henry Nailer, respectively. The dispute between the parties related to the possession of some land ; and the weapons for the intended fight were to be bastons and leathern shields. A plot of ground, 21 yards square, in Tothill Fields, was doubly railed in for the fight, and a stand connected with it was erected for the chief justice, as representing the court of common pleas. Behind it two tents were pitched for the use of the combatants. The Queen was much against the fighting, and the combat did not come off after all, for the champion of the appellant failed at the last moment to put in an appearance, so the plaintiff was non-suited.

Duels of the privileged order naturally survived those of the proletariat. Ashmole MS., No. 856, p. 7, gives " The manner of the challendge made by the Earle of Northumberland against Sir Francis Veare," both by letter dated 24 Apr. 1602, and by inter-messages, until forbidden by the Queen's commandment. (107–111.) Ex. MS. in Bibl' Hatton, and, under the same number, P. 16. " The manner of Donald Ld Rey, and David Ramsey esq. their comeing and carriage at their tryall, upon monday, the 28 of November, 1631, before the Ld of Lynsey, Lord High Constable of England, and others." This is a very full report of the trial. (175-227.) Under No. 856, p. 15. "His MA[ts]: declaration against duells, published at his chappell at Bruxells upon sonday the 24th of November 1658." (172.)

Though practically in abeyance for a long period the law for an appeal to combat had remained on the statute book; and a trial by battle was demanded as late as the year 1817, in the case of Thornton v. Ashford. The judge, Lord Ellenborough, pronounced "that the general law of the land is that there shall be a trial by battle in case of appeal unless the parties bring themselves within the scope of one of the exemptions." The suit was allowed, but the challenge being refused no combat ensued. The law was repealed in the following year (1818).[1]

[1] 59 Geo. III, c. 46.

APPENDIX A

TOURNEY

ABSTRACTS of the Ashmolean Manuscripts, regarding the Tourney.[1]

No. 764.

p. 6.   "Cy sensuyt la façon des criz de Tournois et des Joustes. *Cy peut on à prendre à crier et à publier pour ceulx qui en seront dignes."* 31–43.

On the reverse of the last leaf is a picture of the Joust, whereon two combatants on horseback, bearing their crests, are fighting with lances within the lists.

No. 1105.

p. 9.   Extracts from various records about Tournaments and Knighthood. 200 *et seq.*, 210.

No. 840.

p. 73.   A Justing-cheque, showing how the spears were broken. 298.

No. 763.

II. p. 5.   Rules, etc. 148–149.

"The Ordinaunce, statutes and rules made by John Lord Typtoft, Erle of Worcester, Countstable of England by the Kinges commaundment, at Windsour the 29 of May ao sexto Edwardi quarti, to be observed and kepte in all manner of Justes of pees royall with in this realme of England."

MS. copies of these ordinances are not uncommon, and much differing from each other. They are printed in *Harrington's Nugae Antiquae* by Park ; and in Dr. Meyrick's *Critical Essay on antient armor*, II, 179–186, with valuable notes from the MS. M. 6, in the Heralds' College.

No. 763.

p. 5.   The same Ordinaunce and statutes. 181.
6.   Rules for combatants "At Tornay." 149b.

No. 857.

p. 213.   "Rights due att the tournay. *Firste the Kinge of Armes. . . ."* 506.

No. 1115.

p. 43.   Preamble to articles of tilting, addressed unto the King. 92.

No. 860.   The "Round Table" prohibited, 36 Hen. III, 88.[2]

No. 1109.

p. 191.   Tournament at Windsor, Names of the combatants and judges in a "Course at feild at Windsor the 17th of Nov: 1593, ao regni reginae." 36. 154b.

---

[1] Catalogue by William Henry Black. Oxford. 1845.
[2] Though indexed this item is not in the catalogue.

---

[1] The Marquis of Northampton and others, 14 on each side.

p. 43. The Challenge of four Knights errant, the Earl of Oxford, Charles Howard, Sir Henry Lee, and Sir Chr. Hatton; against all comers, at the tilt, tourney and barriours; addressed unto the Queen for permission to perform the same. 245.

Note that the said challenge was proclaimed by Clarencieux, on twelfth-night, 1570; and that the exercises were performed on 1, 2, and 6 May. 245b.

Written invertedly by another hand. Other papers relating to the same affair are in No. 845, artt. 37, 39. No. 845. II, 36, 37, 38, 39, 40, 41, and at p. 599.

No. 845.

p. 36. Tilting list and cheque, at a tourney between the Earl of Oxford, Charles Howard, Sir Hen. Lea, and Chr. Hatton, challengers, and seven sets of comers; with their arms tricked. 164. See No. 837, Art. XLIIII.

p. 38. A Tilting-list, showing the antagonists of the Earl of Oxford and others. 167a.

p. 37. "These be the names of the noblemen and gentlemen, that for the honor of the Queenes Matie did their endevor at the Tylt at Westminster on the xvijth day of November, being the first day of the xxiiijth yere of the reigne of queene Elizabeth," etc. (1581). 165.

p. 39. "Hastiludium apud Westm' die Solis 6. Decembris 1584, coram Regina, inter nuptos decem et tot coelibes." 168.

p. 37. "The Tourney holden at Westminster, on monday the 15 of May, 1581, when the prince Delphine of Auvergne and other the Frenshe commissioners were here." 166a–5b.

p. 40. Proclamation (in French) of the adjudged conduct of combatants, and award of the prize, at a jousting before Queen Elizabeth. 171b.

p. 41. Proclamation (in English) of the adjudgement of prizes to Don Fredericque de Teledo, and other foreign nobles, on an other occasion. 171a.

Draught of another proclamation (in English) concerning the conduct of gentlemen at the tilt and tourney, not named. 170a.

No. 837.

p. 5. "The manner of the first cominge into the tiltyard, of the most high and mighty prince Charles Prince of Wales, sonne and heir apparent of our sovereign lo. Kinge James, on friday the xxiiijth of March 1619; which was in the most princely and royall manner that had bene sene many yeares before." 129–132.

An original paper, with notes and corrections by one of the Heralds. This art. is recorded in the Heralds' MS., M. 3. f. 1–3b.

No. 1127.

p. XIV. 2. Tournament of the Knight of the Royal Amaranthus. In the first quarter of the 17th century. 198–9b.

No. 1116.

p. 9*. "The manner how the price[1] shall be given at Joustes of peace royall, and for what considercōns it should be forfeited and lost.
First who so breaketh most speeres," etc. 108b.

p. 11*. "A demonstracōn by John Writh alias Garter, to King Edward the Fourth, touching three Knyghtes of high Almayn wch came to do arms in England, with the instruccōns by them geven unto the saide Gartr and the articles of their feates and enterprise." 111–3b. The year must have been 1473.

---

[1] Prize.

No. 763.

 p. 16. "The office of a Kinge at Armes. Fyrst as nyghe as he canne he shall take knowledge and kepe recorde of creastes cognissances and auntient used wordes," etc. 158ab.

No. 837.

 p. 8. "The definition of an Esquire, and the severall sortes of them according to the custome and usage of England. *An esquire called in Latine armiger . . .*" 162a.

No. 1116.

 p. 111. The Names and Arms of the Sovereigns and Knights of the Order of the Golden Fleece (Toison d'or), from its institution in 1429 to the twenty-third festival of the Order, which was holden by King Philip of Spain, 12 Aug. 1559; with historical accounts of the celebration of the feasts, in French. ff. 137b–186.

    The MS. is beautifully written, with the arms tricked (four on each page), by Robert Glover, Somerset Herald.

 p. 88. Lists of the Knights, and notes of the celebration of S. George's feast, in 1589 and 1593, at Westminster. 67a.

 p. 89. Lists of Knights, and notes of the celebration of S. George's feast, in 1584, at Westminster, and 15 Apr. 1585, at Windsor. 67b.

No. 837.

 p. XXVI. "The Office of ye Marshall." 198ab.

No. 1127.

 p. XIII. "The Statutes of the Order of the Golden Fleece" (27 Nov. 1431); and "The Ordinances for the Officers of the Order." 139–166–167–175b.

APPENDIX B

HARLEIAN MS. RELATING TO THE TOURNAMENT

CATALOGUE

EXTRACTS

1. The Proclamation, whereby Six Gentlemen challenged all Comers at the Just-Roiall : To Runne in Ostling-Harneis alonge a Tilt : And to strike 13 strokes with Swords ; upon the Marriage of Richard Duke of York (son to K. Edward IV.) with Anne Mowbray Daughter to the Duke of Norfolk.   After which Proclamation, follow the Articles, & Draughts of the Shields.   1

2. The Challenge of the Ladie Maie's Servants, to all comers, to be performed at Greenwich.

> To Runne 8 Courses.
> To shoot Standart-Arrowe, or Flight.
> To strike 8 Strokes with Swords Rebated.
> To wrestle all manner of Wayes.
> To Fight on Foot with Speares Rebated, and afterwards to strike 8 Strokes with Swords, with Gripe, or other-wise.
> To Call the Barre on Foote, and with the Arme ; both Heavie and Light   2b

APPENDIX C

COTTONIAN MSS. IN THE BRITISH MUSEUM RELATING TO THE TOURNEY

Claudius, C IV.

10. Breve R. Richard I ad archiep. Cantuar. missum, de concessione torneamentorum in Anglia. 233.

11. Forma pacis servandae à torneatoribus, et in juramentis. 233.

Nero, D II.

15. De la creacion et foundacion des heraulz (d'armes). 249b.

16. Les droiz et largesses appartenant et d'aunciennete accoustumez aux rois d'armes, selon l'usance du Angleterre. 251b.

18. L'ordonnance de faire joustes et tournois. 253.

19. Les droiz appartenans aux rois d'armes, et heraulx, en leur absence, en fait de joustes à plaisaunce. 245b.

Galba. B VI.

77. A list of great personages, who probably appeared at a tilt. 109.

Vesp. C XIV.

229. Notes relating to tournaments. 553.

Titus. B I.

35. Judges deputed for the field in the joustes between Guisnes and Andres. 127.

Caligula. D VI.

54. Twenty-three original letters from Charles D. of Suffolk, to Henry VIII, all probably between Oct., 1514, and March, 1515. 147.

APPENDIX D

THE instructions given by the Emperor Maximilian as to the selection of the subjects for the Plates for *Freydal.*

They are set down on Folio 38 of that work.

" Hernach volgt in was zäl die Rennen vnd stechen in den Freytal gemacht sollen werden."

Geschift Rennen.

Item der geschift Rennen sollen XI sein,
Darunnder III fäl, mit ain ander,
Vnnd zwen fäl, das Kaiser besiczt vnnd widerparthey felt,
Die vberigen VI Rennen sollen Sy baide besiczen.

Swayf Rennen.[1]

Item Swayf Rennen sollen VI sein,
Dar vnnder IIII fäl mit ain annder,
Vnd II fäl das Kaiser besiczt vnnd widerparthey felt.

Pündt Rennen.[2]

Item das pünndt Rennen sollen XII sein, dar vnnder sollen zween fäl sein das der Kaiser besiczt vnnd die Wider-parthey felt,
Vnnd die vbrigen X Rennen solln baid besiczen.

Autzogen Rennen.

Item Anczogen Rennen sollen XXV sein,
Vnnd der Kaiser ist albeg den driten tail besessen, vnd sein wider parthey den II tail gefallen.

Teutsch gestech.[3]

Item Es sollen sechs vnnd zwainzig teutscher gestech sein
Die fäl sol Kayserlich Mt noch stymben.

Welsch gestech.[4]

Item Es sollen Acht vnd Dreissig Welscher gestech sein,
Die fäl solle Kyserlich Mt noch stymben.

Tornier (The Tourney).

Item Es sollen sein III Tornier.

Krönl (Krönlrennen).

Item Es sollen sein III Rennen, in der gestalt das ainer ain Krönl der annder ainen scharfen Rennspiess hab,
Die fäl solle Kay Mt noch stymben.

Velt Rennen.[5]

Item Es sollen sein V veldt Rennen
Summa der Rennen stechen vnd Tornier CXXVIII.[6]

---

[1] Another name for *Scharfrennen*.   [2] *Bundrennen*.   [3] German Joust.
[4] Joust at the Tilt.   [5] *Feldrennen*.   [6] 129 ?

APPENDIX E

ASHMOLEAN MSS. RELATING TO JUDICIAL DUELS

DISCOURSES ON LAWFUL COMBATS IN ENGLAND

No. 856.

Par. 9. A Discourse "Of the antiquity, use, and ceremony of lawfull combates in England." 115–125.

12. A Discourse "Of the antiquitie, use, and ceremony of lawfull combates in England, written by Mr. James Whitelock of the Middle Temple." 149–153.

13. "The antiquity, use, and ceremonyes of lawfull combates in England." 154–156.

14. "The antiquity, use, and ceremony of lawfull combates in England." 157–172. "Ex collect' Guil: Dugdale."

No. 865.

10*. A treatise of "The wageing of Bataill between two partyes. First. The quarrell and bills of the appellant and defendant must be pleaded in the court." 258–276.

"*The fee of the Constable is the lystes, the barris, and stagis belonginge to the same.* Thus endeth the wageing of battaill before the King."

1115.

97. Erotulis publicis quaedam annotationes; primo de Militbus Ordinis, et de Windesora; postea de, constabulariis castri Windesorae, de duello, et de insigniis armorum. 225–6b.

Extracts by Ashmole, chiefly from the Patent Rolls and Close Rolls, Hen. III–Ric. II.

No. 840.

47. A short extract by Sir W. Dugdale "Out of a discourse in French concerning the antient manner of Combates." 211.

764.

7. "De la droite ordonnance du Gaige de Bataille par tout le royaume de France. Phelipe *par la grace de Dieu Roy de France a touz ceulx qui ces presentes lettres verront salut.*"

This letter of King Philip IV, written in 1306, limits the practice of wager of battle, and is prefixed to regulations for the whole course of combat. 44–54^b.

856. Order in England, temp. Ric. II.

4*. A book "Of the manner and order of combating within the listes, delivered by Thomas Duke of Gloucester unto King Richard the second." 83–89.

Transcribed "Ex MS. in Bibl' Hatton," *with the listes,* scaffold, and tymber used at the said battaile. 83–89. Compare Art. 23.

16. "The manner of Donnald Ld Rey, and David Ramsey esq. their comeing and carriage at their tryall, upon monday, the 28 of November 1631, before the Ld of Lynsey, Lord High Constable of England, and others." This is a very full report of the trial. 175–227.

824.

V. Another account of the same. 34-46^b.

856. Treatise, temp. Hen. VI.

22. "Loo my leve lordes, here now next folowing is a Traytese, compyled by Johan Hill, armorier and sergeant in the office of Armorye wt kynges Henry ye 4th and Henry ye 5th, of ye poyntes of Worship in Armes that longeth to a Gentilman in Armes, and how he shall be diversly armed and gouverned, under supportacion and favour of alle ye reders to correcte adde and amenuse where nede is, by the high commaundment of the princes that have powair soo for to ordeyne and establisshe. *The first honneur in armes is a gentilman to fight in his souverian lords quarell in a bataille of treason.*" 376-383. A.D. 1434.

23. "And here next foloweth the maner and fourme of makyng of the thre Oothes that every appellant and defendant owe to make openly in the feelde before the Kyng and the Conestable and Mareschal, the same day that they shal do thair armes, both in Frensshe and in Englisshe ; compyled and abstracte oute of a notable Traityes made of the rieule and gouvernance of the feelde in armes, by Thomas of Wodestoke sumtyme Conestable of Englande and uncle to Kyng Richard (the second), to whom he presented the saide traities, submitting it to his noblesse to correct, adde, and amenuse as his highnes best liked." 383-391.

"*La fee du Mareshal est les listes, les barrers, et les estages dycelles etc.*"

6*. "The Earle Marshall's order in the quarrell betwixt Anthony Felton and Edmond Withepole esquires, xxiij May 1598." 105-107.

7. "The manner of the challendge made by the Earle of Northumberland against Sir Francis Yeare," both by letter dated 24 Apr., 1602, and by inter-messages, until forbidden by the Queen's commandment. 107-111.

"Ex MS. in Bibl' Hatton."

8*. A statement of "The French King's edict constitutinge duellos to be punished in the nature of treason, within his dominions." 112-14.

9. A Discourse "Of the antiquity, use, and ceremony of lawfull combates in England." 115-125.

"Ex. MS. in Bibl' Hatton."

10. "Duello foild. The whole proceedings in the orderly disolveing of a designe for single fight betweene two valient gentlemen ; by occasion whereof the unlawfulnesse of a duello is preparatorily disputed, according to the rules of honour and right reason ; written by Lord Henry Howard Earle of Northampton." 126-145.

11. "A Discourse touching the unlawfulness of private combates, written by Sr Edward Cooke Lord Chiefe Justice of England, at the request of the Lord Henry Howard Earle of Northampton." (3 Oct., 1609). 146-8.

"Ex. MS. in Bibl' Hatton."

15. His Ma^{ts}: declaration against duells, published at his Ma^{ts}: chappell at Bruxells upon sonday the 24th of November 1658." 172.

APPENDIX F

HARLEIAN MSS. CATALOGUE OF DOCUMENTS RELATING TO JUDICIAL DUELS

Vol.	Page	Cod.	Art.	
I.	249	424	13.	
I.	492	980	134.	
III.	122	4176	2 *et* 4 *et seq.*	Treatises on Duels.
III.	332	6149	19.	
I.	490	980	36.	Instances of Trial by Duel.
III.	319	6069	66–67.	Tracts on Single Combats.
III.	505	7021	22.	
I.	490	980	46.	Instances of Trial.
III.	322	6079	36.	Between Dukes of Hereford and Norfolk.
III.	370	6495	1.	" Mr. Dan, Archdeacon and Francis Mowbray.
III.	122	4176	2.	James Whitlock. Discourses on Combats in England.

EXTRACTS

I.	249	424	13.	The Way of Duells before the King; with the Office of the Constable and Earl-Marshal, &c. upon such occasions.	42
I.	490	980	36.	Instances of Trials in England by Ordeal & Duel.	ibid.
I.	491	980	46.	What happened to Sir Nicholas de Segrave, anno. 32 Edw. I. who being accused of Treason, offered to justifie himself by Duel; and afterward went over the Sea (without License) to fight with his enemy.	ibid.
I.	492	980	134.	Of legal duels, or Combats.	128
III.	122	4176	2.	Of the antiquity, use and ceremony of Combats in England: by James Whitlock, &c.	12
III.	122	4176	4.	Concerning Duells in Spaine.	37
III.	319	6069	66.	Du Combat appelle Buhort.	113
III.	319	6069	67.	Du Combat appelle Bas ou Barriers.	ib.
III.	322	6079	36.	A Combat between D. of Hereford & Tho. Mowbray first D. of Norfolk, & Marshal of England.	29
III.	332	6149	19.	De Duellis.	164b
III.	370	6495	1.	A Tract with this title, "A tru report of sundry memorable Accidents befalling Mr. Daniel Archdeacon, before and after the Combat appointed betweene him & Francis Moubray. Written first in French, by a faythfull frynd of Mr. Daniel Archdeacon, and sent to another frynd of theirs, and since translated in English by a faythfull frynd to him & to that honest cause." 26 leaves. At the end are some Anagrams & Acrostics in French, on the name of Daniel Archdeacon and a table of the contents of the tract.	
III.	505	7021	22.	A Catalogue of such Combats as have been anciently granted by the Kings of England.	

APPENDIX G

COTTONIAN MSS. RELATING TO JUDICIAL DUELS

Titus. C I.

APPENDIX H

LETTER from Thomas Duke of Gloucester and Constable of England to King Richard II concerning the Manner of conducting Judicial Duels.

In firste the quarelis and the billis of the appellaunt and of the defendaunt schal be pletid in the courte.before the constable and marchall. And when they may not prove ther cause by witnesse.nor bi non other manner but detrmine ther quarell bi strengthe.the ton for to prove his entent up on the tother. And the tother in the same manner for to defende him. The constable hath power for to ioyne that batayle as vecarie genrall undir god & the kynge and the bataile conioynt by the Constable.he schal assigne them day and place.so that the day be not within xl.dayes after the saide batell soo conioynt.but yf it be bi the consentinge of the seyde appellaunt and defendaunt. Than he schall awarde them.poyntes of armes other wise callid wepenes.ayther of them schal have.that is to say.longe swerde schorte swerde and dagger.so that the appellant and defendaunt.fynde sufficianunt surete & plegges that echou of them schal come at his seyde day the appellaunt for to doo his power up on the defendaunt.and the defendaunt in his defence up on the appellaunt. And this to be done.schall be gevyn un to the appellaunt hour terme and soon.for to make his preve and der (sic) and for to bethe firste within the listes. for to quite his plegges. And of the same wise of the defendaunt. And noon of hem schall do hevinesse.ille harme awaite assaute.nor non other grevaunce.nor ennye bi them nor bi non of ther frendes welwillinge.nor bi non other who soo ever it be. The kynge schal fynde the felde.for to feght in. And the (f. 125b) listes schal be made and devisid by the constable. And it is to be considerid that the listes schal be.lx.pases of lengthe and xl.paces of brede in good manner.and that the erthe be ferme stable and harde.and even made, without grete stones and that the erthe be plat.and that the listes be strongli barred rounde aboute and a gate in the este and a nother in the weste with good and stronge barrers of.vij.foote of heyght or more And it is to wite that ther schulde be faux listes withouten the principal listes betwene the whiche the men of the constable and the marchall and s'gauntes of armes of the kynges schulde be for to kepe and defend yf any wolde make any offence or fray azens the cries made in the courte in any thinge that myght be agayns the kynges Roiall mageste or lawe of armes and these men schulde be armed at all poyntes. The Constable schalhave there as many men of armes as he will and the marchall also bi the assignacion of the Constable and ellis not the whiche men schal have the kepynge as is seyde. The s'gauntes of armes of the kynge schal have the keping of gates of the listes and the arestinges yf any schal be made bi the comaudemt of the seyde Constable and Marchall. The day of bataile the kynge schal be in a sege or in a shaffold on heght and a place schal be made for the Constable and marchall at the stayre foot of the seyde shaffold there where thei schal be. And than schal be axed the plegges of the appellaunt and defendaunt for to come in to the listes afore the kynge and present in the courte as prisioners un to the appellaunt and defendaunt be come in the listes and have made ther othes. When the ap (f. 126) pellaunt cometh to his iorney he schale come to the gate of the listes in the Este in such manner as he will feght with his armes and wepenis assignid to him bi the courte and ther he schal abide til he be led in bi the Constable so that when he is comen to the seyde gate the Constable and marchall schal goo thedir. And the Constable schal axe him what man he is whiche is comen armed to the gate of the listes. And what name he hathe and for what cause he is comen. And the appellaunt schal answere I am súche aman. A. de. K. the appellaunt the whiche is come to this iorney &c for to doo &c And than the Constable schal open the viser of his basinet soo that he may playnli see his visage and if it be the same man that is the appellaunt than schal he make open the gates of the listes and schal make him entre with his seyde armes poyntes vitailes and other leuefull necessaries up on him and also his counsell with him and than he schal lede him afore the kynge and than to his tente where he schal abide til the defendaunt be comen. In the same manner schal be done of the defendaunt but that he schal entre in at the weste gate of the listes. The Constable clerk schal write and sette in the regestre the comyge and the houre of the entringe of the appellaunt and how that he entreth the listes on fote.and also the harnyes of the appellaunt how that he is armed and with how many wepenis he entreth the listes and what vitailes and other leueful necessaries he bringeth in with him. In the same manner schal be don to the defendaunt. Also the Constable schal mak take hede that non other before ne behinde the appellaunt (f. 126b) nor the defendaunt brynge more wepin nor vitailes other then were assignid bi the courte. And yf it be soo that the defendaunt come not be time to his iorney and at the oure and terme limit bi the courte the Constable schal comaunde the marchall for to make calle him at the four corners of the listes the whiche schal be done in manner as it foloweth. Oyes. Oyez. Oyez. C. de. B. defendaunt come to yowre Jorney whiche ye have undirtake at this day for to aquite yowre plegges before the kinge the constable and marchall in yowre defence agayns. A. de K. appellaunt of that that he hathe put up on yow. And yf he come not be time he schal be callid the secunde time in the same manner and at the ende he schal say come the day passeth faste and yf he come not at that time he schal be callid the thridde time. But that this be betwixe hye tierce and none. In the same manner as before and at the ende he schal say the day passeth faste and the oure of none is nye soo that ye come bi the seyde oure of none at farrest in pitt that may come. But how soo ever the Constable hathe yevy oure and terme un to the defendaunt for to come to his Jorney never the lesse yf that he tarie un to the oure of none the Jugement schulde not bi right goo agayns him whethir it be in cas of treson or not. But soo is it not of the appellaunt for he muste holde the houre and time limitid bi the courte withoute any plonginge or excusacon what soo ever be it in cause of treson. The appellaunt and the defendaunt entrede in the (f. 127) listes with ther armoure wepenes vitailes and leuefull necessaries and counsell as is seyde and as thei are assigned bi the courte. The Constable schal wete the kinges wille yf he wil assigne any of his noble lordes or knyghtes of worschipe un to the sayde pties and yf he wil that the othes be made afore him or afore the Constable and marchal. And the appellaunt and defendaunt schal be serchid bi the Constable and marchall of there poyntes of armes otherwise callid wepenis that they be vowable without any man disseyte on them and yf thei be other than reson axeth they schal be taken away ffor reson good feythe and lawe of arms wil not suffre no gile nor dissayte in soo gret a dede. And it is to wite that the appellaunt and defendaunt may be armed as sewrely upon ther bodies as they will. And than the Constable schal sende firste after the marchall and than for the appellaunt with his counsell for to make his othe. The Constable schal axe him yf he wil any more protest and that he putte forthe all his ptestacions bi writinge for fro that time forthe he schal make no ptestacion. The constable schal have his clerke redy in his presence that schal ley forthe a masse book open. And than the Constable schal make his seyde clerke rede the bille of the appellaunt enterly on heyght and the bille redde the constable schal say to the appellaunt A. de K. thou knowest wel this bille and this warant and wedd' that thou gave in oure courte.thou schal lay thi right honde here up on these seyntes and schal swere in maner as foloweth (f. 127b). Thou. A.de.K. this thi bille is sothe in all poyntes and articles fro the beginyge contenynge theirn to the ende and that is thine entente to preve this day on the forsayde. C.de.B. so god the helpe and theise halowes and this othe made he schal be led agayne to his place The constable schal make the marchal calle the defendaunt and soo schal be done to the defendaunt in the same manner as to the appellaunt And than the Constable schal make calle bi the marchall the appellaunt agayne and schal make him leye his honde as he did afore up on the masse book and schal say. A.de.K. thou swerest that thou ne haste ne schalt have mo poyntes ne poyntes on the ne on thi bodi within these listes but thei that ben assignid bi the courte that is to say. a longe swerde schorte swerde and dagger nor non other knyf litill nor mekill ne non other instrument ne engyn of poynte ne other wise ne stone of vrtu ne herbe of vrtu ne charme ne expirmet ne karecte no non other inchauntemt bi the ne for the bi the whiche thou tristest the better to overcome the forseyde. C.de.B. thin advsarie that schal come ayens the with in these listes this day in his defence. Ne that thou ne trustest in non other thinge but onli in god and thi body and on thi rightful quarell so helpe the god and these halowes and the othe made he schal be led agayne to his place. In the same wise schal be done to the defendaunt. The whiche othes made and ther chambirleyns and srvauntes put a way. the Constable schal make calle bi the marchall the appellaunt and the defendaunt also the whiche schal be ledde (f. 128) and kepte bi the men of the Constable and marchall before them and the Constable schal say to bothe the pties. Thou A.de.K. appellour schal take. C.de.B. defendoure bi the rigt honde and he the. And we defende yow and echone of yow in the kinges name and up on the pill that longeth therto and up on pill of lesinge yowre quarell the whiche that is founden in defaute that non of yow be so hardy to doo to other ille ne grevauce thirstinge nor other harme bi the honde up on the pill afore sayde and this charge gevy. the Constable schal make yeve ther right hondis to gedir and ther lifte hondes up on the missale sayinge to the appeloure. A.de.K appelloure thou swerest bi the feythe that thou yevest in the honde of thine advsarie. C.de.B. defondoure and bi all the halowe that thou toucheste with thi lifte honde that thou today this day schal doo all thi trewe power and entente bi all the weyes that thou beste may or kanste to preve thine entente on. C.de.B. thine advsarie and defendoure to make him yelden him up to thine honde and creant to crie or speke or ellis make him die bi thine honde to fore that thou wende oute of these listes bi the tyme and the sunne that the is assignid bi this courte bi thi feythe and soo helpe the god and these halowes. C. de. B. defendoure thou swerest bi thi feythe that thou yevest in the honde of thine advsarie A.de.K. appelloure and bi all the halowes that thou touchest with thi lifte honde that to day this day thou schall doo all thi trewe power and entente bi all the weyes that thou beste may or kanste to defende thine entente of all that (f. 128b) that is put on the bi. A.de.K. thin advsarie appelloure bi the feythe and soo helpe the god and all these halowes. And than the Constable schall comaunde the marchall for to crie at the foure corners of the listes in manner as foloweth. Oyez. Oyez. Oyez. We charge and comaunde bi the kynges Constable and marschall that non of gret valew & of litill estate of what condicion or nacion that he be. be so hardy hens fore-warde for to come negh the listes bi foure foote nor to speke nor to crie nor to make contenance nor token nor semblaunce nor noyse where bi nouther of these two prties. A.de.K. appellor &. C.de.B. defendour may take avauntage the ton up on the tother up on pill of lesinge lyf and membre and ther goodes at the kinges wille. And after the Constable and marchall schal avoyde all manner of pepill oute of the listes except their luftenauntz and two knyghtes for the Constable and marchall whiche schal be armed up on there bodies but they schal have nother knyf nor swerde up on them nor non other wepenes wherbi the appellaunt other the defendaunt may have therof any avauntage bi negligence of kepinge of them But the two luftenauntz of the Constable and marchall schal have in there handes outher a spere wtoute yren for to depte them yf the kinge will make them abide in ther feghtinge whether it be to reste them or other thinge what som ever him liketh. And it is to be knowen that if yf any adminstracion schulde be made to the appellaunt or to the defendaunt of mete or of drinke or any other necessarie thinge leeful after (f. 129) that the counsell of frendes and s'vauntz ben put away of the appellaunt and of the defendaunt as is seyde the seyde adminstracion apteneth to the herawdes and also all the cries made in the seyde courte the whiche kingsz heraudes and pursevauntes schal have a place for the assignid bi the Constable and marchall as nye the listes as may goodli be soo that they may see all the dede & to be redy yf thei be callid for to doo any thinge. The appellaunt in his place kepte bi som men assignid by the Constable or marchall & the defendaunt in his place in the same wise. Bothe two made redy and arayed & with feleschipe bi ther kepers above sayde the marchall with the ton ptie & the levetenant of the Constable with the tother. The Constable sittinge in his place above sayde afore the kinge as his viker genrall and pties made redy for the feghte as is sayde bi the comaundement of the kinge. The constable schal say with hye voyce as foloweth. lessiez lez aler. that is to say lat them goo and reste a while. lessiez lez aler and reste a nother while. lessiez lez aler & fair leur devoir depdieu. that is to say lat them goo and doo ther devour in goddes name And this seyde eche man schal depte fro bothe pties soo that they may incountre & doo that them semeth beste The appellaunt ne the defendaunt may nouther ete nor drinke fro that time forthe withoute leve & licence of the kinge for thinge that myght falle but yf thei wol do it bi the consentinge betwixe them. Fro this time forthe it is to be considered diligentli bi the constable that yf the kinge will make the pties feghtinge depte reste or abide (f. 129b) for wham som ever cause it be.that he take good kepe how thei are deptid so that thei be in the same estate and degre in all thinges yf the kinge wil sure or make them goo to gedir agayne and also that he have good harkeninge and syghte un to them yf outher speke to other be it of yeldinge or other wise for un to him longeth the witnesse and the recorde of the wordes fro that time forthe & to non other. And yf the seyde batell of treson he that is convicte & discomfit schal be disarmed in the listes bi the comaunde-ment of the Constable and a corner of the listes broken in the reprove of him bi the whiche schal be drawen oute with hors fro the same place there he is soo disarmed thorow the listis un to the place of iustice where he schal be hedid or hongid after the usage of the cuntre the whiche thinge apenteth to the marchall and to ovrsee and to pforme his seyde office and to put him in execucion and to goo or ride and to be alwey bi him til it be done and all pformed and aswel of the appellaunt as of the defendaunt for good feythe and right and lawe of armes will that the appellaunt renne in the same peyne that the defendaunt schulde doo if he were covicte and discomfit. And yf it happen soo that the kinge wolde take the quarell in his hande and make them acordid withoute more feghtinge Than the Constable takinge the ton ptie and the marchall the tother and lede them afore the kinge and he schewinge them his wille the seedy Constable and marchall schal lede them to the on ptie of the listes with all there pointz and armor as thei are founden and havyge when the (f. 130) kynge took the quarell in his honde as is seyde. And soo they schal be led oute of the gate of the listes evenly so that the ton goo not afore the tother bi no wey in noo thinge for senne the hath taken the quarell in his hande it schulde be dishonest that outher of the pties schulde have mor disworschipe than the tother Wherfore it hath ben seyde bi many aunciaunt men that hee that gooth first oute of the listes hath the disworschipe and this is aswel in cause of treson as in other cause what soo ever it be. The fee of the herawdes is all the poyntes & armor brokin theis pt he taketh away or leveth after that he is entrid the listes aswel of the appellaunt as of the defendaunt and all the poyntes and armor of him that is discomfit be it the appellaunt other the defendaunt. The fee of the marchall is the listes the Barrers and the postes of them.

INDEX